Business-to-Business Marketing Communications

BUSINESS- TO -BUSINESS MARKETING COMMUNICATIONS

Norman Hart

Sixth Edition

**KOGAN
PAGE**

First published as *Business to Business Advertising* in 1971, 1978, 1983
Published as *Practical Advertising and Publicity* by McGraw-Hill in 1988
Published as *Industrial Marketing Communications* by Kogan Page in 1993
Reprinted 1995
This edition published 1998

Kogan Page Limited
120 Pentonville Road
London N1 9JN

British Library Cataloguing in Publication Data

A CIP record for this book is available from the British Library.

ISBN 0 7494 2558 X

Typeset by Saxon Graphics Ltd, Derby
Printed and bound in Great Britain by
Biddles Ltd, Guildford and King's Lynn

To M.D.H.

ACKNOWLEDGEMENTS

In the updating of this book, considerable weight has been placed on contributions from many people and organizations and the author expresses grateful acknowledgement to:

The Incorporated Society of British Advertisers
Institute of Practitioners in Advertising
Periodical Publishers Association
Audit Bureau of Circulation
Center for Exhibition Industry Research, USA
Roper Starch, USA
Farmer's Weekly

In addition, personal thanks are given to Steve Cuthbert, Director General of The Chartered Institute of Marketing, for writing the *Foreword*; to Blackett Ditchburn, Deputy Managing Director of Carat Insight, for writing the chapter on '*New Media*'; to Roger Haywood, Chairman, Kestrel Communications Limited, for contributing to '*Public Relations*'; to David Farbey, Director, Smee's Advertising Limited, for work on the '*Advertising Agencies*' chapter; and, finally, to Peter Russell, Senior Partner, Acorn Marketing and Communications, for casting a critical eye over the entire book.

CONTENTS

Part 6   A LOOK TO THE FUTURE

FOREWORD

Welcome to the sixth edition of *Business-to-Business Marketing Communications*, a practical book for practical people engaged in business-to-business marketing, written by a practical man who's also an expert in the field. This much expanded edition is the latest of a well-established text that has stood the test of time for over 25 years.

Here you will find a substantial amount of practical advice, check lists, and 'shopping' lists covering all aspects of business-to-business marketing communications. There is also a strong emphasis on the importance of defining and focusing on your objectives, and many useful and revealing tables of data to make you re-evaluate your approach. Whether you are relatively new to marketing or an experienced practitioner, there is something here for everyone engaged in the field, with the appropriate theory nicely woven into the fabric of the book.

To get the best out of this book you need to read it cover to cover, and then return to it as a reference guide when you need help to turn a business problem into an opportunity. Experienced professionals and Chief Executive Officers may just choose to use this book to check up on a specific area, or for a second opinion. I'm confident that they will find the answers they are looking for.

In essence, marketing is all about creating and keeping customers. Once neglected, business-to-business marketing is now a recognized discipline in its own right, in part thanks to the work of a dedicated group of professionals, which includes the author. Getting inside the customer's head so you can understand what, how and why he or she thinks as they do is key. This book tells you how to get your message to register with your business customer. As the author himself says, 'a published book is the most permanent and deeply penetrating method of communication yet devised'. In writing this book, Norman Hart has achieved his goal. The rest is up to you!

Steve Cuthbert
Director General, The Charterd Institute of Marketing

PREFACE

The marketing concept is now well accepted by most companies in Britain and Europe even though they continue to lag behind the United States. Indeed, from the commercial area, the idea of 'customer orientation' has spilled over into institutions, government services, charities, social activities and even political parties.

Acceptance of marketing, however, has always been faster among consumer goods companies than in those concerned with industrial/business products and services. Every single function in consumer marketing has developed to a high degree of sophistication: research, product development, advertising, sales promotion, selling, distribution, planning and budgeting – all have become specialist activities with an increasing emphasis on productivity and effectiveness.

Business-to-business marketing has developed at a much slower rate and with some companies is still little more than the old selling function repackaged under a new name. And little wonder, since in contrast with consumer marketing there are few opportunities to learn about business marketing: few courses and seminars, few textbooks, few periodicals and no institution or association dealing with the special needs and interests of executives in this particular sector. Similarly, in the academic world, the introduction of marketing to many business studies continues to concentrate on consumers and mass media, which is after all where public visibility is high and where massive million-pound budgets are commonplace.

When it comes to business-to-business marketing communications this is perhaps the most neglected area of all, a situation which existed when this book was first published. Since that time it has become the accepted work on the subject, both in the United Kingdom and elsewhere. Over a number of editions and reprints it has gathered together such meagre data as have emerged, relying heavily on American research, and it is now presented as a completely updated text, devoted simply to getting the best value for money out of budgets which are almost universally low compared with their consumer counterparts.

Business-to-Business Marketing Communications has been written with the belief that in putting together a promotional campaign there is a need to

consider every channel of communication in order to arrive at a media mix
which will target with accuracy the precise audience that has to be reached
in order to secure action. The book is intended for those managers and
executives who have a responsibility for planning and undertaking business-
to-business marketing communications, ie advertising, public relations, promotion and all the related activities. Students will also find it of value:
indeed it has been a recommended text from the outset for those studying
for the CAM Diploma and the CIM Diploma of Marketing.

Part 1

STRATEGIC PLANNING

1.

Terminology in business-to-business marketing is particularly susceptible to ambiguity and confusion. For this reason, it is necessary at the outset to give some definitions to ensure a complete understanding of the terms used. Evidence of this need is to be found in the United States where 'publicity' is commonly understood to refer to 'free editorials', whereas in the United Kingdom the term is used in an all-embracing sense of publicizing anything for any purpose. It thus includes activities which contribute to selling and may be known as sales promotion, and those which set out to provide information to any of a number of publics and is therefore related more to public relations.

The terms 'publicity' and 'sales promotion' are both subsumed by 'marketing communications' under which heading are included all the various 'channels of persuasion' such as advertising, direct mail, exhibitions and so on. It is not, however, 'the medium' which qualifies an activity as *marketing communications* or *public relations*, but rather 'the purpose for which the medium is employed'.

Public relations is dealt with separately and briefly since its objectives are far broader than simply the promotion of sales, though it must be emphasized that almost without exception the channels of persuasion used for marketing purposes are applicable in some form to public relations.

A good deal of confusion exists about the meaning of advertising; whether this applies only to press and television, or whether direct mail, for instance, is included in the term. For the sake of clarity it will be used only when it relates to press and television; moreover it will be qualified, press advertising.

There is even more confusion on the meaning of marketing. For many people, particularly in the industrial sector, it is taken to be synonymous with selling. For others it means getting a product to market, or simply distribution. Since both these interpretations are incomplete, it is essential to agree at the outset on the meaning of the term when it is used here.

Adam Smith was close to the mark when he wrote, in 1776, 'consumption is the sole end purpose of all production; and the interest of the producer ought to be attended to, only so far as it may be necessary for promoting that of the consumer'.

A more recent explanation has been by L W Rodger, who states that

> marketing has come to be increasingly concerned not merely with the problem of how to dispose profitably of what is produced but also with the much more basic problem of what to produce that will be saleable and profitable, in other words, with nothing less than the profitable matching of a company's total resources, including manufacturing technique, to market opportunities. (See Figure 1.1.)

The Chartered Institute of Marketing goes further by defining marketing as 'the management process responsible for identifying, anticipating and satisfying customer requirements profitably'.

Marketing starts then in the market-place, with the identification of the customer's needs and wants; or perhaps 'requirements' is a better word. It then moves on to determining a means of satisfying that want, and of promoting, selling and supplying a 'satisfaction'. The principal marketing functions might be defined as marketing information and research, product planning, pricing, advertising and promotion, sales and distribution.

It is sometimes argued that while the marketing concept is vital in relation to consumer goods, the situation is so different in the industrial sector that the same concept cannot be usefully employed. It is true that many managements have achieved great success in the past by intuition and brilliant guesswork, and it can also be argued that many areas of industrial or business marketing are quite different and sometimes a good deal more difficult than their equivalents in the consumer field, but a convincing argument against this is given again in *Marketing in a Competitive Economy*.

> The differences between industrial and consumer goods and their respective markets in no way invalidates the applicability of the marketing concept to industrial goods. Indeed because of the high value of unit sales and unit purchases of many industrial goods, and because of the longer manufacturing cycle and high cost of building and maintaining stocks associated with a wide range of such goods, the importance of the marketing concept may be even greater than consumer goods to the extent that the consequences of being wrong – through bad business and sales forecasting, faulty product planning, inadequate or inaccurate information, failure to identify, contact and follow up sales prospects with well conceived sales promotional activity – can be a great deal more costly.

The differences between industrial, or business-to-business, and consumer marketing are not in their concept, nor indeed in their value or relevance. Rather they are to be found in the techniques to be employed, the nature and complexity of the purchasing decision-making, and the size of the budgets available for achieving the objectives. This latter factor, if anything, makes the task a great deal more difficult, especially in view of the continuing lack of data on which to make valid judgements.

The fact of the matter is that with a tight budget one cannot afford to be wrong: hence the need for a well-planned and comprehensive marketing communications programme.

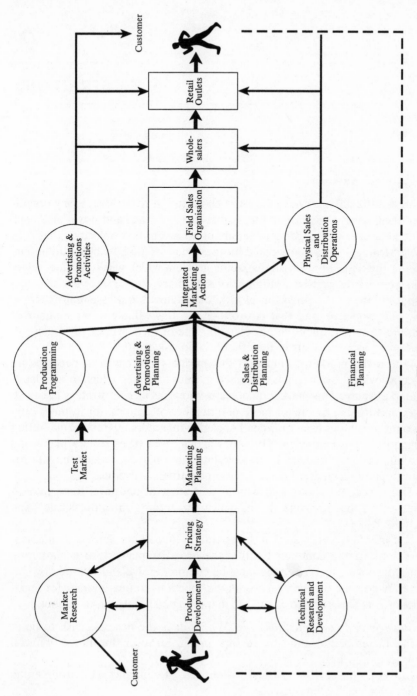

Figure 1.1 The marketing process

2

STRATEGIES

The strategic cascade

There is little need for any confusion about the word 'strategy'. Any organisation will have a purpose in life, namely an objective, and it will also have some idea of how it is going to set about achieving that objective, that is to say, a 'strategy'. So a commercial business may start off its by defining purpose in the form of a 'mission statement', from which will come the objective. There may well be a number of subsidiary objectives, such as social responsibility, or the provision of local employment, but essentially there is only one objective, and that is profit. From this will stem any number of possible strategies aimed at achieving it. One of these will be 'by means of' marketing, as against any of the other functional activities.

Within the marketing function this business strategy now becomes an objective which essentially is expressed in sales turnover, which in turn leads to market share. This marketing objective now has its own strategy to select, and it in turn can be one or more of a number of options, for instance buying out the competition, or indeed engaging in a more aggressive marketing communications campaign. The latter activity now turns from a marketing communications (marcom) strategy into an objective which might, for instance, be to increase the awareness of a particular product.

This procedure shows that what is a strategy at one level turns into an objective at the next one down, hence the term 'strategic cascade'. See Figure 2.1.

It is vital to the efficiency of the operation that all marketing communications activities be conducted within the broad framework of a marketing plan. Moreover, such planning must be comprehensive and written down in a master document which relates all the functions to one another for maximum effect. This key document, the marketing plan, sets out to define:

1. *Strategic and corporate objectives* Where does the business wish to be in five to ten years? Industry sectors, profit, turnover, locations, financial base, employees.
2. *External factors – PEEST* Political, Economic, Environmental, Sociological, Technological.

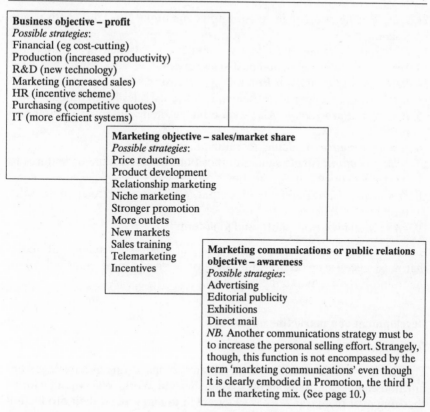

Business objective – profit
Possible strategies:
Financial (eg cost-cutting)
Production (increased productivity)
R&D (new technology)
Marketing (increased sales)
HR (incentive scheme)
Purchasing (competitive quotes)
IT (more efficient systems)

Marketing objective – sales/market share
Possible strategies:
Price reduction
Product development
Relationship marketing
Niche marketing
Stronger promotion
More outlets
New markets
Sales training
Telemarketing
Incentives

Marketing communications or public relations objective – awareness
Possible strategies:
Advertising
Editorial publicity
Exhibitions
Direct mail
NB. Another communications strategy must be to increase the personal selling effort. Strangely, though, this function is not encompassed by the term 'marketing communications' even though it is clearly embodied in Promotion, the third P in the marketing mix. (See page 10.)

Figure 2.1 The strategic cascade

3. *Internal factors – SWOT* Strengths, Weaknesses, Opportunities, Threats.
4. *Marketing objectives* Market share, market/product segmentation, product portfolio.
5. *Sales objectives* Sales targets/forecasts, territory/products, staff motivation.
6. *Communications objectives* Company/product awareness, perception/positioning, sales leads, reassurance, information.
7. *The market* Size, location, trends, decision-makers, international opportunities.
8. *The market need* Customer requirements, buying motives, changes in demand.
9. *Product portfolio* Specifications, benefits, profitability, life cycle.
10. *Competition* Market shares, product specifications, prices, promotions and expenditure, company images, nature and magnitude of selling activities, strengths and weaknesses.

11. *Price* Pricing strategy in relation to competition, special incentives and discounts.
12. *Distribution channels* Retailers, wholesalers, agents, delivery times.
13. *Service* Pre-sales, sales, and post-sales service.
14. *Research and evaluation* Pre and post measurement of markets, awareness, attitudes, copy, advertisements, concepts, sales leads, orders.
15. *Budget and programme* All expense budget items, all income, projected profit, cash flow.
16. *Human resources* Training, recruitment, motivation.
17. *Selling platform* Single selling propositions (SSP), outline of features to be stressed in all selling activities.
18. *Production plan* Build up of output, flexibility and relation to sales targets.
19. *Profit objectives* Both short- and long-term.

Before coming to the marcom plan in detail there is a sequence of events that must necessarily occur if a product or service is to be launched within the framework of a marketing operation.

Development of a marketing operation

MARKET ORIENTATION

The changes that have led to the acceptance of marketing as a management function can be traced as far back as the Second World War when factories changing over from war work were oriented to and around their production capability. The plant and equipment existed: the management problem was how to fill it. This was production orientation and while there were shortages and a lack of sophisticated consumer demand, it was adequate.

With the re-emergence of branded products, and as supply began to overtake demand, managements were faced with an excess of products and the need to find markets for them. This then was a position of sales, or product, orientation. In the first instance the management universe revolved about a production nucleus; in the second case, selling and sales were the centre of the operation. Finally, and following the lead of consumer marketing, the industrial nucleus has changed to the market-place – to the buyer and his or her needs and wants.

It should not be assumed too readily that the marketing concept has become accepted. There are still many companies which conform to product or sales orientation.

MARKET RESEARCH

A marketing operation starts then with an examination of markets and the requirements which exist or can be demonstrably created. Clearly many can be discarded as outside the scope of an organization's activities, but certain opportunities will be identified which can be translated into products or services that appear to meet basic criteria on manufacturing suitability, capital investment, management capability, profit margin and growth potential.

PRODUCT DESIGN

The identification of a potential product is a vital part of marketing development. This involves the services of research and development, design engineering, production and buying departments, all of which, coupled with a viability study, contribute to the evolution of a prototype. In the case of a service it is more likely that a 'concept' is looked at.

If at this stage the project appears to be sound and profitable, there follows a period in which the product is tested on the market to determine whether it provides the necessary benefits to satisfy the market needs. This may be termed compatibility evolution in which all the elements are subject to minor changes – product performance, appearance, price, shape, market segmentation – until there is a match between product and market needs and enough profit to justify the investment.

TEST MARKETING

The proving of the product in the market-place, based upon a prototype or pilot batch, after the policy decision to continue the project, brings the operation to the stage where a full marketing plan is written.

It is more than likely that such a plan will call for further sounding out of the market before the final stage of decision is reached. This is the point of no return for management and the last opportunity to assess the chances of success or failure.

The product must now be test marketed, that is to say given a full scale launching but in a restricted area. This is sometimes more difficult with an industrial product or service than with a consumer product or service, but nevertheless it is possible. Marketing can be restricted to a specified region only, or to a relatively small overseas market. Alternatively, the product can be promoted and exploited exclusively in one industry or market segment. All these activities will provide feedback of essential information which will lessen risk of failure.

DECISION

In the light of the assembled data, coupled with the best experience and judgement which can be brought to bear, the point of decision is reached.

The launch of a product within the framework of a marketing operation resembles a military exercise in which many armaments are brought to bear upon a target according to a carefully produced strategic plan. Furthermore, all the logistics of the operation are provided for, objectives are set, and contingency plans made for unforeseen events: in particular the reaction of the enemy forces.

The marketing strategy is developed into a plan and it outlines in detail the method of launching a product and the means for feedback and research in order to provide intelligence on how the campaign is progressing. Having set sales targets and campaign objectives against which to compare performance, it is vital to provide for flexibility in the organization so that rapid changes can be made in order to intensify or reduce the campaign as this becomes necessary.

ROUTINE MARKETING

Much of this chapter has dwelt on the marketing of a new product but clearly each of the disciplines involved can be applied to an existing product and its future development. Indeed each of the functions described above is essentially of a continuous nature.

The marketing mix

Just as in the recipe for a dish, the ingredients must be specified in quantity and quality, and the ways of mixing them together and cooking them made clear, so in marketing, the mixture must be blended to achieve maximum effect. The marketing mix has been defined as the 'planned mixture of the elements of marketing in a marketing plan. The aim is to combine them in such a way as to achieve the greatest effect at minimum cost'.

A more academic approach to the marketing mix postulates that it comprises what is known as the 4 Ps and S:

1. Product
2. Price
3. Promotion
4. Place

The S stands for service. The balance of ingredients then is made under 4 or 5 heads and depends largely upon the nature of the product and the markets it serves. For instance with petrol, price and place may be the key factors to success. With a new scientific instrument it is the product that counts. For a computer it may be both pre- and post-sales service which secure the sale.

In this book the mix will be considered as it relates to marketing communications in which each component has a communications element. The 'product', for instance, in addition to ultimately providing satisfaction to the customer, also sends out pre-sales messages which contribute to the development of the overall perception upon which a purchasing decision will be made. Its size, shape, colour, weight, presentation and packaging may signal high or low quality, reliability or ruggedness. The 'price' of a product can also have a communications element. In many instances where performance is difficult to evaluate, the price is taken as a measure of quality – the lower the price, the lower the quality. The 'promotion' element of the marketing mix is obviously where the main thrust of marketing communications is to be found. As to 'place', with industrial and business products this usually relates to a combination of distribution outlets and delivery time and is less important as a message source than in consumer marketing where the outlet may be a key factor in the purchasing decision. For instance, who could ever doubt the reliability of a product which Harrods decided to put on display? Finally 'service', pre-sales, sales, and post-sales, sends out a continuous stream of messages which enhance a product, or undermine it. In other words, first-class service can only help to build up a perception of a first-class product.

THE DECISION-MAKING UNIT

It is useful to consider the various people within an organization who might be called upon to contribute to a purchasing decision. These can be categorized under the following six headings:

1. *Specifier* This is simply the initiator or the person who first identifies the need for a purchase. It might for example be a design engineer who specifies that a certain component is required for a piece of equipment which has been newly designed. There may even be a number of people who have had a hand in the design, and this might lead to some debate as to which component, or type of component, precisely is required. A specifier might be persuaded to stipulate a catalogue number, thus in effect identifying who the supplier should be.
2. *Influencer* There will be all manner of people within an organization, especially the bigger ones, who have no purchasing function, but know someone who has. A regional factory manager for instance may have no authority to purchase his own raw materials, but he will more than likely have a point of view as to where the best material comes from. So for that matter might the operatives. Similarly a secretary might not have the purchasing authority for a new word-processor, but she won't be slow in keeping her boss informed of her preferences.
3. *Authoriser* In almost all corporate purchases there will be someone within the system who has the authority to say yes or no. This is very often the chief executive, even for the most trivial of purchases. Added to this may

be the functional head, say the marketing director, and then perhaps the finance director. In fact many of the major purchasing decisions are considered by the whole board.

4. *Purchaser* Someone has to place the order; probably an executive in the purchasing department, and sometimes also the purchasing manager.

5. *Gatekeeper* It is worth considering any possible barriers to communications reaching a target audience. A salesperson calling on a prospect might be impeded by a receptionist. Similarly with a letter, or a telephone call where a secretary might frustrate the connection.

6. *User* There might be one user, or there might be a hundred. For sure they will have a point of view, and this could just be the factor which decides in favour of one supplier as against another.

The point about being so precise in identifying target audiences, as also with segmenting the market, is that purchasing motivations will vary from one person to another according to each individual's interests. That being so, there is not just one selling message to be delivered but several depending on the audience being addressed. Not only must the message be fitted to the target audience, the media also must be similarly selected so as to get maximum impact.

A further factor in selecting the optimum audience is what has been called the 'buy class'. If for instance the purchase is a repeat of what has been a routine supply for some time and there is no change in the product, and say no change in the supplier, then the whole decision-making unit is hardly likely to be involved. Given a situation in which a supplier has failed in some way and is required to be replaced then the procedure is likely to become more involved with perhaps a few more people having a hand in the selection of a new supplier, ie the DMU will become larger. This is referred to as the 'modified buy' as opposed to the 'straight rebuy'. Come now to a 'new buy' and the size of the DMU increases yet further, and the higher the value of the purchase, the more people are likely to be involved.

CHANNELS OF PERSUASION

From the definition of the market, distinct groups of prospects will emerge whom it is desired to influence. To achieve this object, a number of methods of communication are available, such as personal selling, exhibitions and advertising. These are channels of persuasion, and the extent to which any of them is used must depend on the nature of the market and how far each communication channel fits in.

It is useful to consider each typical prospect in a given segment of a market and then to examine each channel of persuasion to determine if it is relevant. An 'impact diagram' (Fig. 2.2) can be developed in which the promotional mix can be demonstrated simply and visually. From this can be

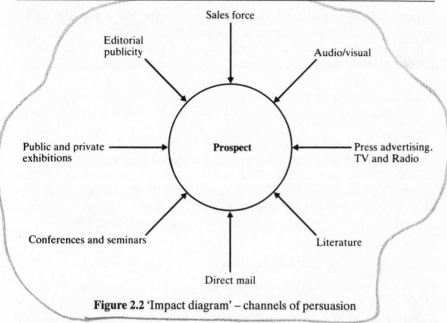

Figure 2.2 'Impact diagram' – channels of persuasion

developed the timing, intensity and interrelationship of each individual item (see Chapter 3, Figure 3.3).

The appropriation as between one channel and another is changing rapidly as the cost of personal selling increases at a faster rate than any of the non-face-to-face media. Hard evidence for this comes from the United States where selling costs have risen by over 200 per cent in 10 years. This compares with the consumer price index increase of under 150 per cent over the same period. Looking at each of the non face-to-face media, costs have increased more in line with the price index.

In the United Kingdom the average cost per 'industrial' sales call is well over £200 and rising. The outcome of this fact must lead to a completely new approach to what may be termed the media mix. For instance, in comparison with a salesperson who can influence say three or four persons a day, a publication can reach thousands or indeed millions of people in the same time. The message in an advertisement must necessarily be shorter and the percentage of readers upon whom the message will have any impact may be of a low order but the impact can be increased by various devices such as the number of appearances, size of space and so on. To be effective, a salesperson must first find the prospect and then secure an interview. With an advertisement this is not necessary: prospects need only be defined in general terms and a publication by virtue of its blanket circulation will ensure a large coverage of a potential market. The cost of delivering a particular message is also relevant since for a salesperson it may amount to a factor of 100 compared with an advertisement.

Since the nature of relative media costs is vital, not only in examining press advertising, but in the chapters which follow, it is worth considering in a little more detail.

Recent research in the United States has shown that the cost per sales call is rising at a rate approximately double the rate of that of advertising space.

In order to make a comparison with press advertising, another piece of American research has been taken, and here a sales call costs around 500 times that of an 'advertising contact'.

While the above data relate to the American market, it should not be difficult for any advertiser to produce his own figures in relation to his own company. These can be examined using the same criteria as in Chapter 3.

The role of marketing communications

The detailed role of marketing communications within the marketing mix is examined in the next chapter, but at this stage it is useful to consider it from a strategic point of view. The following table lists the respective functions of marcom, sales force, and the product itself:

Table 2.1 The five stages of the business-to-business selling process

Stage of selling process	Marcom role	Sales force role	Product or service role
Awareness	Very high	Relatively low	None
Comprehension	High	Relatively low	None
Preference	Medium	High	Some
Trial	Low	Medium	High
Satisfaction	Almost none	Very little	Very high

Source: Business Marketing

Setting targets

It is now time to examine in more detail the way in which the various promotional elements fit into the marketing plan.

It cannot be over-emphasized that in progressing towards more efficient and effective management, it is necessary to set objectives and to quantify them: to identify targets that are attainable and can be measured. Only in this way can exact courses of action be planned and progress compared with objectives.

The marketing strategy, in addition to outlining the plan of action, must set targets for each component part of it to achieve. There must be sales targets, production targets and profit targets. Such targets do not only deal with the short term, but cover as many years ahead as the nature of the business requires, sometimes up to five years, and, for capital-intensive industries, even longer.

Targets and forecasts differ in their nature and their purpose. A forecast can be considered to be an estimate for the future, assuming a number of constants and given an adequate amount of historical data from which to make an extrapolation. It is based upon the assumption that the past pattern of development is likely to continue in the future, subject to the influence of current events and possible future occurrences. A target, on the other hand, is a positive statement of intent backed up by whatever plan of action is judged to be necessary to achieve it. It may or may not have its basis in historical data or other guidelines.

To be effective a marketing plan must include a quantitative and qualitative statement of objectives to be achieved by promotion. It is not enough for a campaign only to provide 'a general background of support for the selling operation'.

As will be seen later, such campaign objectives may or may not include a direct relationship with sales targets. It is most important to discriminate between 'communications goals' and 'sales' since the former can well be achieved, and the latter not, due to other factors such as price, service or product performance.

An authoritative statement on advertising objectives comes from *Managing Advertising Effectively*.

- If advertising is to be effective and handled with the maximum efficiency it is necessary to know what it is intended to achieve. Hence the need for advertising objectives.
- Advertising objectives need to be expressed in clear, precise, appropriate, attainable and written terms.
- Advertising objectives must be distinguished from marketing objectives, but must be compatible with both these and the overall company goals.
- The process of setting precise advertising objectives is an invaluable management discipline which focuses thinking on the service or product.
- Objectives ensure that management are aware of the assumptions being made and consequently know the degrees of risk involved.
- Precise objectives assist in determining advertising budgets.
- Setting objectives aids the appraisal of advertising plans and control of ongoing situations by top management.
- Written objectives help the advertising and research agencies to prepare and evaluate relevant plans for advertising practice.
- Setting advertising objectives permits meaningful measurement.

The particular goals of a campaign will vary from time to time and company to company. A piece of research on this in the United States identified six major goals of advertising programmes, and these are shown in Figure 2.3 overleaf.

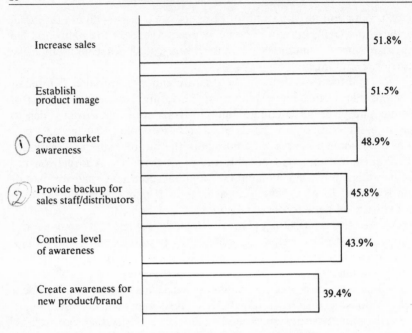

Figure 2.3   Advertising goals

Marketing communications strategy

A prerequisite of a promotional strategy and a plan of action is a detailed set of targets upon which the success of the marketing operation depends just as much as the capability of the factory to produce the goods.

If sales leads are required, a marketing plan must state how many; if product awareness is to be built up, this must be represented as the percentage of the potential market it is required to influence.

For example, a new branded range of electric switches is to be launched. It can be defined in advance whether they should become known as quality switches with built-in reliability, or whether as very cheap and easy to replace. Given the market share which it is required to achieve, a figure can be set for the number of buyers who must recall the brand name and be able to associate the product with the company name after a given period of time.

A further example might be the requirement in a large potential market, say for internal telephones, to identify the proportion of potential buyers who have an active interest at that particular moment; in other words to build up a live sales-call list. This may demand a campaign which will bring in large numbers of enquiries: the number can be quantified in advance. Given an existing conversion rate and knowing the sales objectives, the quantity of enquiries can be calculated. A further calculation as a double check will be the number of calls per salesperson, multiplied by the number of salespersons, minus the number of calls on existing accounts, which will equal the number of new sales leads.

If such targets are calculated for, say, a year, then split up into weekly figures based upon the build-up of the campaign and perhaps seasonal factors, it is possible within a very short time to determine whether the promotional mix is right and whether the campaign is producing the desired results.

Just as in the marketing plan there needs to be an optimum mix of the 4 Ps and S, so in marketing communications the media mix must be carefully formulated to ensure optimum performance. The appropriateness of each medium must be assessed methodically in relation to such factors as the potential market – its size, nature and location; the degree of competition and thus demand; the nature and availability of the media themselves.

The strength of each medium, therefore, must be considered and then each element brought to bear on the target in relation to the campaign as a whole. It is only at this stage that the cost of achieving the results can reasonably be considered. Matching costs to desired results is commonly known as the 'task method' of budgeting (see Chapter 3).

Running parallel with the selection of media and budgeting will be the interpretation of the selling message in terms that fit the various media to be employed. The two inevitably interact. A complex message may not be suited to posters or even sometimes to press advertising. Alternatively such a message may require large space advertisements to cover all the points adequately: or a series of small advertisements taking one point at a time may be more suitable. The number and form of direct mail shots will be influenced by the sales message and vice versa.

Finally an essential feature in any properly planned campaign is a predetermined scheme for measuring results and feeding them back quickly for corrective action (see Figure 2.4.)

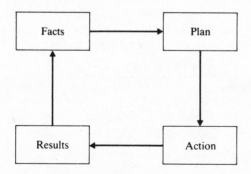

Figure 2.4   Feedback of results

Creative strategy

It is not the intention of this book to examine the creative aspects of industrial publicity in any detail since this is a specialized subject worthy of a book in its own right, but it would be wrong in this chapter on strategies to ignore the essential planning element which can be applied to the creative function.

It is in fact rare to come across the application of a disciplined approach to creativity. One agency has developed what is known as the 4D approach which, while devised largely in consumer terms, has equal relevance to business-to-business advertising. 4D is an abbreviation for four dimensions which break down as follows:

FIRST DIMENSION

Pinpoint the single selling idea – the particular consumer need that the brand satisfies

1. Understand the consumer needs and attitudes in relevant product fields.
2. Appreciate what competitive brands are offering in each field and all that our particular brand can offer.
3. Select and define what our brand will offer and to whom.

SECOND DIMENSION

Create the most effective and appealing expression of the idea

1. Recognize the real problems of gaining consumer attention and what is already competing for it.
2. Make sure the selling message is clear, distinctive, believable and convincing in consumer terms.
3. Create in all material an equally clear, distinctive total identity and underline the brand name.

THIRD DIMENSION

Find the most efficient media to communicate the idea

1. Select the media that reach the right people.
2. Choose the media best capable of carrying the message.
3. Use the media with the greatest impact, economically; with understanding of competitive strategies.

FOURTH DIMENSION

Eliminate uncertainty as far as possible before and after the advertising appears

1. See whether research can help, and understand just what is to be measured.
2. Be creative and forward-looking in the use of research.
3. Present results clearly, to help decision-making.

A methodical approach such as this does not set out to replace creativity, but merely to channel the creative process through each stage of development in a minimum of time and with maximum effect.

Checklist

1. Has a marketing plan been prepared?
2. Does the marketing plan set specific goals to be achieved by marketing communications?
3. In formulating a promotional strategy, has consideration been given to
    (a) Identifying the potential market?
    (b) The selling platform and the advertising message?
    (c) The most effective media?
    (d) Timing in relation to other sales activities?
    (e) The budget to achieve the objective?
    (f) Feedback, and measurement of results?
4. Has the usefulness of each of the following media been evaluated in order to arrive at an optimum media mix?
    (a) Press advertising
    (b) Direct mail
    (c) Exhibitions
    (d) Literature
    (e) Audio-visual
    (f) Photography
    (g) Editorial publicity
    (h) Conferences and seminars
    (i) Sales aids
    (j) Posters and display
    (k) Point of sale and packaging
    (l) Gifts and novelties
    (m) Television and radio
    (n) Brand name
    (o) Special events
5. Has the marketing communication strategy been developed in conjunction with the advertising agency?
6. Is marketing/sales management fully aware of its contents and purposes?
7. Has the cost per sales call been calculated together with the average number of calls required to secure the first order?

3

PLANNING AND BUDGETING

The need for a marketing strategy, encompassing all the elements of marketing and their interrelationships, was emphasized at the beginning of the book. From this overall strategy stems a plan of action for marketing communications which uses and integrates the channels of persuasion which are applicable.

After assessing the advantages and limitations of each medium, and the extent to which it can be used, a quantified media mix emerges. Expenditure figures can be put against each of the media on the basis that the total deployment of these forces will result in the objective being achieved. Thus the budget is compiled. In practice it is not simple, and the difficulties likely to be encountered will be examined in some detail later.

Planning

One aspect of marketing communications that needs to be touched on now is the time-scale. There is clearly an interrelationship between the start of a campaign and the receipt of the first order. Hence production planning must be related to sales planning and in turn it will be evident that sales will influence the timing of raw materials purchasing, tooling, finance, labour, up to the end of the whole business operation.

The chart, Figure 3.1, shows how certain key functions may relate to each other on a time and quantity basis. Here an investment of £500,000 is shown at a certain point in time. This is intended to represent a piece of capital equipment for the production of a new product. Soon after the initial investment, a publicity campaign begins – way before the equipment becomes operational. Start-up of production is shown to coincide with the first order being received. This planning is essential if adequate funds are to be available at each stage of development. Moreover it follows that having laid down such a plan it is necessary to build in accurate feedback in order to identify deviations as soon as they occur so that corrective action can be taken.

The time-scale of some industrial developments can be of a very long-term nature. Obviously it takes time to build a factory and to install new plant, often a year or two. It is equally important to remember that it can take fully as long to build up a demand for a product. The idea of beginning

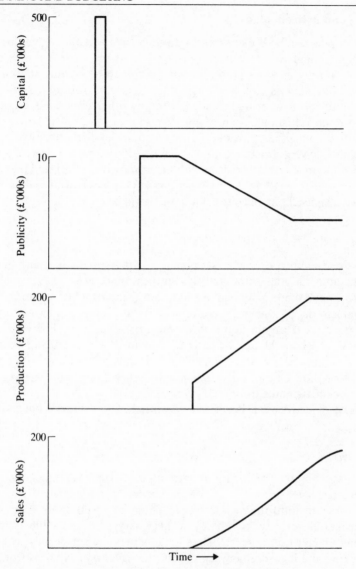

Figure 3.1 Timing of publicity in relation to capital, production and sales

a campaign two years before the product becomes generally available may be rare for some managements but for certain products and services, this is the length of time involved. This is not only true of a new product launch. For existing products there is a good deal of evidence that the sales of today are largely the results of efforts made months or years before and this is a significant factor in determining the promotional budget.

The ten-point marcom plan

A marcom plan can be broken down into ten discrete steps as given below. Some might argue that the opening stage should be *research* rather than *objectives*, and that is a fair point. If, then, all the necessary information for compiling the plan is not available, it is clearly important to conduct research into the market and, indeed, into any other topic as is required. Also, in the introduction, it is useful to give the overall context of the communication plan, eg the business objectives and/or the marketing objectives.

NB. The following structure is the same for a PR plan as for a marcom plan. The only difference is that one deals with the *product* (marcom), and the other with the *organisation* (PR). In actual fact, this structure is equally valid for the marketing plan itself but, of course, the content will be quite different.

STEP ONE – OBJECTIVES

These should comprise a clear statement of the aims of the plan, having regard to both the marketing and the business objectives. They should be simple to understand, unambiguous and, most importantly, quantified. So many plans in the past have set out to achieve 'an increase in awareness' of a given product or organization. What must be asked is by how much, by whom and by when. There is clearly no way in which a campaign can be evaluated unless there is a tangible, and thus measurable, objective. Furthermore, how can a budget possibly be set without knowing precisely what the benefit is going to be?

Marcom objectives can be many and varied. The principal ones are as follows:

1. Awareness

In a particular market segment, amongst a particular DMU category, what is the present level of awareness 'of the product', and what is the desired level in order to fulfil the task in hand? These may well be no more than well-considered guesses thought to be necessary to support the ultimate marketing objective but, nevertheless, figures must be set, if only to facilitate tracking and measurement, eg to raise the level of awareness from the current 20 per cent to 70 per cent within one year.

2. Perception

Again, with a similarly well-defined target audience, the level of awareness may be very high but it might be that the perception is substantially negative. So the task might be defined as to create a perception amongst those who are aware of the product that is at least 75 per cent positive, again within one year.

3. Information

Another marcom task is to ensure that there is an adequate flow of information to enable recipients to acquire the required positive perception.

4. Persuasion/Create Desires

It is no use having completely passive information sent out: it must be designed to lead ultimately towards purchasing. So it must be persuasive and create a desire to purchase.

5. Sales Leads

Very often in industrial marketing communications, a major role is to act as a filter and to identify those prospects who are likely to become customers within the foreseeable future. In other words, to avoid the wasting of time by the sales force by presenting only 'warm' or even 'hot' leads. These are usually in two stages. The first stage is to generate the maximum possible number of genuine enquiries which will be used to update or add to a database. These are then classified into those which represent short-term business, and those which are likely to come to fruition at some later date. At this stage, it is also useful to categorise them in terms of their sales potential, both short and long-term. It is here that the concept of lifetime customer value is introduced (see Chapter 19, 'Relationship Marketing').

6. Reassurance

Customers may well, after a sale has been concluded, begin to have second thoughts as to whether their decision was as good as they originally supposed. This is well illustrated by the fact that the largest readership group of car advertisements are people who already own the car in question, but are seeking reassurance that their purchasing decision was correct. This phenomenon is known as cognitive dissonance or post-purchasing dissonance, and must be allowed for in any campaign. In fact, 'reassurance of existing customers' is a fast-growing marketing activity, and is the basis of relationship marketing, where 'retention' is given a high-priority by comparison to 'acquisition' or 'transaction' marketing.

7. Correct Misconceptions

Within any business there is a continuous process of improvement involving all elements of marketing activity. It may be that in order to gain a competitive edge, a company promises a vastly reduced delivery period. Plainly, this will have no impact until it is both put into operation and *known* to be in operation.

8. Remind

It is not just that new people are continually joining the decision-making units; existing people need to be reminded of a product's existence so that at the next occasion when a purchase is to be made, it is in the forefront of the buyer's mind.

Primary Objectives

The foregoing might be said to be primary objectives, of which the most important are:

1. Awareness
2. Perception
3. Enquiries
4. Qualified leads

Secondary Objectives

Over and above the primary objectives, there are any number of secondary objectives which can be said to be subsidiary to the primary or core objectives. They might comprise, for instance:

1. Visitors to exhibitions or events
2. Delegates to seminars or conferences
3. Number and frequency of press releases
4. Number of editorial mentions (press cuttings). Also column inches
5. Number of feature articles
6. Audiences for VCR and audio tapes

The setting of targets for such activities will come only after the media plan has been developed, but they have a place in objectives as well as in the Measurement section.

NB. Profit, market share, and sales are not marcom objectives, since these criteria are also affected by other factors such as product performance, price, delivery and selling activity.

STEP TWO – ISSUES

The question here is, are there any issues, internal or external, which could undermine the achievement of the objectives? Or, alternatively, are there any which could contribute to achieving objectives? The state of the economy might be an important factor, as might unhelpful staff attitudes. If the communications objective is to establish a firm as the technological leader in the field, this will be to no avail if one of the product range has a poor performance. Indeed, it may be necessary to change the objectives in view of the existence of certain issues. It is useful for internal issues to refer to a SWOT (Strengths, Weaknesses, Opportunities, Threats) analysis, and for external issues to use a PEEST (Political, Economic, Environmental, Sociological, Technological) analysis.

STEP THREE – STRATEGY

There should be no confusion here of the difference between objectives, strategy and plan. Quite simply, the objective is what we aim to achieve, the strategy is how we intend to achieve it, and the plan is the details of the programme of activities which are to take place. The strategy, then, sets down in brief the policy for reaching the objective, ie 'by means of'. This should be no more than a sentence or two.

STEP FOUR – AUDIENCES (EXTERNAL AND INTERNAL)

In order to achieve maximum cost-effectiveness, there are two essential considerations. First, there is a need to fine-tune each market segment or niche market into those narrow groups which have the same homogeneous characteristics, and in industrial or business markets this means identifying the people belonging to the decision-making unit, not just the organizations. The second, and equally important, ingredient is to quantify the people concerned. The reason for this is that it will help in defining the media to be used.

For any campaign there are eight target audience categories, each of which might be further subdivided into ten or more categories to allow for the individual members, for instance, of a DMU (decision-making unit).

1. Existing customers (specifiers, internal influencers, authorizers, purchasers, gatekeepers, users)
2. Potential customers (specifiers, internal influencers, authorizers, purchasers, gatekeepers, users)
3. Past customers (specifiers, internal influencers, authorizers, purchasers, gatekeepers, users)
4. Intermediaries (retailers, wholesalers, agents, business partners)
5. External influencers (press, professional bodies, trade associations, consultants, academics)
6. Customer-facing employees (internal and external sales force, service personnel, telephonists, reception, secretaries)
7. Other employees (all others, regardless of status or position)
8. Future players (education) (universities, colleges, schools – students, lecturers, teachers)

STEP FIVE – MESSAGES

It is important to understand that these should not be a statement of the 'attributes' of the product or its function or performance. Rather, it is a matter of identifying customer benefits. After all, engineers can be said not to buy drills, but holes. One can even argue that customers only buy 'perceived benefits'; so if a customer *thinks* he or she is getting satisfaction, then to all intents and purposes he or she *is*. Thus, messages must be transmitted to satisfy the 'needs' or 'wants' of a prospect, which more usefully might be termed 'requirements'. Messages need to be prioritized and tailored to fit each person in the DMU.

Organizational buyer behaviour is obviously determined by a complex series of factors, both seen and unseen, known and unknown, and which may or may not be amenable to influence by external stimuli such as advertising. In so far as they are, there is a myth to be disposed of in the field of 'industrial buying'; namely, that decisions are mostly objective and are based upon price, delivery, performance and service.

Irrational Buying

There is very little evidence to support the contention that any purchasing decisions, even consumer, are largely irrational. Purchases are made to provide a perceived satisfaction and, as long as they do just that, such an action can hardly be held to be irrational. What they are, in fact, is subjective, but that is quite a different matter. The confusion arises out of the basic purchasing motivation. What we have had drilled into us is that people buy things to satisfy their 'needs'. This is not so. They actually make purchases for the most part to satisfy their 'wants', a fundamentally different human characteristic. What a person 'wants' is a highly subjective matter and varies from individual to individual, regardless of whether the decision is within the framework of a family purchase or a company (organization) purchase. Indeed, since the number of people known to be involved in the latter is so much larger, so also is the likelihood of decisions being all the more subjective, and complex at that.

The change from a philosophy of 'needs' to 'wants' can have quite a profound effect throughout the marketing process – in product design, in market research formulation, in pricing strategy, in selling, but, above all, in advertising propositions and in advertising media. This is not to say that objective factors do not enter into purchasing decisions. Quite the opposite, they enter into all such decisions to a greater or lesser extent. What is argued, however, is that there is also a high degree of personal motivation – to satisfy the self in all purchases whether for company, family or, indeed, self.

Purchasing Motivations

The whole basis of messages is to identify the critical purchasing motivations which apply in any given situation. The following are typical examples:

Additional supplier
Advertising/commercials
Availability/delivery
Brand image (product image)
BS 5750
Business gifts
Celebrity endorsement
Charity link
Cheapest
Colour
Comprehensive – no hidden costs
Contra-deal
Convenience
Corporate culture, corporate ethics
Corporate hospitality
Corporate image, reputation
Country of origin
Depreciation (slow)
Directed by boss
Dissatisfaction with competitors – cognitive dissonance
Durability
Early adopter (being the first)
Easy to purchase
Ego – snob value
Environmentally friendly
Ergonomics
Fashion
Investment (future growth)
Guarantee/warranty
Habit
Hard sell
I need it
I want it
Ignorance
Impulse
Incentives
Laziness
Literature design
Loyalty
Membership of trade/other quality organization
Most expensive
No alternative – unique
Packaging and presentation

Part of a series/range
Past experience
Post-purchase rationalization/reassurance
Post-purchase service
Prejudice
Pre-sales service
Pressure – peer group
Price/discount/terms
Product performance, attributes, benefits, quality – real and perceived
Promotional offer
Recommendation
Reliability
Safe purchase – fear
Sale or return – trial period offered
Salesperson – personality, knowledge, enthusiasm
Sales service
Size
Stockpile for use in future
Technology
Xenophobia (dislike of foreigners)

A final point to be considered is that the 'unique selling proposition' (USP) is becoming redundant since, as more and more products are undifferentiated, it follows that there is an absence of uniqueness. USP should be replaced by SSP, ie 'single selling proposition'. Whilst the idea might not be 'unique', it will be the most important benefit of the particular stage of a campaign. It also becomes the basis for the copy platform in advertising, and the basis of all other messages coming out from a company.

In summary then, it might be said that industrial purchasing decisions will take in all the objective and measurable criteria, to which can be added any number of other factors. Principal amongst these will be three:

1. The fear factor – 'No one was ever fired for purchasing an IBM' sums it up nicely. Making a safe purchase is to be preferred from the point of view of one's career progression.
2. The ego factor – What will other people think? This applies every bit as much amongst the decision-makers as in consumer purchasing motivation, and more so since the sums of money are likely to be much larger and there are so many other people to influence.
3. Personal preference – Quite simply, 'I like doing business with this company or, indeed, this person'. Furthermore, 'Since I am the decision-maker, why shouldn't I?' After all, it is easy enough to rationalize that the chosen product or service is as good as that offered by the competition.

Prioritizing messages

The starting point, having set down the customer benefits and then the relevant purchasing motivations, is to formulate every possible message. These must be related to each of the specific audience categories. A simple device is to produce a table with audiences on the left-hand side and messages across the top. For each audience, the messages which apply are identified and, having done that, the procedure is to prioritize all the messages for each target group. This will identify the 'single selling proposition' for a particular period of time, although it is likely to change as a campaign proceeds.

STEP SIX – MEDIA PLAN

Here we deal with the the channels of communication through which the messages are to be sent to the target audiences. These are the guts of the marcom plan, showing how each of the component parts relates to the others in both time, messages, and what might be termed brand identity. They will be matched to each of the target audiences for minimum wastage. Again, a table can be useful to show which media are intended to reach which audience.

By far the most important medium in industrial marketing communications is the trade, technical and business press. These journals comprise basically two parts, namely, paid-for space, ie advertising, and the rest, namely, editorial. Editorial breaks down into three categories – news, features, and comment. (More of the latter in Chapter 10 on 'Editorial Publicity'.) The usefulness of the press lies in the fact that any publicity secured in the editorial columns represents by far the best value for money of any medium. The other reason for its importance lies in the fact that more money is spent on journal advertising than in any other medium.

In all, the media spread is very wide, and growing. The following list gives no less than 46 external media, nine 'people message sources', and 25 internal media. This makes a total of 80 possible choices; and this does not include the sales force.

46 External Media

Aerial advertising
Audio/visual material
Books
Business gifts
Case studies
CD-ROM

Cinema
Competitions
Complaints
Corporate hospitality
Customer training
Customer user panels
Dealer panels
Direct mail
Directories and year books
Disks
Editorial publicity (press releases, features, visits)
E-mail
Events
Help lines
House magazines (internal, external, audio)
Internet
Letters
Literature – leaflets, brochures, catalogues, price lists, technical papers
Magazine advertising – consumer, trade and technical
Mailing – ads and press releases
Newsletters
Newspaper advertising – national, regional, local
Outdoor/poster
Packaging and presentation
Point of purchase
Presentations
Private exhibitions and receptions
Public exhibitions and trade shows
Radio
Road shows
Sales aids
Sales service actions
Samples
Seminars and conferences
Social events
Sponsorship
Telephone
Television
Video conferencing
Works visits

People as Media

Agents
Business partners
Consultants and academics
Customers
Employees
Journalists
Other outside influencers
Retailers
Trade associations and institutions

25 Internal Media*

Annual reports
Attitude surveys
Award ceremonies
Big boss visits
Campaigns presentations
Company magazines
Congratulations boards
Information on personal computers
Intranet
Literature
Local newspaper articles
Manager/employee team talks
Mass meetings
Notice boards
Pay packet inserts
Posters
Senior management presentations
Special competitions
Special launch brochures
Specialist consultants
Sports and social activities
Static displays
Trades union representatives
Training sessions
Videos/audio cassettes

*NB. Many of the external media channels can also be used as internal media, eg press releases can be sent to employees.

The above list of media is by no means exhaustive, as will be seen from Chapter 14 on 'Public Relations' which itself lists 100 'message sources'.

Broadly, it can be said that all media fall into one of two categories: above-the-line and below-the-line. These particular pieces of jargon have very little to commend them, and certainly no logic. Simply stated, above-the-line media comprise all those which pay a media commission to advertising agencies, such as print periodicals, television, radio, cinema and outdoor (posters). The remaining media will fall largely into the below-the-line category and include exhibitions, direct mail, editorial publicity, literature, etc. The inclusion of 'people' as media reflects the fact that they can often be one of the most powerful sources of promotional messages.

Each medium has its own strengths and weaknesses; those of the main media are discussed in the following chapters. For the purpose of planning, it is perhaps useful to examine here the 20 most used channels of communication:

INTER-MEDIA COMPARISONS

Medium	Strengths	Weaknesses	Comments
External communications			
Editorial publicity	High degree of credibility. Medium gives implied endorsement. Can provide widespread coverage of a market. Up to five times the number of readers of advertising. Free. Greater reach than advertising. Suitable for inexpensive reprints.	No control over appearance, positioning, timing or accuracy or whether it will ever appear. Cannot be repeated.	Very important for educating the market and providing widespread coverage.
Press advertising/ advertorials	Can provide widespread coverage of a market. Can control timing, size, colour, positioning, accuracy, message and media where it appears. Can be repeated.	Comparatively expensive. Fewer readers. Obviously biased.	Important to ensure repetitive exposure and to generate enquiries. Advertorials should first be offered to editors as exclusive features and also used as mailers.
Exhibitions	Very good for meeting people on a face-to-face basis. Buyer approaches the exhibitor.	Difficulty in getting prospects to attend. In competitive environment. A lot of distractions.	Also very good for corporate image.

Medium	Strengths	Weaknesses	Comments

External communications

Medium	Strengths	Weaknesses	Comments
Exhibitions (*continued*)	Can allow demonstration. Many times more cost-effective than visiting prospects.	Availability and timing of relevant exhibitions is not always suitable.	
Direct mail	Can be accurately targeted and allows considerable creative scope. Can provide a high level of response. Sample testing is possible. Can be progressively rolled out. Competition cannot monitor.	Inaccuracy of many databases. Difficulty of defining the decision making unit. Direct mail can give a poor image.	A newly emerging core medium.
Telemarketing	It permits direct contact with a prospect which can have a high level of impact and attention. It is also very fast. It can be designed to respond differently depending upon circumstances encountered. It can gather information as well as fix appointments for sales calls, etc.	It can be expensive. It needs trained operators to run effectively.	Vital for following up enquiries and to pull sales through dealers. It is also an important tool for gathering market information.
Audio/visual material	Very good for demonstration of complex products or concepts, especially where a personal demo is not possible.	Can be expensive.	This could be useful medium for seminars and conferences.
Business gifts	Can help prompt awareness and can keep a supplier name in front of a prospect.	Can be expensive if used indiscriminately. Can be seen as a bribe.	This could be a good means of maintaining a name in front of prospects during a lengthy

continued overleaf

INTER-MEDIA COMPARISONS (*CONTINUED*)

Medium	Strengths	Weaknesses	Comments
External communications			
Business gifts (*continued*)			decision-making process, provided the gift is appropriate and tasteful and contains a relevant sales message.
Case studies	Good for showing doubtful prospects how other businesses in a similar situation have benefited from a product and its application which helps build confidence and trust.	Selected businesses need to be genuine case studies and should have quantifiable benefits. Cannot be done for new products which are yet to be proved.	Case studies should play a vital role once the product starts selling and customers are available to provide information. Should be used in press articles, in literature form for use by sales force and in mailings and possibly as advertorials, as well as being used as subjects of seminars, presentations, meetings, etc.
Customer training	Ideal for ensuring customers can use products properly and are consequently satisfied and loyal users.	Only practical for products which have fairly limited sales and which are technical and need demonstration or training.	Useful competitive feature.
Customer user panels	A good means of obtaining feedback from customers on strengths and weaknesses of products and for stimulating new product development.	Can be used by customers as a product-bashing forum.	Vital and very cheap form of customer research.
Directories and yearbooks	Useful when a prospect is looking for a supplier.	Many are never used. Reactive and will only be consulted	Not considered relevant at a strategic level,

Medium	Strengths	Weaknesses	Comments
External communications			
Directories and yearbooks (*continued*)		once a prospect has made up his mind. Usually a highly competitive environment, with rival entries all together.	although some directories might be useful in specific situations. Entries may be free.
Help lines	A good means of maintaining contact with customers and prospects and helping to ensure that they do not have problems with a product.	People only use if/ when they have a problem. Cannot always resolve the problem over the telephone.	Good for selling to markets with relatively low technical expertise and where help can be vital in ensuring success of product.
Newsletters and house magazines	Useful for building understanding and trust in a company and confidence in its products. Can be very cost-effective.	Need a proven database of prospects and a continuous stream of news.	Could be very useful as a means of maintaining contact and building confidence.
Literature (leaflets, brochures, catalogues, price lists, technical papers, etc)	Good for conveying technical information and for more complex products and for where there is a lengthy gestation period for the purchase.	Can be too technical for the audience.	Essential for a technical product.
Presentation/ private exhibitions/ receptions/ seminars/ conferences	Good for communicating with small groups of people like journalists, etc.	Only practical for small groups and cannot therefore cover a large market. Can be expensive and requires administrative efforts to organise.	Ideal for communicating with journalists, dealers, buying groups, chambers of commerce, etc.
Road shows	Ideal for demonstrating products to a small group of people.	Many people agree to attend but do not turn up, especially in small retail	Always worth considering.

continued overleaf

INTER-MEDIA COMPARISONS (*CONTINUED*)

Medium	Strengths	Weaknesses	Comments
External communications			
Road shows (*continued*)		businesses which can be difficult to leave. Can be difficult to organise. Can be costly.	
Sponsorship	Especially good for strengthening loyalty to a known product or for enhancing a brand image by associating it with a sponsored event or activity.	Does not convey information about a product.	Not seen as especially important during the launch phase, although it might be considered once the product is becoming established.
Internal communications and communications with business partners			
CD-ROM/ E-mail/disks/ Internet	Good for computer-related products where facilities are available. It has novelty appeal, especially to technophiles.	Not everyone has CD-ROM, e-mail or computer facilities yet.	Not important for end users at this stage, but vital for internal and dealer communications.
Corporate hospitality	Very good for building relationships with selected contacts. Personal, and can be responsive to individual requirements.	Is only practical with a limited number of contacts. Can be expensive. Can create ill feeling among people who are not invited.	Useful for building relationships with key business partners and long-term customers.
House magazines	Good for communicating within an organization, especially where people are on remote sites and not in regular face-to-face contact.	Often seen as propaganda or as being too trivial.	Could be a good means of communicating with local offices in other countries and help overcome poor internal communications. Also with business partners.

RESPONSE MECHANISMS

An increasingly important discipline is to ask of any advertisement, editorial, direct mail shot, etc exactly what action it is intended to stimulate. There is a growing tendency to invite enquiries which, in turn, can be converted into qualified sales leads and, more particularly, added to a database for subsequent promotional activity. This, therefore, requires something more to be offered than simply 'Ask for further information'. Attractive response mechanisms are, then, of growing importance, ie what offering is likely to induce a prospect to take some action by way of making contact?

Advertisers and agencies in the UK have been very slow to recognize the benefits of using all types of advertising to obtain the names and addresses of potential customers. Enquiries generated from advertising may well lead to hot sales leads. But even if they don't in the short term, the fact that a prospect has made contact means that the company name and the product will achieve a firmer place in the memory bank. Even more important, with the growth of direct marketing, such enquiries add to and update the database. Another factor is that responses can be counted and their origin traced. This forms an important element in measuring effectiveness.

Obtaining a response, then, cannot be guaranteed simply by including the words 'For further information, write or 'phone...' in the body copy. This is really missing an opportunity. Two factors need to be taken into consideration. First, the invitation to make contact must be signalled boldly, eg a cut-out coupon. This can be coupled with all the other methods of contact, such as freephone, fax, E-mail and, of course, Internet. A particularly effective way of making it easy to respond is by using the Royal Mail 'Freepost Name' scheme. This is intended mainly for TV, cinema, radio, posters, etc, and only requires the consumer to remember the brand name. But it is equally useful for business marketing.

The second factor which has been picked up by many financial services organizations, amongst others, is quite simply to offer something which prospects would like to acquire. The offer may not be unique (though there is no reason why not), but it should certainly not be one of the cliché offers such as an alarm clock, key-ring or ballpoint pen. So what will achieve a good response? Here are some ideas that have been known to work:

A competition with attractive prizes

An independent guide to whatever business you are in (maybe specially commissioned by you, and preferably by someone who is well regarded)

A statistical guide to future industry growth

A specially produced booklet on safety, first aid, security, fire precautions, driving, personal finance, insurance, leisure, health, exercise, dieting, wines and spirits, etc

History of an industry or trade

World trends in whatever business you are in

Business tips on overseas travel in particular countries or regions

Foreign language phrasebook

Relevant dictionary or glossary, or any other textbook

Free magazine subscription

Free voucher, eg £100 off the next purchase

Free seminar on relevant or interesting subjects

Case histories

Samples

Research reports

Video or audio tape, CD-ROM or disk

Helpline

Business guides, eg 'Writing a Marcom Plan'

Demonstration

Free trial/sale or return

There is nothing wrong with offering an important piece of company literature if it can be made out to be something which people would like to
acquire. And if it is at all possible, let the offer be illustrated. It is no exaggeration to say that the addition of a good response mechanism can lead to
a ten-fold increase in enquiries. Finally, it is worthwhile piloting any ideas to
see what the response is likely to be or, alternatively, put it to your 'customer panel' or 'focus group'.

NB. It may well be that whatever is chosen as a response mechanism can
also be used as a business gift.

STEP SEVEN – TIMETABLE

This usually spans one year, which can be on a rolling basis. A shorter
timescale might be employed, but it is certainly useful to give some indication of a longer period ahead. In practice one can see how a direct mail
campaign will support an exhibition and how a press release can be timed so
as to avoid being scooped by an advertisement carrying the same story. The
use of a GANT chart is recommended, as is making provision for periodic
reviews.

A useful addition is an action schedule showing the various actions to be taken on a month-by-month basis in order to have the material and media ready in time for implementation.

A typical GANT chart is shown in Figure 3.2. It begins with a press conference and is followed by the campaign launch which reinforces the editorial publicity, with trade press advertising and an intensive direct mail operation backed by advertising in the national press. The sales force is held back in this plan in order to achieve sales leads which will enable it to operate more efficiently and with greater impact.

Trade press advertising, personal selling and editorial publicity are shown to be continuous with periodical sales review meetings. A second intensive phase is centred around a trade exhibition when direct mail and national press are re-introduced.

Campaign evaluation research is timed for the end of the first year, though there will be continuous feedback of results weekly or monthly against targets in respect of enquiries, quotations, visits and orders throughout the year.

STEP EIGHT – BUDGET

The basis upon which a marketing communication budget is established must clearly be the 'objective' in view or the 'task' to be done. This has been summed up well by the Institute of Practitioners in Advertising:

> Advertising expenditure must be related to the marketing objectives which the company aims to achieve. Therefore the company should start by forming a realistic marketing plan. Such a plan needs to be based on the knowledge of the overall size of the market, the company's share of the market, the economic trend of industry in general, and the trend of the company's own particular market. It should be shaped to take account of the weak as well as the strong points of the product and its probable life cycle, and the same competitive products. It should pin-point who buys the product and why, and the several influences on the buying decision that may exist at various levels from the factory floor to the board room.

In view of the good sense contained in this statement, it is surprising to find that on the evidence of some researchers and in the experience of many experts, the 'task method' of budgeting is often not used in industrial marketing. The same IPA publication makes a statement which seems too far-fetched to be believable were it not supported by many similar views – 'Think of a number. Halve it. Then decide what your advertising has to do. This is not the exaggeration that it may seem of some companies' way of deciding how much to allocate for industrial advertising.'

Another authority, Harry Henry, has written,

> Since British industry is currently spending upwards of £1,800 millions a year on advertising, it might be expected that the companies and organisations responsible for such expenditure would take reasonably seriously the problem of deciding

	Jan.	Feb.	Mar.	Apr.	May	June	July	Aug.	Sept.	Oct.	Nov.	Dec.
Sales conference / Sales review meetings	X				X			X			X	
Press conference / Press releases		X	X	X	X	X	X	X	X	X	X	X
Private exhibition			X									
National press advertising		▭	▭								▭	
Trade press advertising		▭	▭	▭	▭	▭	▭	▭	▭	▭	▭	▭
Direct mail		X	XX	XX						XX	XX	
Sales literature / Sales aids	X											
Trade show		X									X	
Personal selling			▭	▭	▭	▭	▭	▭	▭	▭	▭	▭
House magazine feature article												
Campaign evaluation research												X

Figure 3.2 Detailed scheduling of promotional media

just what ought to be the size of their advertising budgets. Whether or not this is invariably the case, examination of the variety of methods used for the purpose, and the wide divergence often found between what an advertiser thinks he is doing and what he actually does in practice, indicates that this is an area of managerial activity replete with confusion.

An enlightening piece of research work on this subject is to be found in McGraw-Hill's *Special Report on Buying and Selling Techniques used in the British Engineering Industry*. This analysed the various methods of arriving at a promotional budget (see Table 3.1).

Table 3.1   Basis of advertising budgets (1)

	Percentage of respondents
(a) Percentage of last year's sales turnover	7
(b) Percentage of this year's expected turnover	17
(c) Percentage of last year's actual and this year's estimate	4
(d) A fixed target without specific reference to sales	39
(e) No known basis	29
(f) Other formulae	4

A later piece of research conducted by the author provided data which are given in Table 3.2. This brought to light the fact that many industrial companies are now using techniques which approximate to the task method.

Table 3.2   Basis of advertising budgets (2)

	Percentage
% sales turnover	4% (17)
Cost related to objective	68% (53)
Arbitrary sum	14% (30)
Other	14% (NA)

Note: See Appendix

Since the data in Table 3.2 were derived from the larger industrial advertisers, they are probably not typical, but they can certainly be regarded as indicative of a more rational approach to the matter.

It is perhaps useful to examine briefly each of the bases upon which a budget is arrived at.

Percentage of last year's turnover

This has the advantage of being simple to arrive at and indeed may be valid in circumstances in which a market is static both in terms of total demand and competitive activity. It makes no provision for a company to use promotional expenditure to improve its position, neither does it take into account any change in products, economic conditions, customer requirements or competition. It must therefore be regarded as a hazardous method of determining the level of promotion.

Percentage of this or next year's anticipated sales

At least this has the merit of being related to future events and at the same time being easy to calculate, but it does not face up to the reality of the marketing situation. If the demand for products has suddenly increased, a promotional budget based upon a fixed percentage of forecast sales may be higher than necessary, and indeed may result in orders being received which cannot be satisfied by the production capacity. Conversely if market demand enters a period of decline a higher percentage expenditure may be required to produce the required sales results. Furthermore, to use next year's sales as a basis ignores the fact that for some capital goods, the gestation period for promotional activities is more than one year.

In any case to use a percentage of anything presupposes that one can obtain from some source the optimum percentage level for efficient expenditure. That this is not so is evidenced by the wide range of percentage expenditures in different industries. An example quoted in the appendix to the IPA publication mentioned above shows the range of expenditure in the United States (see Table 3.3).

Fixed figure unrelated to sales

The kindest observation that can be made on this method of fixing the budget is that it may be supposed that over a period of years it has been found by trial

Table 3.3 Advertising as a percentage of sales

Industry	% of industrial sales expended for industrial advertising	
	High	Low
Paper	4.0	0.2
Printing and publishing	1.65	0.1
Chemicals	9.3	0.003
Rubber and plastic products	8.0	0.1
Primary metal industries	3.0	0.0004
Fabricated metal products	16.2	0.003
Machinery	18.5	0.001

NB. Even where specific product groups are examined, wide differences occur.

and error that a given expenditure results in a level of sales and profit which is regarded as satisfactory. This method, however, can hardly claim to have any place in modern marketing, or, indeed, in modern business management.

Competitive advertising

Some companies are known to base their publicity on what their competitors are doing. While this has the advantage of at least countering competitive activity, it assumes that it is possible to measure competitors' expenditure with some degree of accuracy: it also assumes that the competitors know what they are doing and have arrived at their budgets on a sound basis. Both assumptions are unlikely.

The 'task method'

This involves defining the objective, or the task to be done, then determining the best media mix to achieve it. From this a budget can be drawn up which will represent the best estimate of the optimum promotional expenditure. (See Figure 3.3.)

In a comprehensive review of budgeting methods Harry Henry lists ten other possible lines of approach:

Intuitive, or rule of thumb This is someone's subjective assessment of 'what should do the job', and is an amalgam of hunch and experience (experience being what has been done before, not necessarily having regard to its outcome). It is very dependent upon the person making the decision: should he be replaced, a different view may be taken.

Figure 3.3 'Task method' of budgeting

The affordable method   This method, spending 'as much as can be afforded' (which means what is left over after all other cost and profit requirements have been met) is not one which many firms claim to follow. But the attitude towards advertising which this approach reflects does in practice often emerge as a constraint on a good many other methods of budget determination, including those which on the face of it are rather more logical.

Residue after last year's profits   Often regarded as being a ploughing-back of profit, or as re-investment in the future, this approach concentrates on the source of funds rather than on the purpose to which those funds are devoted.

Percentage of gross margin   This keeps advertising expenditure in proportion to turnover and profits, but begs the question of what advertising is for, or how its cost-efficiency may be improved.

Fixed expenditure per unit of sales   Although expressed in different terms – 'so much per case for advertising' – and born of standard costing procedures, this method is not all that different in its effect, in the short term, from the percentage of sales method.

Cost per capita   In this approach, which is used mainly by industrial advertisers, the advertiser calculates the advertising cost per head for his present customers and, when he wishes to gain more, increases his expenditure pro rata.

Matching advertising to brand share   This is an apparently sophisticated approach, based in fact on rather simplistic analysis. It is essentially a development of matching competitive advertising.

The marginal return approach   The cost of an extra unit of advertising activity is compared with the increased profit which is expected in consequence. A standard technique in direct response advertising, it becomes very complicated when there are other factors in the marketing mix, and has to be used in conjunction with marketing models.

Marketing models   These are designed to describe the relationship between sales or profit and the main elements in the marketing mix – including advertising – and from these relationships it is theoretically possible to determine the optimum advertising budget. The technical problems involved in gathering and interpreting the necessary data are, however, formidable.

Media weight tests   The theory behind this approach is that if, in a test situation, a given weight of advertising expenditure produces a particular level of sales, the level of advertising in the total market which will produce a required level of sales can be deduced. For a variety of reasons, the theory rarely works in this way.

Cost of advertising

As has been indicated, the cost of advertising in relation to the overall marketing expense and to turnover varies considerably, and particularly between one industry category and another.

In drawing up budgets, it is important to make provision for every element of expenditure and to relate it as far as possible to each product group or profit centre.

A good example of the various items which might be included in a typical publicity budget is given below

1. Advertising programme:
    (a) Space costs
    (b) Production
    (c) Service fee
    (d) Agency commission
    (e) Pulls for internal circulation
    (f) Research
2. Other media:
    (a) Direct mail
    (b) Exhibitions and trade shows
    (c) Postage
    (d) Sales literature
    (e) Customer publications
    (f) Films and AV
    (g) Photography
3. Public relations
4. Department's expenses:
    (a) Salaries (plus extras)
    (b) Travel and entertainment expenses
    (c) Office equipment and supplies
    (d) Telephone and cable costs
    (e) Rent, light and heat for department
    (f) Subscription to associations, news services, magazines
    (g) Press cutting services

To allocate each of these items to profit centres may be difficult and will certainly involve a degree of estimating, but the procedure is necessary if a true level of profit is to be calculated. Perhaps the biggest obstacle is attitude of mind which tends to allocate publicity expenditure as part of the general overhead rather than an intrinsic part of the cost of 'production and distribution'. A cost accountant, however, will find that the breakdown of publicity costs is no more involved or inaccurate than the breakdown of works supervision or even of machine time and expense on the shop floor.

ANALYSIS OF MEDIA EXPENDITURE

The allocation of expenditure to the various media varies a good deal as between consumer and industrial publicity (see Figure 3.4).

The results in Table 3.4 based on the author's own research show press advertising at the head of the list, with sales literature featuring predominantly. On the whole, the breakdown between principal media groups has shown very little change over time. Further confirmation is given in a study by MIL Research which is reproduced in Table 3.5.

The promotional mix will of course vary considerably from one company to another and the above data are simply averages for industry as a whole.

Financial appraisal

The failure of the task method of budgeting to gain the widest usage in business can be explained in two ways. Firstly it involves a great deal more work, and a considerable measure of expertise. Given that this is available, the second reason may be the belief that, having arrived at a budget by 'scientific' means, it is now sacrosanct and regardless of any other considerations cannot be changed. It must be emphasized that the only element of science

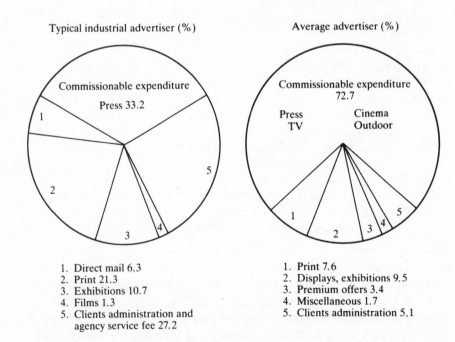

1. Direct mail 6.3
2. Print 21.3
3. Exhibitions 10.7
4. Films 1.3
5. Clients administration and
   agency service fee 27.2

1. Print 7.6
2. Displays, exhibitions 9.5
3. Premium offers 3.4
4. Miscellaneous 1.7
5. Clients administration 5.1

Figure 3.4 Comparison between industrial and consumer appropriations (*Source*: IPA Forum 19, Institute of Practitioners in Advertising, London)

Table 3.4 Analysis of media expenditure

	Percentage
Press advertising	33% (40)
Sales literature	28% (27)
Exhibitions	13% (15)
Direct mail	14% (9)
Public relations	13% (9)

Note: See Appendix

Table 3.5 Expenditure on business-to-business media

	Percentage
Business press	34.5
Brochures, catalogues	14.4
Exhibitions	14.1
Direct mail	8.1
PR	6.0
Directories	5.5
Regional newspapers	2.9
National newspapers	2.8
Videos/AV	2.8
Premiums	2.1
Point of sale	1.5
Posters	1.4
TV	1.2
Sponsorship	1.0
Radio	0.5
Others	1.2
(Base 807 advertisers)	100.0

in the task method of budgeting is its methodology. The essential 'mixture' is still a matter of judgement, and can be accurate or inaccurate.

Most important of all is that a budget, arrived at in this way, must now be subjected to appraisal in terms of its relationship to the total sales expense, and in particular to the projected turnover and profit. It is more than likely that adjustments will have to be made, not only to the marcom budget, but to the sales expense and turnover before a profit margin is arrived at which is satisfactory in business terms.

An advertising campaign may be expanded or cut back providing the implications are known, and it is not done blindly. As with any investment, the returns are seldom linear, and it may be found that a reduction in advertising expenditure, say, of 40 per cent will result in a reduction in effectiveness of only 15 per cent or a reduction in sales turnover of only 2 per cent. A planned initial approach to the budget enables revisions to be made from a sound base which is likely to produce results closer to target than a blind guess.

Finally it is interesting to note how the budget breakdown compares with that in the United States (see Table 3.6).

Table 3.6 Media expenditure, United States (*Source*: McGraw-Hill Research Report 8009.4)

	Percentage
Press advertising	36
Sales literature	24
Exhibitions	20
Direct mail	8
PR	5
Other	7

STEP NINE – MEASUREMENT

Campaign evaluation is both vital and simple, providing the objectives are clear and quantified. Furthermore, it is important to carry out some form of tracking in order to make adjustments to the campaign if targets are not being met. It is necessary to stress that the only relevant criteria are the communication objectives as opposed to, for instance, the marketing objectives.

STEP TEN – RESOURCES

This relates to human resources, both in terms of the number of people to be involved in implementing the campaign and in their professional capability and motivation to carry out the work involved with maximum efficiency. They must obviously have the time needed to do the job and the necessary talent and motivation. There may be a case for providing some kind of incentive: financial perhaps, or a new job title, or simply the opportunity to broaden their experience. This part of the plan should also take in the use of outside services, such as advertising agencies and PR consultancies. Here also is where any training needs and expense should be covered.

NOTES ON THE MARCOM PLAN

1. Research

Should any essential factors be unknown, provision should be made for initial research over and above that which will be conducted at the 'evaluation' stage.

2. Quantifying

Particular attention should be paid to quantifying objectives and target audiences, as well as a media breakdown.

3. Budgets

Budgets should be task-oriented bottom up rather than top down, using an arbitrary figure. The actual media to be used should be indicated – in advertising, for instance, define the publications, frequency and size of the ads. If a direct mail campaign, think about how many shots, to whom and with what response mechanism. With seminars, consider how many delegates, how often and where.

4. Media Plan

This should represent the main body of the report and list the media in detail, and also the rationale for using those chosen and for those rejected.

5. Executive Summary

It is always useful to include at the beginning or end a short summary of the proposed actions and the reasons behind them, together with the intended outcomes. Also, include an introduction, the costs and background notes.

6. Tables and Charts

These should be used where possible. In particular, a GANT chart is useful for the timetable.

CONTENT OF THE MARCOM PLAN – THE TEN Ps

The ten-point marcom plan gives a structure which takes each activity in turn, and follows a logical progression. As to the content, it might be supposed that this simply takes in the mainstream media as encompassed by above- and below-the-line. This, after all is provided for in the classical Four Ps, where the third P stands for promotion.

Before examining the role of promotion as such we should look at the message cues that might be transmitted by the other three Ps – product, price and place.

1. Product

The fundamental marketing concept postulates that a customer does not buy a product but rather a produce performance or, more to the point, a satisfaction. Furthermore, the customer bases purchasing decisions upon the perceived benefits that will be received as against the actual physical product attributes.

The total product offering is not what the supplier offers, but what the customer sees to be on offer. It may well be that packaging and presentation constitute the key factor in a purchasing decision, particularly with the increasing number of undifferentiated products. Indeed, with some of these – for instance, cigarettes, cosmetics, and drinks – it could be argued that the package is the product. Increasingly, what comes inside the pack is identical as between one brand and another and, where that is so, the package is the single most important purchasing influence. With products that sell in supermarkets, this is particularly important.

An interesting example of packaging and presentation concerned a range of divan beds where the mattresses were finished in a variety of fabrics from the traditional to the very modern. A further variable was that the choice finishes on offer were between of a soft plain surface, a quilted finish, and the rather old-fashioned button-type fixing. The customers unhesitatingly chose a quilted finish in the traditional fabric, notwithstanding the fact that all the mattresses were physically identical.

Research evidence shows that the buyer is influenced to a critical degree by the size of a product and its shape, colour, weight, feel, typography, and even smell. The successful package is the one that appeals to both conscious and unconscious level of the consumer's mind. The conscious mind recognizes just the product, whereas the unconscious mind is motivated by the package.

It must not be supposed that 'presentation' of product applies only to the consumer field. The study of 'organizational buyer behaviour' shows clearly the many subjective factors that enter into a purchasing decision. Gone are the days when a handful of components was bundled into a black box, and all that mattered was that the performance matched the specification. The appearance of an industrial product sends out signals. The design, shape, colour and so on all combine to create an impression on the one hand of a dynamic, innovative, go-ahead company or, on the other, of a traditional or maybe a backward one. It is important to realize that it usually costs no more to put a conscious effort into good product presentation, whereas to create the same effect by means of conventional promotional media is often very expensive.

Consideration must further be given to the brand name as part of the total product offering. Any product is going to be called something by its customers and users, so it might as well be a name of the company's own choice, and one that brings with it certain positive attributes. Does it have or imply a favourable connotation? Is it short and memorable? Can people actually pronounce it? Does it support the claims being made of product performance? And then there is the graphic symbolism or the associated logotype: a good brand name can evoke a feeling of trust, confidence, security, strength, durability, speed, status, and the like.

2. Price

For many if not most products, the signal given by price, and thus the effect on purchasing, follows the economist's normal law of demand. As price falls, so demand increases. With everyday products, where price levels are common knowledge, the message conveyed by price is indicative of good or bad value for money: hence the success of supermarkets in being able to offer heavily branded products at a lower price than the local grocer and, going one stage further, the success of own-label products which undercut the established branded ones.

For some products, however, the normal rules do not apply, as is shown for instance in Figure 3.5. In this case, price is taken as signalling quality or prestige and, within limits, creates a desire to acquire which increases as the price increases. Without delving into the ethical considerations, the fact is

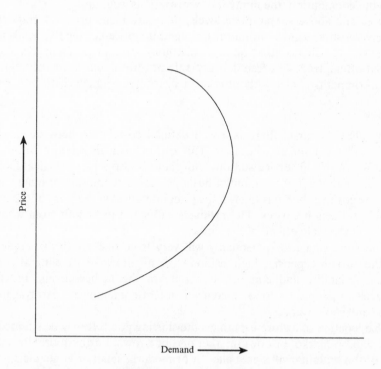

Figure 3.5   Where price is taken as signalling quality or prestige

that in some circumstances a reduction in price will signal a reduction in quality and vice versa. This is particularly so where the customer is unable to make a judgement on any other basis – a watch, for instance, or a hi-fi set, or cosmetics in general. There are other factors, of course, such as appearance and availability, but in the main the assessment of quality in such items will be based heavily upon price.

The same price–demand relationship is found in products that are purchased as gifts. Here a higher price may be paid largely as a compliment to the receiver of the gift, or for that matter to enhance the prestige or satisfy the ego of the giver. Once again, it is a matter of perception on the part of the buyer. It matters little what message the seller intends to convey: the purchase will be determined by the way in which the buyer interprets the message.

An example in the field of services was in a programme of seminars where, in order to attract larger numbers to a particular subject area, the price per day was dropped progressively over a period of years: the numbers decreased. In desperation, the sponsor offered the seminar free of charge. No one attended. At the other end of the scale, an advanced course of instruction was offered at a much higher price than hitherto, and higher than the competition: the number of registrations went up.

Over and above simple price levels, there are many price offerings that can give positive signals without resorting to the price-cutting that leads to a price war. Credit facilities, quantity discounts, prompt payment discounts, special offers, trade-ins, free delivery, sale or return, and so on can all provide a competitive edge without necessarily incurring a high cost.

3. Place

Physically, of course, there is a well defined correlation between market share and the number of outlets. This can be seen in car hire firms, for example, or petrol service stations. But there is also a psychological factor, and that is that every retail outlet has a perceived reputation or image, and if this is positive then it is likely to bear an influence on the sales of the individual products it carries. The products will stand to benefit from what is known as the 'halo effect' of the store.

The store image or personality will vary from one group of people to another. So an expensive high-fashion store might evoke a feeling of confidence, reliability and comfort to people in the higher-income bracket, whereas to people on lower incomes it might communicate extravagance, waste and snobbishness.

The location of a store is perhaps the starting point. It may be situated in either an up-market or down-market part of a town. Furthermore, the exterior of the building will signal ancient or modern, small or large, elegant or drab – even the name and fascia will convey an impression. The interior of the store is even more important. The size of gangways, displays, colour, sound, smell, temperature, decor, and lighting will all play a part. Added to this is store personnel, all of whom will be transmitting messages depending upon their age, sex, race, speech, product knowledge, friendliness, and helpfulness. In the personnel field it is most easy to swing from a very positive perception to a very negative one due simply to lack of staff selection, training, and motivation.

In putting together a marketing communications mix, the question here is to what extent might 'place' be important in enhancing a product perception in such a way as to increase sales? Let us take an example of two extremes. In one case take a new Albanian wristwatch being offered by a soap-box salesman in Woolwich market. He claims that its accuracy is greater than any other watch owing to the application of new technology. The price is at a bargain knock-down level of £49.00 including gold bracelet. Now take the same watch and the same claims and price, and put it in the window of Harrods in Knightsbridge. Which 'place' is likely to be most successful? An interesting reflection on the reputation of Harrods is that, referring to the previous section, if the price of the watch were put up to £149.00, the sales might well increase.

4. Paid-for advertising

This category refers to all above-the-line media, ie all those offering a media commission. Take any product advertisement, and it might be supposed that its sole purpose was to send a selling message. It may do this well, or not so well, but whatever the case it will also create an impression of the organization behind the advertisement. Thus it has two tasks, and both messages will contribute to the marketing objectives.

5. Promotion

As would be expected in a marcom plan, all the other deliberately placed, or active, message sources must be included, ie below-the-line – sales promotion, merchandising, exhibitions, publicity, etc.

6. Personal Selling and Service

A peculiarity of the way in which marketing and marketing communications have developed lays down that selling is a sub-set of marketing but not marketing communications. So what is it doing in a marcom plan? The answer is very simple, namely that whilst the marcom function does not control selling, which after all is the responsibility of sales management, it is nevertheless vital that the two be integrated. The same messages must come from both face-to-face sources (sales force) and from non-face-to-face sources (advertising). Timing must be co-ordinated in order to be mutually supporting, and even synergistic. This category, then, takes in the field force, the back-up internal selling function, estimators, technical sales, telesales, service engineers, merchandisers, demonstrators, transportation and delivery.

7. Publicity

The fourth of the active message source channels has to be publicity, that is to say, mentions in the press, whether news, features or comment.

8. Third Party Messages

Arguably the most important single source of persuasion, the endorsement by a credible message source such as a customer is something which is often overlooked, but must surely be provided for. There may be a feeling that there is not much one can do to stimulate the transmission of favourable messages by third parties, but this is not so. This is something that can easily be encouraged and assisted by a continuous stream of information about the product and the company, so that any supporter is well provided for with the latest facts. The information will also act as a continual reminder.

9. People

With the development of relationship marketing, more and more attention is being given to the messages which are sent out by employees at all levels. Simply, they can be favourable, passive, or unfavourable both about the product, and also the company. Increasingly, it is seen that for a company to operate within a total marketing concept, *all* employees have a marketing role to perform; it is only a question of whether they are customer-facing, or providing some kind of service or contribution to those that are. We need to give proactive consideration to verbal and non-verbal communications, knowledge, motivation, enthusiasm, and so on.

10. Passive Messages

Message sources which were never intended to communicate but do, eg smoking policy, factory/office building, dress code, culture, company cars, layout of correspondence and response time, etc.

Checklist

1. In timing a promotional campaign, is there a clear understanding throughout the company on the length of time between starting marketing communications and seeing results in terms of sales?
2. Is a master schedule produced, as a routine for each campaign, to show the relationship between all the various media and including sales force activities?

3. Is budgeting for promotion based upon the 'task method'? If not, is top management aware of the shortcomings of other methods?

4. Is the advertising agency committed to 'task method' budgeting, rather than accepting a sum of money and recommending the best way of spending it?

5. Has any attempt been made (a) to monitor competitors' expenditures: (b) to obtain inter-firm comparisons – in particular the proportion of promotional expenditure in the marketing expense budget, and as a percentage of sales?

6. Has a strict system of budgetary control been established?

7. Is this broken down into shorter control periods than a year?

8. Has provision been made for each item of expenditure to be set against product groups?

Table 3.7 Budget outline

	Product 1	Product 2	Product 3	Total
Marketing services				
salaries				
overheads				
expenses				
Advertising agency				
PR consultancy				
Press advertising				
space				
production				
Direct mail				
database				
production				
distribution				
Exhibitions				
space				
design				
standfitting				
transport				
staff				
miscellaneous				
Literature				
creative				
production				
distribution				
Photography				
Video and AV				
production				
distribution				
Research				
Editorial publicity				
Posters				
Point of sale				
Packaging				
Conferences and seminars				
Sales aids and manuals				
Gifts and Christmas cards				
Miscellaneous (enumerate)				
Contingency				
Total				
Sales forecast				
% Promotion to sales				
Other marketing expense				
Total marketing expense				
% Marketing expense to forecast sales				

Part 2

ELEMENTS OF MARKETING COMMUNICATIONS

4.

PRESS ADVERTISING

Press advertising relates to any form of advertisement which appears in a publication and is paid for. It is viewed primarily from the point of view of selling a product or service, though clearly it can have other aims such as building goodwill, establishing confidence in an organization, or recruiting personnel.

Purpose

The purpose of press advertising, as of any other channel of persuasion, is primarily to communicate a selling message to a potential customer.

The starting point is what is known as a 'target group audience' (TGA) or a defined market or public, i.e. a number of people whom it is wished to influence. A proportion of this public will be exposed to the advertising pages of various publications and, depending upon the impact of an advertisement, a proportion of these will take note of a message.

Press advertising in the industrial sector has come in for a good deal of criticism on the grounds of its ineffectiveness, relative to the money spent on it. Much of this has arisen from the inadequacy and inaccuracy of media selection and the incompetence of some advertisement design and copywriting. Often the failure, however, is traceable to different reasons, namely that the purpose of advertising has not been defined in advance or, if it has, it has been lost sight of.

For example, there is the sales manager's view when he or she sees some hundreds of thousands of pounds being spent on press advertising, and relates this to the number of additional salespeople that could be put on the road for such an expenditure. If, however, the purposes of these two channels of persuasion have been pre-defined, the one to provide active sales leads, the other to clinch the sale, they become mutually dependent and not competing alternatives.

The position of press advertising within the broad communications framework must be established at the outset, and its strengths and weaknesses analysed. The following criteria examine press advertising in relation to other media.

1. *Market size*   The total size of a market segment and all of the people that go to comprise it must be the starting point of media choice. With a market size of ten units there is clearly not much room for more than personal contact supported by whatever back-up might be required. Move to 100 units and the situation hardly changes. At 1000 the personal contact must become selective, and here one can add direct mail, specialized press, editorial publicity, literature, maybe sponsored video and AV, local demonstrations and perhaps telephone selling. At 10,000 personal selling falls away and press advertising and most other non-personal media take over. Exhibitions have a particular merit here, combining unit economy with the benefits of face-to-face contact. Direct mail sometimes starts to become difficult to handle. Editorial back-up is of course well worth full exploitation. At 100,000 one starts to move into mass media with television, radio, national newspapers and posters replacing or heavily supplementing the other media already listed. The following grid can be used to evaluate the whole range of media in relation to the size of the audience.

AUDIENCE SIZE GRID

	100	1,000	10,000	100,000	1 M
Personal contact					
Letters/DM					
Telephone					
Demonstration					
Seminars					
Conference					
Private exhibition					
Public exhibition					
Literature					
AV					
Editorial publicity					
Press advertising					
Radio advertising					
TV advertising					
Poster advertising					
Sponsorship					

2. *Intrinsic impact*   The extent to which an advertising message is transmitted, received, stored and able to be recalled with accuracy is vital. Each

medium has its own intrinsic impact potential. Clearly a medium which facilitates two-way communication is top of the list, and so personal selling, exhibitions, demonstrations, telephone selling are all worthy of a high rating. Direct mail, properly conceived, can expect to perform well here, as can editorial publicity, sponsored videos and literature. All the research evidence we have on page traffic and Starch measurements would indicate that press advertising performs least well in achieving impact.

3. *Message*   What is the nature of the selling message? Is it simple or is it a reminder? Is it complex, technical or innovative? In the former case, press advertising, point-of-sale, posters and radio will do well. For a complicated message, however, the need is for demonstrations, seminars, feature articles, literature, videos, and the sales force.

4. *Coverage and penetration*   This is the breadth and depth of a medium's capability. In breadth the question is what proportion of the target audience (i.e. people within a market segment) is covered by readership as opposed to circulation? In other words, will they have an 'opportunity to see' (OTS)? In direct mail the answer could be 100 per cent, with a national newspaper perhaps 60 per cent but with great wastage. Generally, one is looking for coverage of around 80 per cent. Turning to penetration, certain media are known by long-standing practice to penetrate decision-making units even where the actual names of the people involved cannot be identified: a major trade fair, for instance, or a weekly trade magazine that has to be seen by anyone who is anyone in order to keep up to date.

5. *Negative characteristics*   Some people resent some advertising and it is as well to check out in advance of using a particular media group whether your intention could be counter-productive. Most people in the United Kingdom dislike selling messages on the telephone or at the front door or on the street corner. They also dislike loose inserts, direct mail that is too intensive or repetitive, and for many, radio and television commercials are intrusive. On the whole, however, press advertising does not suffer from 'intrusion'.

6. *Positive characteristics*   We are looking for an added plus which comes over and above the basic advertisement itself. Examples are with an ad in a very prestigious publication where to be seen in good company lends an extra credibility to an advertising proposition. Similarly a strong editorial base helps. With an exhibition stand a comfortable lounge can be a welcome oasis after the formal business has been completed. An in-house exhibition or seminar may draw together people with common interests who have not met for some time and who welcome the chance of informal discussion almost as much as the event itself.

7. *Cost*   There are two costs – and also the price – to be considered. The

first cost is the total capital investment involved and whether this is compatible with the cash-flow position, and also the other major capital expenditures in marketing activities. Then the cost per contact must be evaluated, ranging as it does from the latest estimated call cost for an industrial salesperson of over £200 to just a few pence for press advertising. Media planning decisions are often made on the outcome of aggressive media buying, and this is where price comes in. All rate cards have their price, and 10 per cent or more off quoted rates can be a lot of money.

8. *Speed*   Under pressure, television, radio, newspapers and direct mail can all be transmitting messages within 24 hours or less, and to very large audiences simultaneously. The sales force can respond even more quickly, but at a rate of just a few people a day. At the other extreme it may be two years before an appropriate trade fair takes place. Thus, if the time for activating consumer/customer behaviour is a critical factor then choice of media must be influenced by this.

9. *Complexity and convenience*   Nothing could be simpler than taking half a million appropriation and allocating half of it to a single commercial network on television, and the other half to full pages in national newspapers. Such a media strategy may even be right. As against this can be compared the complexity of a multi-market multi-shot direct mail campaign, coupled with regional presentations tied in with local editorial back-up, sales visits, regional press, supporting literature and posters with a culminating business gift. Media choice just might be influenced by ease of use (idleness), coupled with such other non-professional factors as good or bad agency commission. Is there any possible justification for some media paying commission and others not? Media choice within an agency must therefore have some regard to the amount of effort required to service each medium (a cost) in relation to the income and aggravation it is likely to receive. Specialized trade press and small spaces may be very effective but they can be complicated to handle and with only 10 per cent media commission are expensive for an agency to handle.

10. *Feedback*   Examine any advertising medium and you will find that the greater majority of advertisements invite no explicit response in the way of a direct feedback, and thus they receive very little. Hence press advertising, and television, are essentially single-channel communication systems. Since impact is greater where a dialogue can be established, there must be an intrinsic advantage in all the face-to-face media, and even with direct mail and editorial publicity where there are some instances of feedback. It is worth noting that many of the popular sales promotion techniques draw heavily on the customers' participation.

11. *Creative scope* Should a medium be chosen for its creative scope? Increasingly this is regarded as a major factor but within the rather strict limits of availability of colour or movement. What is meant here is the opportunity for some quite novel or extraordinary approach to be made entirely as a result of the medium being used. In press relations the creative opportunities to set up an extremely newsworthy event are limitless, and needless to say this would be done in such a way as to involve the product or company inextricably. With direct mail there is complete freedom on material, size, shape, colour, smell, timing, audience and frequency. Exhibitions also have an almost infinite variety of creative opportunities. Where the product itself is mundane, the choice of media where creativity can be exploited fully is especially relevant. Clearly creative opportunities are somewhat restricted in press advertising.

12. *Data availability* There is a somewhat naive idea in industrial advertising that since the amounts of money to be spent are relatively small the need for information about what one is buying is not therefore very great. This is a quite extraordinary and quite illogical situation since the advertising task may well be of the greatest importance to the company; the fact that the cost of achieving it may not be astronomical does not mean that the media-buying operation should be incompetent.

With any media that overlap into consumer marketing a good deal of information is likely to be available, but otherwise it is hard to find. The technical press is rarely able to provide reliable readership data and exhibitions are way behind the press. Some advertisers set up their own sources of audience information and it may be that in respect of 'data' media choice should be biased towards those channels from which the most reliable facts can be obtained.

13. *Subjective factors* So far, the factors being discussed on media choice have been largely objective and quantitative. In practice of course there are many other sources of influence, apparently trivial, but perhaps of far greater significance in the media-buying decision than many people either realize or are prepared to admit. Why else do advertisers opt for a particular medium? Here are a few reasons:

(a) Good service from the publisher or media house.
(b) Good salesmanship – hard selling – pleasant personality.
(c) The buyer's ego trip – he likes his products to be seen in a particular medium.
(d) Good lunches, Christmas presents, and all forms of what might kindly be termed 'grace and favour'.
(e) Because the managing director says so.
(f) Competitors use it.
(g) The title of a publication, also its format; with exhibitions, location is a factor.

(h) Inertia – we've always done it this way.
(i) Personal prejudice and ignorance.
(j) The good reputation of a medium; with publications, the quality of their editorial.
(k) Hunch.
(l) The agency gets a better service or higher commission.

While the above criteria do not in any way lead to scientific media planning, their evaluation in relation to press advertising and all the other media can lead to a systematic ranking of each of the channels of communication. Figure 4.1 provides a simple grid leading to an effective media mix.

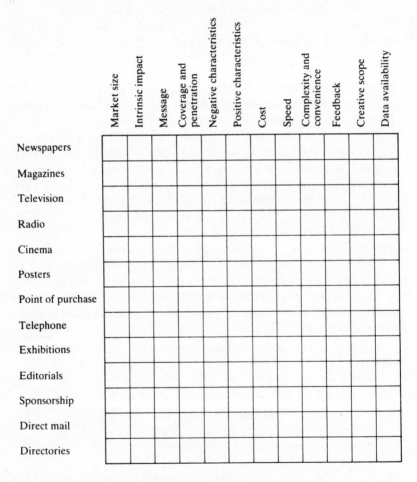

Figure 4.1 Criteria for media choice

Effectiveness

A very early survey of sources of information, *How British Industry Buys*, indicated that advertisements in the trade press had a relatively small part to play in providing information which influenced the purchase of industrial products. The highest category was 'operating management' of whom 32 per cent cited press advertising as one of the two most important channels of communication. Perhaps the most important category, board members, scored only 14 per cent.

There is good evidence in this survey that respondents are not always willing to admit even to themselves what are the outside factors they allow to influence them in reaching purchasing decisions. Sales engineers' visits for instance were rated at 66 per cent by board members, yet elsewhere in the survey only 18 per cent of board members ever saw a sales engineer! Since the first figure is an expression of opinion and the latter one of fact, 18 per cent is more likely to be the accurate figure. If not from sales engineers, where did board members obtain the information upon which to make decisions? Advertising may well in fact deserve a higher rating than these respondents were prepared to admit.

In the United States a good deal of work has been done to relate on a very broad basis the effectiveness of press advertising to sales.

A survey published by McGraw-Hill showed that in 893 industrial companies, when the ratio of advertising to selling expense is higher, the ratio of selling expense to sales turnover is lower. On average it was found that 'high advertisers' (where advertising accounted for more than 20 per cent of selling expense) had a 21 per cent lower overall selling cost than 'low advertisers'. The trend was found to be consistent regardless of the volume of sales and of product groups. In the former case, 'high' advertisers in each of four sales size groups had average selling expense 16 to 30 per cent lower than the 'low' advertisers.

For the machinery group (all special industrial machinery such as machine tools and construction machinery, motors, instruments and controls, transport and communications equipment) the sales expense ratio was 25 per cent lower on average among 'high' advertisers than among 'low' advertisers.

For the materials group (raw materials and ingredients such as steel, industrial chemicals, rubber and plastics, structural products) the difference was 27 per cent. For the equipment supplies group (maintenance and operating supplies such as furniture, paper products, lubricants, tyres, valves, machine tool accessories, paint, lighting fixtures, electronic components) the difference was 15 per cent.

It can be argued of course that these data are of a general nature and will hide wide variances. The conclusions, however, are important enough for industrial advertisers to take steps to obtain information relating to their own particular business, maybe through their trade association using inter-firm comparisons.

There are wide differences in the amount of investment in industrial advertising even among firms in the same industry. This is only to be expected but it is unfortunate that the reasons for such differences are often subjective or illogical. They are sometimes based on a philosophy of 'I don't believe in advertising', a comment which has as much rational justification as not believing in raw materials. Or perhaps the sales manager thinks he knows exactly who his customers are, calls upon them at frequent intervals and therefore does not need advertising – a proposition which can almost always be disproved on methodical investigation. Too often sales staff and managers completely underrate the importance of the corroborative function of industrial advertising. Because they may not be able to point to sales or worthwhile prospects obtained by advertising they assume that their advertising is not effective. In fact, however, a company's generalized reputation is most important; and although advertising is only one factor in building up this reputation it is a vital one. This is discussed further in Chapter 14.

The industrial and business press

Publications can be broken down into six main groups:

1. National dailies
2. Provincial dailies
3. Sunday newspapers
4. Local newspapers (weeklies)
5. General interest and class magazines
6. Trade and technical publications

The primary concern of industrial or business advertisers is in the very many trade and technical publications. These journals are diverse and complex. They encompass a comprehensive range of activities, vary greatly in size, scope, authority and in the method of circulation. In recent years there has been a good deal of rationalization in the industry which has led to a large proportion of the total publications being produced by a relatively small number of publishers. Many changes have taken place, some of which have been to the benefit of the advertiser, for example the availability of research services. Fundamentally journals have tended to move away from an editorial basis where a brilliant editor published material about a particular subject in which he was an expert, to a marketing basis where the whole concept of a publication is to provide information and a service to meet the needs of a particular market or specialized group of people. This matter is dealt with in greater detail in Chapter 16 on publishing.

The advertising schedule

The starting point once again must be a written definition of the people it is desired to influence. For example it is not uncommon in the development of a campaign to aim at four groups – the people who specify a product, often the engineers, designers or technologists; the people who have contacts with the suppliers and place the order, usually the purchasing officers; the user; and most important, the authorizers, often the board of directors. To these can be added two further categories – 'influencers' in the making of decisions and 'gatekeepers' eg a secretary or a receptionist/telephone operator. It is essential to establish at the outset which of these or other groups it is required to reach. Moreover it is necessary to take the analysis further to include factors such as geographical location, age, sex and so on.

The selection of the most effective publications is vital, for even a poor advertisement in the right journal has some chance of success, whereas a first-rate advertisement in a quite inappropriate publication is absolutely useless. It follows then that time and effort invested in the methodical selection and final evaluation of media is a very worthwhile investment. In practice the data available from publishers are usually grossly inadequate, often misleading and sometimes blatantly inaccurate. Media research is a growing activity in industrial advertising and is dealt with at length in Chapter 13.

Given a potential market, there will be a number, often a large number, of journals whose circulation will cover part or all of it. Circulation, however, is not the real criterion since it is only readership and, in particular, effective readership, that counts. One journal may have a high 'pass on' factor in relation to its circulation, but are the recipients also effective buyers? Furthermore it is not enough for a magazine to appear on a desk, it must be read in order to be effective.

The total circulation or readership of a journal is usually of no great significance in itself. If for example the brief is to reach 1000 chemical engineers in the food industry it will probably be of little value that a journal also reaches 10,000 chemical engineers in plastics, petroleum and other trades in which food has no application. In assessing media and in making comparisons the aim must be to isolate the readership that is directly relevant to the marketing objectives.

Quite often it will be found that there will be numerous publications all having good coverage of the market. The question is whether to concentrate on a limited few, or whether to spread into all publications to secure the widest audience. This judgement must be made in the light of knowledge of readership duplication and also the impact which a campaign is required to achieve. It is generally true in press advertising that after the first two or three publications in a specialized field, any additions will add only a few per cent more to the coverage (reach) of a market (see Chapter 13).

COST-EFFECTIVENESS

The cost per thousand total circulation basis, so popular with publishers and agency media departments, is quite inadequate for effective media assessment. Equally unrealistic as a rule is cost per order originating from a given journal, since the number of traceable contracts is usually of such a low order as to be statistically unreliable.

Cost per reader within the defined market segment is probably the most effective basis of assessing a publication, though in some instances cost per enquiry can be an even better guide. This latter factor necessarily depends on whether enquiries are what an advertisement is designed to achieve. A study of packaging media for instance showed the cost per thousand circulation to vary little between one publication and another. When the required readership for a particular type of pack was examined, the cost per reader varied from £1.50 per thousand to £20 per thousand. Moreover, after the top two publications had been added together, further additions made no significant difference to the number of readers reached. In this instance it was found possible to reduce the number of publications from eight to two, increase the concentration and level of advertising, and thus impact, while reducing expenditure.

CIRCULATION AND ADVERTISING RATES

When the overall economics of publishing are considered it is generally found that advertising rates are reasonably geared to production costs. Within any specialized sector it is usual to find the forces of competition have caused the cost per thousand copies of one journal to be much the same as another. Indeed so far as the absolute level of cost per page is concerned it may be argued that the rates in general tend to be too low to enable a publisher to provide a good enough all-round service to maximize the marketing efficiency of his publication.

The important differences between rates begin to emerge only when readership 'segmentation' is considered and here the advertiser is at a great disadvantage. Accurate and authentic data on total circulations are beginning to emerge, but circulation breakdowns are usually no more than a publisher's statement and the bitter fact is that these must be treated with reserve. Until circulation breakdowns are subject to independent audit as in the US it is unwise to pay any serious regard to them since the basis on which they are compiled is unknown and they cannot be subject to comparative study.

Nevertheless the work done in the UK by the Audit Bureau of Circulation in developing and promoting audited circulation data represents a very important advance in providing a quantitative basis for media selection.

Given the difficulty of determining cost/readership effectiveness, there are still opportunities for significant savings on the basis of rates alone. For instance in determining how many publications to place on a schedule in relation to how many insertions in each, graduated scales of charges are worth examining since quantity reductions in page rates can effect major economies. Long-term contracts can enable further savings to be made, and notwithstanding the existence of published rate cards, many publishers are prepared to negotiate prices in order to increase their share of business.

A growing trend among publishers is to offer discount rates based on the total business placed in certain groups of publications. Another variation is to consider financial concessions related to the time of year.

An alternative to looking for special rate reductions is to look for special services from a publisher. There are many facilities which can be placed at the disposal of an advertiser which will help to make his campaign more effective. Progressive publishers are recognizing this and are prepared to co-operate, for instance in split runs, inserts, and joint research. One questionable service is the occasional offer of editorial preference in consideration of the placing of advertising. If a journal is willing to do business on this basis it can only mean that it is prepared to forfeit its editorial independence in order to make short-term gains at the expense of the reader and therefore the advertiser.

An interesting term in the publishing business is the 'numbers game'. It is a reflection on the gullibility of some advertisers that the journal most likely to be chosen as number one on a schedule is that having the greatest total circulation. Before the introduction of free-circulation journals, this might have been a valid criterion in a homogeneous market, but where it represents, as is now sometimes the case, simply an expression of the print order, its claims are quite misleading.

Over the past decade a large number of publications have appeared, almost always given away, with circulation methods which are sometimes not controlled with any degree of effectiveness. Such journals have had circulations inflated by a factor first of two, then three and then four – each publisher going one better in quoting a higher number. Rates for such journals expressed in relation to circulation totals have seemed reasonable, but any company librarian will quote example after example of the inflow of duplicate copies of such journals which serve to benefit the printer, papermaker and publisher, but not the advertiser.

In numerous readership surveys there is ample evidence of magazines quoting massive circulation figures but receiving extraordinarily low readership ratings. The moral, as always, is let the buyer beware, and verify all facts by independent audit.

While page rates in relation to circulation may be fairly standard, this is by no means so of special positions, rates and concessions. The advertising value of such positions may be questionable, but all the same, there is a good deal of scope for skilled media buying.

Wide variations between one publisher and another will be found in respect of facing matter, covers, additional colours, bound-in and loose inserts, and bleed pages. The combination of these factors can entirely change the economics of an advertising schedule and this points the need for a very close liaison between media buyers and the creative staff of agencies in order to achieve the maximum cost-effectiveness. Some journals for example make no charge for bleed whereas others have a high premium: cover positions in particular are susceptible to variations quite unrelated to their advertising value which in itself is questionable.

Skilful media planning and buying is therefore a high priority though many advertising agencies greatly underrate it for technical advertising. This is often because with the complexity of the task the client's 'intimate' knowledge of the trade is allowed to predominate without a critical examination.

Media selection

Intra-media comparisons in the trade and technical press are particularly difficult with the relevant facts often unknown and sometimes misleading. Although this makes the task more difficult, it does not provide a reason for ignoring it. Some of the principal criteria in selecting media are:

1. Total circulation
2. Total readership
3. Segmented circulation
4. Segmented readership
5. Standard rates in relation to 1, 2, 3 and 4
6. Reductions and premiums in relation to special circumstances
7. Credibility of publisher's data
8. Editorial excellence
9. Journal's reputation
10. Format, paper, printing
11. Method of circulation
12. Frequency
13. Special services from publisher
14. Readership duplication
15. Enquiries
16. Experience

In the limit, of course, given adequate research, and feedback of information, the sole criterion is the extent to which a publication serves as a means of achieving the written specific advertising objectives in terms of the market to be influenced. This hinges largely on the extent to which an advertiser has access to reliable research data. Chapters 12 and 13 deal with this in some detail.

It is necessary at this stage to touch briefly on other criteria which are often employed but which in general are less helpful in assessing media.

Probably the biggest single misleading factor in media selection is the use of reader reply cards. This is a service introduced largely by 'controlled circulation' journals as a means of securing a maximum of enquiries. Viewed in this light alone, and provided the specific campaign objective is to secure the maximum of enquiries without qualification, then these cards can be said to provide a useful service. However, from an examination of advertisements in the technical press the conclusion must be reached that the principal purpose of many advertisements is not to secure enquiries, since so few offer an incentive, either specific or implied, to make an enquiry. If this is so, reader reply response is not specially valuable.

It is the quality of enquiries which is of prime importance in most cases of a campaign to obtain sales leads. Here reader reply cards will be found to need scrutiny in two respects: firstly there tends to be a higher proportion of enquiries from people lower down the scale of purchasing influence; secondly the very ease with which one can make an enquiry using a reader reply card makes such an enquiry less serious, and more casual than would otherwise be the case. Evidence of this is to take at random returned cards in a publisher's office and examine the number of ticks per card, sometimes so many as to be ludicrous. It is not unknown for a card to be received on which every number has been ticked, including all the spare ones against which no advertisement or editorial item has appeared. While it is important to be cautious, the plain fact is that reply cards on balance provide a valuable service to advertisers and to publishers, but more to the point it is a service which is applauded by the readers as can be seen in Figure 4.2.

Reader reply cards in respect of editorial items are also used as an argument for the advertising effectiveness of a journal. This may be valid in some instances, but it is open to considerable doubt. Consider the timing of an editorial on a new product. The first journal in a specialized field to publish a new product item will tend to mop up the enquiries of those having immediate interest. Subsequent appearance in a competitor journal may pull significantly less because of the later timing. Furthermore a brief notice editorially about a new product giving only a few of the necessary facts will tend to pull more enquiries than an editorial which gives a full and detailed description. Indeed the journal which is so interested in a product as to give a full-scale article on the subject can be fairly sure of pulling virtually no

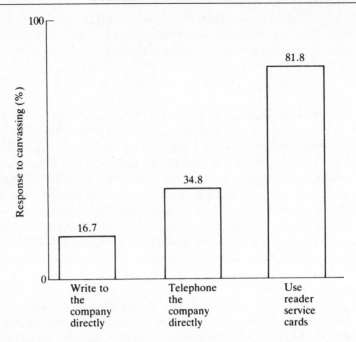

Figure 4.2   Use of reader service cards (*Source*: Cahners Research Report No. 240.1)

enquiries at all. This interesting fact should be considered in relation to copywriting for an enquiry-getting advertisement.

The number of advertisements carried by a journal is by and large evidence neither for nor against its value as an advertising medium. The argument that many advertisements mean less exposure of one's own advertisement, or conversely that few advertisements mean greater exposure and therefore greater effectiveness, is unsupported by evidence. Likewise the inclusion of competitors' advertisements in a publication is only indicative of its value in advertising terms if an advertiser is confident that his own assessment of media is inferior to that of his competitors!

The list of irrational reasons for selecting media is long. It includes personal views influenced by the salesmanship of the media representative, the views of company employees assessing editorial content from an entirely different viewpoint than the customer, the opinion of the sales force or any other department.

There is in fact no substitute for objective media readership analysis and since this requires an investment in terms of formal research, whether desk or field, it is unlikely that an advertising budget which does not set aside a significant sum of money to evaluate its advertising will secure maximum value for its total advertising investment. It can be argued that in industrial advertising, a research budget of say 10 per cent total publicity expenditure is the minimum required to explore methods for maximum efficacy.

Impact in press advertising

The first requirement of an advertisement is to have the power to stop the reader – to secure attention. From that point on there occurs a series of mental processes which determine the degree of impact achieved. Factors such as advertisement size, novelty, position, frequency and subject matter will affect the impact on a person's mind. It is all too easy for advertisers who are very conscious of their own advertisements to suppose that their impact is likely to be of a much higher order than is actually the fact. From the research work carried out in the United States and to some degree in the United Kingdom there is evidence that advertisements in the trade and technical press are noticed, on average, by only a relatively small percentage of readers and that real impact is achieved with perhaps as few as 2 or 3 per cent. In some studies described in Chapter 13 on research there are indeed instances of advertisements consistently scoring zero in their readership rating. It is essential therefore to examine continuously methods of obtaining maximum effectiveness, and here the following criteria have some bearing.

CREATIVE EXPRESSION

There can be little doubt that all other factors being equal, the creative expression of the sales message – the customer benefit – is paramount. Equally this factor is the most difficult to evaluate and quantify. As an example of this a new range of fluid power equipment was produced for which six selling features were identified. These were thought to be equally important in terms of satisfying buyers' needs, but applying the 'single selling proposition' a series of six advertisements was designed, each featuring one sales point. The advertisements were couponed and designed specifically to pull enquiries. The result was that one advertisement pulled far more enquiries than any other and from this the conclusion was drawn that this selling feature must be the most important to buyers. A new campaign was designed centring on this one feature, but the result was a disastrous failure. The simple fact was that the successful advertisement had achieved its success due to its creative excellence in attracting attention, not to the selling feature.

The advertiser therefore must look to the copywriter and visualizer for those touches of inspiration which cannot be defined and yet are so decisive in the success of a campaign. There may be little an advertiser can do to stimulate such inspiration, but at least a serious effort can be made to establish a good rapport with the creative team, and to provide a full and adequate brief.

Many attempts have been made to effect some measurement of 'creative expression', particularly as perceived by readers of advertisements, namely, buyers. One of the most extensive was by G McAleer of Florida Technological University. This examined four industry groups to determine the extent to which specific advertising propositions were regarded as valid by advertisers on the one hand and purchasers on the other. The market segments selected for study were consulting engineers, electrical contractors, architects and building contractors. A list of 48 advertising appeals was drawn up in a questionnaire and mailed to both parties in the four groupings. Respondents were asked to use a numerical scaling between +5 and –5 to indicate the extent to which they felt that each proposition had validity to them personally in their professional capacity.

Clearly if both parties showed a similar score (as indicated by comparing arithmetic averages) then there would be a good understanding by advertisers of the needs of their customers. Alternatively, if the ratings for a particular proposition were significantly different then there was good reason to suppose that advertisers were not as aware as they should be of the motivating factors relating to their customers. Table 4.1 is an extract from a very comprehensive listing of items, some of which have similar ratings between the two groups, and others differences which are significant.

The conclusion of the survey was that 'advertisers to each of the market segments studied did not correctly perceive the influence of advertising appeals upon the market concerned'. Such a conclusion does not imply that all companies are operating with such a lack of understanding of their customers nor indeed that in other countries the data have a direct validity. It does, however, lead one to give consideration to carrying out a review of selling propositions to check their correct relevance.

Table 4.1 Creative expression as perceived by advertisers and buyers

Advertising appeal	Advertiser (av. mean)	Customer (av. mean)
Ease of installation	2.05	1.87
Low maintenance cost	2.30	2.61
Physical features	2.88	2.40
Reliability of the seller	2.35	2.34
Ability to keep delivery promises	1.67	2.32
Newness of product	0.63	–0.43
It is widely specified	2.53	–0.53
Testimonial by a supplier of the product	1.96	–1.08
Easy to repair	0.40	2.65
Announcement of new installation	1.51	–0.24
Automatic operation	–1.00	2.52
Increasing output	–0.48	2.76

PRE-TESTING ADVERTISEMENTS

The wider implications of advertising research will be considered later in Chapters 12 and 13. At this stage, however, serious consideration should be given to testing the 'creative proposition' to ensure that what may appear to be highly compelling and lucidly persuasive copy really is just that.

It is commonplace in consumer campaigns to pre-test advertisements, and experience has shown that there is a good correlation between such research findings and actual performance. With industrial advertising there is a widespread point of view that pre-testing is unnecessary, too complicated, and anyway costs too much. Such an argument is fallacious in that the task of an advertisement is to communicate a selling message to a potential market irrespective of cost, and if that message is not adequately received then a vital part of the marketing communications process is missing, perhaps with a disastrous effect on sales.

SIZE

The size of an advertisement must clearly influence the impact it produces. Research in this field gives some evidence, however, that this is not a linear relationship, and thus large and particularly multi-page advertisements need to be justified by other considerations. Factors which properly enter into the selection of large spaces are the nature of the sales message, the pictorial content required, prestige, and the nature of the publication and the advertisements it carries. There is no doubt that for some products and services a quarter page can be as effective as a whole page.

The importance of bleed has often been neglected. The additional cost is minimal whereas the additional area available is substantially greater. There is some indication from field research work that bleed advertisements score disproportionately higher than non-bleed, perhaps because they are so rare. Another option to consider is the use of a loose insert. Some will hold that with more than, say, one insert the readers become antagonized to the extent that they either ignore the advertising message or even build up resentment to the advertiser. Again looking to American research data, there is some evidence as in Figure 4.3 that advertising readership increases significantly by the use of inserts.

POSITION

A great deal of inconclusive and misleading research has been conducted on the importance of the position of an advertisement in a publication. In newspapers there is probably scope for being particularly selective in the positioning of an advertisement. In the trade and technical press there is little evidence to justify paying the premiums demanded for special positions

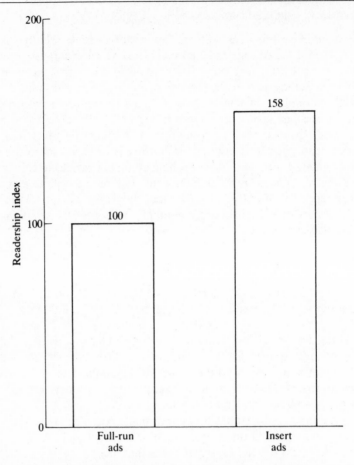

Figure 4.3   The influence of inserts (*Source*: Cahners Research Report No. 117.1)

even where a journal is carrying a hundred or more pages of advertising. The same doubts should also be raised about cover positions which, while undoubtedly having a high prestige connotation, may turn out to have a very low page traffic rating, particularly front covers where so often a circulation slip is attached by the librarian before a journal is circulated in a company.

FREQUENCY AND DUPLICATION

Once again there has been research in the United States which seems to indicate that if the first appearance of an advertisement is seen by, say, 10 per cent of readers, the second appearance will also be seen by 10 per cent but of substantially different readers.

This is probably an area in which a great deal more research should be carried out, particularly to establish how often an advertisement should be changed. There is a general consensus that three appearances is a good minimum and that up to six can be justified. This is borne out by advertisements which set out to get enquiries and therefore enable a response rate to be traced.

Frequency and duplication must often, at this stage in advertising knowledge, depend upon experience and intelligent guesswork having regard to the market share aimed for, the speed with which the message needs to be delivered, activities in other media, the frequency with which orders are placed, reminder advertising and the overall impact which it is desired to achieve. Some hard evidence is provided by an example from the States of an advertisement which was repeated 41 times over a period of 11 years and produced an apparently ever-increasing number of enquiries as shown in Figure 4.4.

COLOUR

The effect on impact of colour depends very much upon the circumstances and as a general rule is not nearly so important as creative expression and product illustration. In a magazine full of colour advertisements a black-and-white design can obtain a very high score. In a publication with no colour at all, a multicoloured advertisement will clearly have an advantage.

Limitations and advantages

The limitation of press advertising is that, due to the excessive number of publications and the lack of precision in defining readerships, there is a strong risk of wasting large sums of money without ever realizing it.

The advantage is that extensive coverage, even saturation, of a market can be obtained with a minimum of effort – often influencing purchasing units which cannot be reached easily in any other way; which are often indeed not even known to exist.

STRENGTHS AND WEAKNESSES

Since the most significant medium in industrial marketing communications is the trade press, in considering the specific strengths and weaknesses of advertising, it follows that this will be largely in respect of editorial publicity. Other media, of course, are also related.

Strengths

Complete control of:

- when the ad appears

**Ad repeated 41 times
and still working**

The Ludlow Corporation has demonstrated, by counting enquiries,
and by running the same ad over eleven years in
Engineering News-Record that an ad can be successfully
repeated at least 41 times.

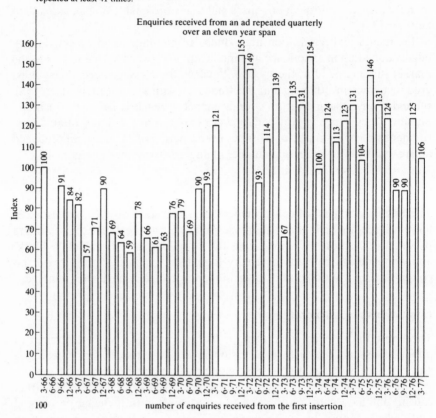

Figure 4.4   Repeat of advertisement (*Source*: McGraw-Hill Research Report No.
3043.2)

- How often
- In which publications
- Size and shape
- Words and illustrations
- Choice of colours
- Response mechanism
- Will penetrate the DMU
- Always positive
- Easy to organize and administer
- Up-to-date database

Weaknesses

- Expensive
- Lack of readership data
- Low page traffic
- Few people will read it
- Those that do won't believe it
- Lack of impact
- Limited reach

Checklist

1. Has the potential audience for an advertisement been defined in terms of

   (a) Size (numbers of DMUs and their purchasing powers)?
   (b) Location?
   (c) Market segments?
   (d) Individual's job categories?
   (e) Special characteristics?
   (f) Purchasing motivation?

2. Have the proposed media been selected (a) on the basis of the information from item one and (b) in relation to authenticated readership data?
3. Has readership duplication been considered?
4. Does a particular advertisement or series (a) have a tangible objective, (b) can this be measured, (c) does it fit in with the overall marketing strategy?
5. Has a full and written brief been prepared?
6. Does the brief include

   (a) Advertisement size?
   (b) Frequency?
   (c) Position?
   (d) Number of colours?
   (e) Essential illustrations?
   (f) Action required?
   (g) A means of media identification?
   (h) Provision for measuring effectiveness?

7. Have the number, frequency and timing of advertisements been scheduled in relation to other parts of the marketing mix?

5.

DIRECT MAIL

Direct mail means the use of the postal services to carry a persuasive message, in any form, to a prospect. The mailing piece can be as simple as a sales letter, or a postcard. Alternatively it can be as sophisticated as a major catalogue, a complex gimmick or an expensive sample. For practical purposes, items which are distributed door to door by a commercial organization will be included under the term direct mail.

Referring back to the basic impact diagram in Chapter 2 (Figure 2.2), direct mail is one of the major channels of persuasion available to a company for reaching a prospect and achieving maximum impact. Its importance in the marketing mix will clearly vary, depending on the nature of the product and market, from being of paramount significance (eg drug promotions to doctors) to being almost useless (eg promotion of nuclear power plants to a government agency).

During the past few years, direct mail has suddenly come of age, and in the UK represents some 10 per cent of the total advertising spend – somewhat more than that of the business and professional press. Consideration must also be given to faxes and to e-mail.

Special advantages

Direct mail enables the user to aim a message at a precisely defined prospect, and to place the mailing piece in front of that prospect at the exact time required, and, indeed, as soon and as often as is wished. Moreover a mailing piece has an advantage over a press advertisement or editorial item in that for a moment at least it occupies a solus position, gains greater attention and therefore greater impact. There is no absolute restriction on size, number of words, colour, illustrations or quality of reproduction. Hence there is a good opportunity to put across an argument in full. A further benefit is that since it can be addressed directly and personally it can be so designed as to produce a response, and where this is a particular objective a very high rate of replies can be obtained.

Direct mail is a versatile tool which can be varied widely in magnitude, direction and frequency; can be brought into use virtually overnight and sometimes most important of all, can be an extremely cheap method of communication.

Disadvantages

The advantage of direct mail, that it aims at a precise target, is also one of its limitations. In Chapter 2, dealing with strategy, the importance of defining the market in detail was stressed as was the large number of purchasing influences likely to be involved in the placement of an order. For direct mail to be fully effective it is essential to be able to define precisely the audience to be influenced. This means broad market categories, companies within these categories, plants within the companies and people within the plants.

Definition of target audiences cannot be overstressed. Just as with press advertising, it is pointless to develop a first-class proposition if it is placed in front of a non-prospect.

A further limiting factor in practice is the lack of experience which promotion people in general have of direct mail, coupled with the fact that it is complex, difficult to set up, easy to go wrong, and perhaps not yet developed to the state of relative sophistication found in other media. While this generalization cannot be applied, say, to the promotion of pharmaceuticals or to certain specific products, for instance *Reader's Digest*, it is nevertheless true of most industrial operations. Here, however, is the opportunity to gain the edge on competition. There can be little doubt that in trade and technical campaigns, direct mail is going to play an increasingly important role.

Databases

Establishment of an effective database is the prerequisite of a mailing campaign, and upon it will rest the success or failure of a promotion.

The marketing plan will have defined the markets, their sizes and locations, their relative importance, and the key people to influence. The marcom plan will have defined the role of direct mail and which of the various targets it is to be used to attack and with what intensity. Most important, it will also have defined exactly and quantitatively the objectives of the direct mail operation.

It will be useful to identify the principal sources of databases, but while doing so it is important to stress that there is usually available in any campaign a wide range of special sources which a creative mind can explore. Careful thought and consultation can be most rewarding here.

SALESPEOPLE'S CALL LISTS

Where a direct mail campaign is required to support a field selling drive it is vital to incorporate the salespeople's call lists. Indeed with some product groups in which the market is compact and easy to define, the call list may be all that is required. If so, however, it is still necessary to have a foolproof system of feedback from the sales force covering changes immediately they occur, and to achieve this the full co-operation and sympathy both of sales managers and sales representatives is required.

The limitation of such a list is that salespeople, however good, cannot always unearth all prospective companies, far less determine accurately which individuals in an organization influence purchasing decisions. Even if such people can be identified, a salesperson may not be able to make contact with them and accordingly they may not be on the call list.

ENQUIRIES

From the marketing communications activities in which a company engages come a variety of enquiries. These are usually obtained at considerable cost and are a major source of contacts for a mailing campaign. They often serve to supplement the sales call list by identifying within a prospect company individuals who while not strictly 'purchasers', are very much 'influencers'.

It is not uncommon to include the need for enquiries as a means of list building as one of the objectives of a campaign. An example in press advertising is to include a specific offer of a brochure or a sample; similarly at exhibitions to record meticulously all callers on a stand whether they have some immediate requirement or not.

CUSTOMERS

The nature of a campaign may not require that existing customers shall be included but in other circumstances they must head the list as a top priority. Once again, it is not just the person that signs the order who must be reached, but all the other individuals who contribute to the purchasing decision.

DIRECTORIES

These are particularly useful when entering a new market where a body of knowledge and a range of contacts do not already exist. There may be severe limitations since all directories are well out of date before they are published, many of them are not comprehensive, and some of them are substantially inaccurate. An example of how easy it is to waste money here is with the use of what is probably the best-known business directory to promote a particular training programme to marketing directors and the like. In one of the lists supplied 53 per cent of the names and addresses had an error in them, ranging from a wrong spelling to a person who had left the company five years previously.

Where names of executives are included, this can be of great value: where they are not, a good deal of research is probably going to be necessary to personalize the list in order to make it effective.

EXHIBITIONS

A list of exhibitors is an excellent supplementary source of prospects within a given market. This can very usefully and easily be extended by setting up a survey in which visits are made to each stand and representatives questioned as to who in a certain company is likely to be interested in a particular product. The degree of co-operation that can be achieved, particularly at a slack time, can be very high, almost total.

A new opportunity which is being created by certain exhibition organizers is to invite each visitor to identify himself by filling out an enquiry card. This builds a bank of purchasing influences which is likely to be more extensive than any other method, but a fairly disciplined scrutiny of job category is necessary here.

HOUSE MAGAZINES

From the point of view of direct mail a benefit of external house magazines is that over a period of time they build up a circulation list which often includes many people behind the purchasing scenes whom a company wishes to influence. Additions to the circulation of a house magazine should automatically be considered for addition to the promotional mailing list.

PUBLISHERS

An increasing number of publishers are exploiting their circulation lists by hiring them to advertisers and others for direct mail. As with all lists it is important to be cautious about their value and, as far as trade and technical journals are concerned, the circulation lists are not always as extensive and accurate as is sometimes thought. Many are often directed to libraries, academics, students – indeed to all manner of non-commercial people.

TRADE ASSOCIATIONS AND INSTITUTIONS

Such bodies often publish, or will provide, a comprehensive list of members.

NEW APPOINTMENTS AND NEWS

A large number of publications carry news items of new appointments which clearly identify prospects for a mailing list.

DIRECT MAIL AGENCIES

There are a number of commercial organizations which provide an extensive service for direct mail users. The service usually offers some hundreds of specialized lists which are in effect available for hire; the mechanics of addressing, enclosing, franking and posting the mailing pieces; a creative design studio; also sometimes a research unit to help in list building if one is not already in existence.

There is little doubt that with the right degree of co-operation and understanding, a direct mail house is very useful; indeed sometimes almost essential. It is necessary, however, for a client to realize that with many campaigns in hand at any one moment it is not possible for a direct mail company to give the kind of attention to minute detail that the client would himself, and it is therefore important to give a most thorough briefing with written confirmation in order to avoid misunderstandings.

Finally it should be realized that with very few exceptions a mailing house has access to only the same sources of lists as anyone else. Given time a company can usually produce a better list itself. What it probably cannot do is process it more efficiently.

COMPUTER SERVICES AND LIST BROKERS

With the widespread availability of computers and word-processing machines the use of direct mail is becoming more widespread. This is because the development and maintenance of in-house mailing lists has become much more simple, as has the reproduction of personalized letters. Coding and fast retrieval are now available to companies with only the most elementary equipment.

Computers have also become part of the standard equipment for direct mail houses which have become more sophisticated in the storage of, and access to, their mailing lists. Some outside services have specialized to the extent that they handle only mailing lists. Such list brokers in practice are in the business of simply selling labels.

UNUSUAL SOURCES

For each product group and each market there may well be a variety of unusual sources of lists. Announcements of births and marriages for instance, or graduations at university. Co-operation with complementary trades can provide a source such as the names of people buying turfs as a sales lead to a company selling lawn-mowers. Other useful sources might be shareholders, rating lists, return guarantee cards and records of companies.

Campaign planning

Having defined the market and identified the names and addresses of people who will influence the purchasing decision, it is now necessary to consider the form which the campaign should take. A number of factors need to be examined in order to formulate the most effective campaign mix. The number of shots is going to depend on how complex the sales message is and also the percentage return which is set as a target. If 3 per cent is required (a common but highly misleading norm) then one shot may be adequate. Two shots would possibly bring 6 per cent, or maybe 5 per cent, since the law of diminishing returns clearly applies, particularly on a short time base. If there are six major selling features, and these are not well known, it will be necessary perhaps to send out six shots.

The same general guidelines as used in a press advertising campaign clearly apply but with the additional opportunities of attention, space and colour. In the end it is experience which determines the final plan. This is not the subjective experience of whim or fancy, but rather the building up of a set of data relating to the reaction of prospects to a given mailing technique. One of the interesting characteristics of a direct mail operation is the opportunity to carry out test mailings to small samples of a given list. In this way the likely reaction of the entire list can be determined before becoming committed to the total campaign or indeed the total expenditure.

A direct mail shot can vary from a cheaply duplicated circular to a personally signed letter, to an impressive colour brochure, to a bottle of whisky, to a quarter-sectioned hydraulic cylinder weighing fifty pounds and costing rather more. It is all a matter of deciding what impact it is required to achieve and what is necessary in order to achieve it. Given adequately experienced and able creative people, there is considerable scope for novelty and therefore impact, particularly in comparison with press advertising which is limited in size and material. In direct mail, one can select from a number of materials, choose from a variety of sizes, use three dimensions, and even sound, smell and chemical reaction. A further extremely useful aspect of mailing is that an actual sample can be sent out of the product itself.

The use of the mail is not fundamentally a requirement of direct mail. Circular distribution has already been mentioned though this is clearly more relevant to consumer promotions. Maybe the industrial equivalent is to use e-mail or fax for distributing an advertising message. This is fast, accurate and likely to have high impact. Care needs to be exercised as recipients could regard this as intruding on their privacy, much as they react to telephone selling.

Whatever form a shot may take, however, it must be emphasized that it does not begin to achieve purchasing impact until it reaches the right person.

An undirected leaflet in a personally addressed envelope may be put in the right file in the mailing room, but without the envelope the leaflet is directionless and will end up who knows where? An individually typed letter addressed to ICI and starting Dear Sirs, may just as well not be sent at all. Similarly a letter to the Chief Buyer of Unilever is hardly likely to reach the person one is trying to influence. It is essential to determine carefully and precisely whom the message is to reach, whether by name or job title, then to address both the envelope and the enclosure to that person.

TIMING

As with press advertising there is an opportunity to achieve a cumulative build up of awareness by sending out a series of shots. The actual number will be determined by factors mentioned earlier. A further consideration is the period of time over which the campaign is likely to extend. If for a year, and if continuity is required, then it may emerge that a monthly interval is an optimum time. If for a longer period, say several years, then perhaps a quarterly interval is adequate, as with a house magazine. Even less frequent mailings can be effective: for instance a calendar or a diary once a year.

It may be necessary to achieve results quickly and in this case the campaign can comprise a series of rapid shots at weekly or even at daily intervals. When considering this kind of saturation it is useful to recall the personal nature of direct mail. One of the pitfalls, which is also one of the strengths, is the fact that the recipient of a direct mail piece tends, rightly, to regard it as an individual and personal communication from the sender. Consequently the receipt of five letters from the same firm on the same subject on five consecutive days may achieve impact, but may well alienate the prospect. Similarly a generalization which does not apply to a particular person in a press advertisement may well cause offence if written into a letter. For instance, a letter inviting an existing customer to try out a product which he or she has been using for years is a good way of losing the business which already exists.

In calculating timing it is useful to put oneself in the place of the buyer and consider the most likely reaction to a proposed plan.

A good deal of emphasis is sometimes placed on the best day of the week and the best time of the year to send out direct mail. It is argued for instance that Monday is a bad day both psychologically and because it is a heavy day for incoming post; also that Friday is a bad day because people's minds are turning towards the weekend. Another argument is that August is a bad month and, of course, Christmas time is poor. In modern marketing there is little place for conjecture. It is the function of a direct mail practitioner to accept such theories as possible, but to test them, to verify them or reject them; Christmas time, after all, is a very good time for Christmas trees.

COST

Costs, absolute and relative, are vital factors when establishing the advertising and indeed the marketing mix.

A full page in a technical magazine for instance might cost £2000 given a circulation of 10,000. This would be a cost per copy of 20p.

There may well be more than one reader per copy which brings the cost down to say 8p per reader. It is known, however, that a 10 per cent 'noted' rating is a reasonable average, ie only one in ten readers will actually notice the advertisement, and of these perhaps a third will read most of the copy. This can put the cost of real communication up to £2.40 per prospect.

Going to the other extreme, the cost of getting a selling argument across by means of a salesperson may well be £200 per prospect, or more. An exhibition may produce results at a lower figure, but both these situations afford the opportunity of face-to-face selling, which is likely to be more effective.

How does direct mail stand up in comparison with other channels of communication? Distribution of a cheap circular to households can be done at around 30p per unit. Using the postal services and a well-produced letter, maybe including a simple leaflet, the cost is going to be of the order of 50p. Thereafter the costs rise as the mailing increases in quality and sophistication.

If a campaign is designed largely to obtain sales leads a different set of figures will be obtained. It is not uncommon in press advertising of capital goods to find the cost of an enquiry ranging between £5 and £50. With direct mail a 5 per cent response where the unit mailing cost was 40p would result in a cost per enquiry of £8.

It may fairly be said that, all things being equal, there is not much to choose between press advertising and direct mail in terms of cost. If this is so, however, it is strange that so many promotional budgets allocate very much larger sums of money to press. One reason may be that direct mail is a good deal more complex and difficult to set up and that it is far more likely to go wrong. Another reason is simply that insufficient attention has been given to the value of this medium in relation to others and that its results have not been so carefully measured and analysed. And anyway it doesn't pay agencies a commission.

Setting targets

Before the position of measuring and assessing results can be reached, it is necessary to set targets. Just as, in an efficient business, management by objectives is an accepted way of operating, so in direct mail the starting point must be to define the objectives – in measurable, meaningful terms.

As with press advertising, the objectives must be realistic. There will be occasions when an increase in sales can result directly from a mailing operation, but more often in industrial promotions the effect on sales is going to be indirect and less tangible. Thus it is necessary to set a target which can be more directly related. Perhaps the intention is to get sales leads which, in turn, will enable the sales force to convert them into orders. In this situation it may be unrealistic to measure the efficacy of the direct mail campaign in terms of sales. The product may not be right, or the price; alternatively the leads may not be followed up efficiently. If the primary objective is to secure sales leads, then the campaign must be assessed in these terms.

In the course of time it will be possible, for a given type of campaign, to establish norms of performance. These will vary considerably between one product group and another, and between markets, but even if a norm has not been established it is nevertheless valuable to set a figure against which performance can be measured.

A mailing campaign to a thousand prospects may take as an objective 'to secure a hundred sales leads'. This gives to the executive concerned, and the copywriter and visualizer, a clear statement of what the operation is all about. It also indicates to marketing and sales management exactly the role this campaign is intended to play. It facilitates a cost comparison with other media and this has a long-term value in shaping future media mixes. As the campaign proceeds it becomes apparent whether or not the objective is likely to be achieved or whether the operation needs to be strengthened, cut back, or indeed stopped, to avoid wasting money either because it is totally successful or a complete failure.

Obtaining sales leads is perhaps easy: a campaign designed to strengthen a company's reputation may be more difficult. This does not, however, lessen the need for setting targets. Indeed, with image-building campaigns, unless a plan is made beforehand to measure the results, it will be impossible to begin to evaluate the effect of the expenditure. In the case of such a campaign the objective must be quantified even if very broadly, for instance 'to be rated among the top three suppliers of industrial paints'. This will necessitate a minimum of two investigations: first to find out the present rating and then in due course the change in position after the campaign.

A campaign may set out to establish a realization among buyers that a certain brand-name connotes a particular product – and often a product with pre-defined benefits. This is a classic softening-up operation before the field force goes in, and calls for a saturation campaign which will continue until the objective has been achieved.

For every direct mail campaign then there must be a specific purpose, formally stated and in terms which can be measured. The methods of measurement to be adopted will be an integral part of the plan.

IMPROVING DIRECT MAIL RESPONSE.

Direct mail is clearly becoming a mainstream medium for both industrial and consumer products. It is certainly the fastest medium and folklore has it claiming an average of 3 per cent response. This latter figure is just not true. Response can be anything between 0 per cent and well over 100 per cent depending on how attractive the response mechanism is. There are instances of the incentive to reply being so strong that recipients tell their friends and colleagues who, despite not having received the mailing, reply nonetheless, thus resulting in a response greater than the mailing.

Given that the response mechanism is sound and the direct mail shot itself has a high creative impact, there are a number of other factors which will increase the return. A recent study has shown how six actions can lead to significant increases of anything up to 26 percentage points:

Table 5.1 Industrial mail surveys: techniques for inducing response (*Source*: Jobber, D and O'Reilly, D (1996) *Market Intelligence Planning*)

Treatment	Response increase over control (percentage points)
Prior telephone calls	19
Monetary incentives	
10c	17
25c	19
$1	26
20p	15
Non-monetary incentives	
Pen	12
Pocket knife	15
Stamp business reply	7
Anonymity (in company)	20
Anonymity (external)	10
Follow-ups	12

As can be seen in the above table, a phone call prior to a mailing can increase the propensity to reply quite significantly, possibly because it enhances the perceived importance of the mailing. Similarly, a pre-paid financial incentive in the initial mailing can increase the response rate. The value of the coin is irrelevant, but people are unwilling to pocket it without doing something to justify it; namely, respond to the mailing. Small gifts will increase response, but it may be that in future they will need to be more imaginative than a ballpoint pen. The reply envelope is a necessary accompaniment, but will work better if there is a real stamp. When the mailing comprises a research questionnaire, assurance of anonymity leads to a higher response and, finally, one or more follow-ups will always increase the outcome.

STRENGTHS & WEAKNESSES OF DIRECT MAIL

Strengths

Targeting to named individuals
No geographic limitations
Carries complex message
Flexible timing
Fast
Piloting is possible
Response mechanisms work better
Telephone follow-up
Creativity
Samples can be sent
High 'noting' and impact
Natural medium for existing customers – three times more effective, ie read it
Easy measurement
Competition doesn't know and cannot measure

Weaknesses

Inaccurate databases – give poor responses and incur bad will
Limited frequency of mailings
Cheap image
Good designers difficult to find
Doesn't reach everyone in the DMU
Requires special writing skills because people take the message personally

DIRECT RESPONSE MARKETING

There is some confusion as to the difference between direct mail (DM) and direct response marketing (DRM): indeed some people regard the terms as synonymous. This is unfortunate since they are fundamentally different.

Direct response marketing is an activity in which prospects are invited to place an order directly as a response to an offer in an advertisement or a direct mail shot. The order is placed directly with the marketing organization without a salesperson as intermediary, and it is dispatched directly to the customer by post or freight without the intermediary of a retail outlet. There is also another term in use, direct response advertising, which refers to any advertisement that seeks to secure an order directly.

Direct response marketing is said to be the fastest growing sector of marketing activities, and many examples are to be found in the Sunday colour magazines and in the Saturday editions of national newspapers. These, however, are all in the consumer goods field and so far there is not much evidence of its suitability for industrial goods.

A growing problem is the use of the terms 'database marketing' and 'direct marketing'. Users of the terms usually intend them to be synonymous with direct mail. A useful description of the term is provided by Royal Mail:

DATABASE MARKETING

The roots of database marketing lie in the continual development and increasing level of sophistication of direct marketing.

Direct marketing can be described as:

> An accountable form of marketing which uses a range of communications to build relationships directly with customers and prospects.

The choice includes:

- Direct mail
- Direct response press
- Direct response TV
- Direct response radio
- Door drops
- In- and out-bound telephone marketing
- Sales promotion

Direct marketing's prime objective is to sell direct, or get the prospect/customer to respond to an offer, so that the organization can learn more about them and is therefore in a better position to make a sale next time. The advance in computer technology and decrease in hardware and software costs have allowed companies to store this detailed information in one place. We can now store and process large volumes of data, at speed, at low cost. Software has become more sophisticated, allowing us to structure information in databases, providing a high degree of flexibility to support the changing needs of the marketeer. This marketing data is stored in a marketing database.

Database marketing can therefore be described as:

> An accountable form of marketing, based on a detailed knowledge of the target market stored in a marketing database, and used to drive targeted communications through a range of media directly to customers and prospects.

The objectives of database marketing are that it goes beyond a one-off sale or enquiry, by building up information on the individual, and using the information to develop knowledge and strategy and drive activity.

Checklist

1. Have the target audiences been defined?
2. Are adequate databases available?
3. Can the people be (a) named, or (b) designated?

4. Do you plan to use a direct mail agency. If so, have you checked (a) the origin and (b) the nature of their lists, and (c) whether they are up to date, accurate and comprehensive?
5. In producing the brief have you defined
   (a) The objective of the campaign?
   (b) The number of shots?
   (c) The form they should take?
   (d) Frequency and timing?
   (e) Use of reply-paid material?
   (f) A follow-up to a reply?
6. Is there a system for names to be deleted from the list as replies are received?
7. Have quantified targets been set?
8. Are the means for comparison of performance clearly specified?
9. Has the field force been given advance notice of the campaign?
10. Has consideration been given to an initial test mailing?

EXHIBITIONS

Exhibitions vary considerably in size and scope from a small show with perhaps 20 or 30 modest stands to vast international fairs with a thousand or more exhibitors covering a product range across the entire industrial sector.

The significance of exhibitions in the industrial promotional budget may not be great but, looking at some of the larger events, it is evident that the individual expenditure on many stands is of a high order indeed. While a budget of a hundred or so pounds may be possible with some of the smaller exhibitions, the costs rise easily into tens of thousands and more with the bigger shows.

It is strange to find that so little is known about the usefulness of exhibitions, that they are so often an expression of faith rather than fact, with such factors as size of stand and budget determined intuitively by some senior executive. Evidence of this is to be found by discussing the matter with exhibitors and is confirmed by the random way in which in one year a company invests in a substantial stand, next year pulls out altogether, then later comes back with an even larger display.

There tends to be a progression in the evolution of a particular exhibition rather like the life-cycle of a new product. Initially an exhibition satisfies a need which as it grows causes the exhibition to expand. This attracts more visitors and thus more exhibitors, producing a cumulative growth. A further variable at work is the force of competitive prestige. In order to impress customers, exhibitors vie with each other to have the grandest and largest stands and, as this factor develops, so the expense rises until a few of the leaders suddenly realize that the whole thing is uneconomical, and drop out. The example having been set, others follow suit, and the exhibition goes into a period of decline in which it may stagnate, disintegrate, fragment or disappear altogether.

There is probably more money wasted at exhibitions than in any other medium, a paradox since fundamentally the concept of an exhibition is to save money by getting face to face with large numbers of buyers in greater numbers per salesperson-day than could ever be achieved on the road.

The exhibition industry itself may be partly to blame. It breaks down into three broad groups: the organizers, the venue proprietors and the contractors.

Exhibitions are arranged by a wide variety of organizations ranging from commercial exhibition companies to trade associations, publishers and learned bodies. Their function is to hire a hall, then let out spaces to exhibitors at a rate which will bring a profit. Beyond this they may involve themselves in conducting pre-publicity and providing some service during the show. Only the most progressive organizers will set up facilities for providing intelligence for exhibitors on the number and nature of visitors, their length of stay, their attitudes towards different stands and exhibits, their wants and criticisms. Furthermore there is little effort to discipline exhibitors into containing costs by, for instance, restricting stand sizes or imposing shell schemes, as is common practice in the United States. Exhibition organizers sometimes play a passive and short-term role which is not helpful to exhibitors and in the long term does not help themselves.

Exhibition halls are often inadequate, and this, though perhaps not the fault of anyone in particular, points the need for exhibitors to assess carefully the value of each venue. Exhibition contractors, the people who construct the stands, are involved in very high labour costs, with the result that a stand built to last for a week will often cost more than a luxury house. There is considerable room for improving the cost-effectiveness of exhibitions and there is little doubt that the exhibition industry as a whole could make an important contribution. This is largely outside the control of an individual exhibitor, but this should not preclude collective action by groups of companies. Moreover, to be aware of areas of high expense at least enables a company to exert maximum control and scrutiny in obtaining good value for money.

Exhibitors

Before turning to the positive role of exhibitions in the marketing operation, it is unfortunately necessary to press this negative theme a little further by extending it to the exhibitor. Earlier in this book it has been pointed out that much in marketing communications has hitherto been intuitive, without any logical objective, and without any data to support decisions. Exhibitions are equally susceptible to this danger, as is borne out by a booklet from the Institute of Directors in which what it terms dangers and temptations to exhibitors are set out.

1. An exhibition should not be looked upon as an isolated event.
2. Never enter an exhibition – no matter how inexpensive it appears to be – unless it fulfils some clearly defined marketing objective.
3. An exhibition is not the occasion for giving a once-off opportunity to polish up a tarnished corporate image.
4. Prestige is never a sufficient reason for appearing at exhibitions.
5. Don't base exhibition plans on the theory 'if the competitors are there, we have to be'.

6. Don't try one exhibition just 'to see how it goes'.
7. An exhibition should not be looked upon as an opportunity for senior members of the company to have a free holiday or a booze-up with their old cronies – it is an occasion for the people in the firing line, no matter how junior they may be, to do a hard-hitting job of work.
8. Don't exhibit at all if you have to do it on the cheap – in money or executive time. This is not to say that many exhibitions are not inexpensive – but be sure you assign adequate money for the job expected to be done.
9. Remember – it's ten times easier to start exhibiting than to stop, once you have an exhibition programme under way.

To the above 'rules' we can add a number of other points worthy of consideration with a view to increasing the effectiveness of an exhibition.

10. Regard an exhibition stand as a three-dimensional advertisement.
11. Build in really effective corporate identification.
12. Pay special attention to lighting the key points of the stand and to the writing of copy panels.
13. Design a single focal point visually and in terms of traffic flow.
14. Allow for staffing at the level of approximately two people per 10 square metres.
15. Plan in advance for fast post-exhibition follow-up.
16. At each show make a formal evaluation of competitors' activities.

Inter-media comparisons

An exhibition is simply a channel of persuasion which is available as an ingredient in the marketing mix. It must therefore fit into the marketing plan and have a specific purpose, or not be used at all. It has certain characteristics which make it more or less attractive depending upon the requirements of the campaign. It is useful to examine these and in so doing relate them to other media with which it will be required to combine.

SELLING EFFICIENCY

Fundamentally an exhibition should be highly efficient in selling terms since it assembles in one place maybe tens of thousands of buyers who if they can be attracted to a stand will facilitate a 'call rate' far in excess of normal. A salesman on a stand may well talk to 40 or 50 buyers in the course of a day – a factor ten times greater than the norm. And think of the psychological advantage of the buyer calling on the salesforce and asking for information. A recent study in the US showed that customer contact could be seven times greater on an exhibition stand than in the field. See Figure 6.1.

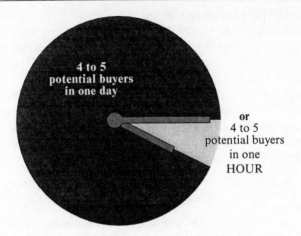

Figure 6.1 Trade show exhibitors accelerate qualified sales lead development by as much as seven times the number of prospects reached through normal field sales techniques (*Source*: Trade Show Bureau)

IMPACT

Compared for instance with press advertising, impact is obviously higher, since an exhibition has the opportunity to compress into one activity the whole selling operation – attention, interest, persuasion, desire to purchase and indeed the placing of an order.

DEMONSTRATION

Here an exhibition scores even over sales visits, since with heavy equipment in particular the opportunity exists to give far more comprehensive demonstrations than can ever be achieved by a travelling salesperson.

TIME-SCALE

This acts in two ways: firstly one may well have to wait a year or two for an exhibition to take place; secondly, setting this factor aside, an exhibition can provide the chance to influence a very large part of a market in a very short space of time.

MARKET PENETRATION

Having regard to the complex nature of the decision-making units in industrial companies, exhibitions often bring to the surface many of the hidden influences in the purchasing process – the engineer, chemist, designer, factory manager, as well as directors.

COMPANY IMAGE

The company can be presented in all its aspects at one and the same time, enabling a customer to see it as a whole – its products, manufacturing facilities, subsidiaries and associates, and most important its senior management.

MARKET DEVELOPMENT

A unique opportunity is presented for uncovering a wide variety of uses for products which lead to the identification of new markets. Similarly an interchange of views on products often leads to modifications which give rise to the development of new products.

US RESEARCH

Two pieces of research in America add further to our knowledge of the strengths of exhibitions in relation to other media. Figure 6.2 shows how 1000 decision-makers rated various media for 'Extremely useful sources of

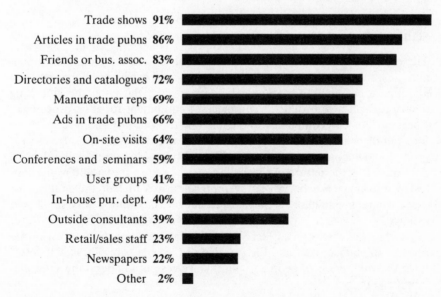

Figure 6.2   'Extremely useful' sources of purchasing information (*Source*: Trade Show Bureau)

purchasing information'. Table 6.1 compares the roles of exhibitions to advertising and direct mail.

Table 6.1 Which marketing tools are most effective

Most effective for	Exhibitions	Advertising	Direct mail
Generating sales leads	38.8%	27.4%	19.9%
Introducing new products/services	41.7%	23.8%	27.6%
Taking orders	11.9%	4.9%	8.3%
Promoting brand image	41.8%	43.4%	18.7%
Promoting company image	32.9%	31.8%	22.0%
Entering new markets	27.7%	24.8%	24.5%

Source: CEIR: 'The Power of Exhibitions' II (1996)

COST

It is important to cost an exhibition fully, to add together rental, stand construction, staff, promotional material, entertaining, pre-publicity and so on. An unsophisticated show costing a few hundred pounds can have a very high degree of cost-effectiveness. One costing say 70,000 or 80,000 pounds needs a great deal of justification. The real cost however is the unit cost, that is, the cost per enquiry or the cost per contact and this needs to be assessed in relation to the unit costs of other media.

Setting the objectives

These must be set down in writing as part of the overall promotional plan and must incorporate targets that are precise, and capable of being attained and measured. For instance, an exhibition may be chosen as the launching platform for a new product, say a piece of equipment for food processing. There may be 500 companies who could buy this product and, with perhaps four people likely to be involved in the buying decision, one arrives at a total of 2000 people to be contacted. The setting of the target will in fact be determined by the nature of the exhibition, in that a popular and well-established one may well be visited by representatives of half the industry or more whereas a smaller or untried one may attract only a very small percentage.

Further factors in setting targets in this instance are the interest in the product or service itself and the prestige of the company. These will determine the willingness of people to put themselves out to attend the show and visit the stand.

In the light of such factors and perhaps with previous experience, the first target may be to make face-to-face contact with 500 people who represent potential customers and to secure an entrée for a subsequent sales visit. A secondary goal could be to obtain the general goodwill of the industry as a whole by distributing to interested parties 5000 leaflets describing a new piece of equipment.

Over and above the primary objective of an exhibition stand will be a number of supplementary requirements which should be catered for only so long as they do not act as a distraction or as a negative influence. The broad range of company activities may need to be put across to show how it backs up a new product. The extent to which modern plant and machinery is used may be another feature, with examples of accuracy, reliability and quality control. Provision may be made for conducting marketing research; perhaps entertaining facilities are needed for customers in other product categories.

At the other extreme, the need may be to provide first-class entertainment for only a small number of very large customers. Such an example could be the Farnborough or Paris Air Shows where, frequently, there is little emphasis on products, but rather a very well set up 'soft sell' operation in

Table 6.2 Objectives of an exhibition

Whilst sales leads are the most popular goal, there are many other objectives as the following US research shows. Exhibitors went into exhibitions in order to:

Generate qualified leads	71%
Maintain an image	63%
Intensify awareness	60%
Establish a presence	56%
Introduce a new product	31%
Generate immediate sales	25%
Judge reaction to new product	13%
Provide dealer support	8%
Discover new applications	5%
Stimulate secondary markets	4%
Recruit distributors	3%

Table 6.3 Reasons for visiting an exhibition

As against exhibitors' motives, the following were the reasons attributed to visitors for attending a show:

To evaluate new products	56%
To see specific products or companies	23%
To obtain product information	13%
General interest	10%
To attend seminars	6%

which VIP customers are provided with pleasant facilities to relax and enjoy
the display with hard business left to another time and place. The objective
in this instance may be to provide an opportunity for 150 top customers to
meet the chairman and to spend one of a number of agreeable afternoons
with him.

Planning an exhibition

Having defined the objectives of an exhibition in quantitative terms it is necessary to build into the event a maximum of efficiency in order to achieve
the required result at least cost. This can be planned by examining every
stage in the development of an exhibition promotion.

Certainly a primary factor in participating in an exhibition is to capitalize
on what may be described as a captive audience. The audience, however, is
rarely captive in the sense that cinema viewers are: indeed their movements
along a gangway are often fleeting and transitory; an attractive stand helps
somewhat to overcome this.

It is worthwhile to regard the established visitors, who will come anyway,
as a bonus which adds to the effectiveness of the operation, but the essential
task for an exhibitor is to take all possible steps to ensure that the key
prospective customers are notified in advance of what will be on show, how
much their presence will be welcomed, and the ways in which they will stand
to benefit.

An exhibition stand can justify a separate campaign of its own, designed
to obtain visits by the right people defined in the marketing plan. This calls
for the usual letter stickers, advertisement inserts, preview editorials and a
plan showing where the stand is located, but this is what everyone else is
already doing. A good deal more is required if the full benefits are to be
obtained, and this calls for a campaign of its own using all suitable channels
of persuasion – invitations from a director, backed up by personal contact
from the sales force, special press advertising, a direct mail build-up and
some special incentive.

The fact is however that many firms do little individually to publicize
their events. Evidence of this is to be found in a piece of research conducted
in the United States but with general application anywhere (Figure 6.3).

Just what is required will depend on the objectives of the exhibition
stand, and as has been said earlier, these will be quantified, thus providing a
basis for developing the campaign plan, and also eventually a mark against
which the exhibition can be evaluated.

It is only when 'to have 500 potential buyers call upon our stand' has
been written down and agreed that the size of the task becomes apparent.
The exhibition campaign plan can only then be put in hand and tailored
carefully to match the need – no more and no less.

PRE-SHOW PROMOTION

It might be said that the principal role of the exhibition organizer is to build attendance at the show as a whole. It must be for the individual exhibitor, however, to promote the company stand. The task is to get the company name on the 'must see' list. The following is a list of some pre-show promotions which have proved to be successful:

- Pre-show mailers
- Dedicated advertisements
- Posters
- Telemarketing
- Sales calls
- Exhibitor guest tickets
- News releases
- Press party
- Pre-show receptions
- Speciality business gifts
- Media packs

SITE AND SIZE

An examination of any exhibition hall will bring to light the fact that some areas are popular while others are not. What are missing are factual data on

Pre-show promotion techniques (83% of all companies did some pre-show promotion)

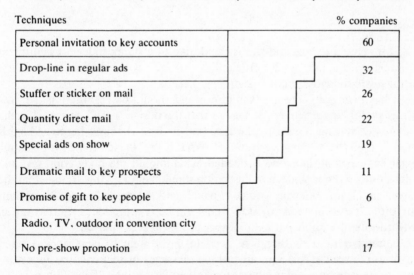

Techniques	% companies
Personal invitation to key accounts	60
Drop-line in regular ads	32
Stuffer or sticker on mail	26
Quantity direct mail	22
Special ads on show	19
Dramatic mail to key prospects	11
Promise of gift to key people	6
Radio, TV, outdoor in convention city	1
No pre-show promotion	17

Figure 6.3   Pre-show promotion techniques in the United States
(*Source:* Trade Show Bureau Research Report Study No 4)

the traffic flow at various places in a hall at various times. This is vital and one should look to exhibition organizers to supply such information. In its absence, it must rest with the exhibitor to extract his own information, such as traffic flow in main and subsidiary gangways, and in upper floors as compared with the ground floor. Interviews with visitors can for instance establish whether they visited the gallery, how much time they spent in the hall altogether and how valuable they found the exhibition. Research can easily be extended into determining what other channels of persuasion they are exposed to, for instance which trade magazines they read. Such information enables one to judge the relationship between a given exhibition and other media including, of course, other exhibitions.

As to the size of a stand, the answer is simply to make it as small as possible consistent with the laid-down objectives. Too much regard is probably paid to highly subjective comparisons with the size and appearance of competitors' stands, a factor which is probably much less significant to the visitor than the exhibitor. If, of course, the objective is primarily to impress upon people that a company is the largest and most important in the industry, then a large and impressive stand could be justified.

It is important to begin by listing what facilities are essential and what are the minimum areas required, rather than first determining the square footage and then fitting things in as best one can. The shape of available sites is often an important consideration, and the number of open sides can be a vital factor, if only because an island stand has up to four times the display area of a wall stand.

DESIGN

Closely related to size and site is the design of a stand: indeed it is difficult to see how a stand can be efficiently conceived without some regard first being given to layout if not design.

It has been said that an exhibition stand should be regarded as a three-dimensional advertisement. It follows that the design should be tested in the same way, having regard to the fact that its cost can well be considerably greater than that of an advertisement. What is the 'single selling proposition', what eye-catching headline is needed, what should the body copy say, and who should write it, and what illustration should be used? It is strange that the layout of a stand, the words on copy panels and the products and illustrations are often left to in-company staff to determine and produce, whereas for an advertisement a whole battalion of specialists will be employed.

A number of skills therefore need to be brought to bear since a stand involves construction, décor, advertising messages or selling copy, display, as well as an optimum environment for face-to-face selling. Too often it is evident that only a number of these aspects has received adequate consideration, for example, the large number of people who will walk past the stand, but will not be prepared to step on it and thus become exposed to the attention of sales staff. For these people, usually the majority, it is vital that the design be in the form of a three-dimensional advertisement. It must incorporate a means of attracting attention, it must convey at a distance, and at a glance, a good selling message which will stimulate interest, and it must follow this with descriptive and selling copy which will cause a person to want to read more and to enquire for further information. To a person concerned with advertisement design, such an approach may be second nature and in any case there will be close co-operation with a copywriter whose very function it is to express selling messages in a crisp, compelling manner. Exhibition designers may sometimes be primarily specialists in architecture and décor rather than advertising, and the copy is more often than not written by a sales manager or a member of the advertising department who would not lay claim to being an expert copywriter. Yet the space to be filled will cost considerably more than an equivalent press advertisement, or even a campaign.

The layout of a stand is critical to its success in terms of its laid down objectives. Does the stand need to be designed so as to attract a maximum of visitors to it? In that case it must be open and inviting. Does it alternatively have to function primarily as a meeting point for important customers who will relax and refresh themselves in the convivial company of senior members of staff? That may call for a largely closed-in stand where access is open to a carefully selected and screened number of people. Perhaps a major objective is to distribute a large number of leaflets to visitors, in which case it just isn't good enough to lay out the leaflets in whatever vacant space there happens to be. No, the whole stand design in that case must be built around making it as easy as possible for the passer-by to pick up a leaflet. It's the equivalent of a reply-paid coupon in an advertisement.

For designers to have the best chance of producing a stand which will be effective it is important that their briefing should be brought fully into the overall objectives of the exhibition and be provided with a complete list of facilities required, products to be exhibited, displays to be featured, and finally every single word of copy with an indication of emphasis and dominance of each part.

The sequence of events which should be followed is agreement on layout, visuals, a model if necessary, then working drawings and specification. Each stage must be considered and approved in detail if extra costs are to be avoided. If top management are going to express a point of view, it is now that this should take place before any construction is started.

STAND ADMINISTRATION AND STAFFING

It will be found most effective to designate one senior executive as stand manager for the whole period of the show, and for that person to have a written brief. The job will entail achieving the written objectives and it is only fair therefore that he or she should be involved at an early stage in the development of the stand. Such a person will in effect be the captain of the ship, responsible for motivating sales staff, maintaining discipline, looking to stand cleanliness and maintenance, ensuring an adequate supply of litera-ture, and the hundred and one things that go to make the stand a dynamic part of a marketing operation.

It is surprising how often the staff are not given an adequate briefing on their responsibilities and functions. It is enlightening to go to any exhibition and visit a series of stands in order to assess the level of sales service. It is unlikely that any attention will be given in anything other than a minority of cases and generally speaking the larger the stand the poorer the service. Yet it is elementary to include in the exhibition briefing the instruction (always assuming this is desirable) that everyone stepping on to a stand should be greeted with an offer of help, indeed that anyone even showing an interest from the gangway should be given some attention.

The failure of sales staff to perform effectively on an exhibition stand has been well explained in a feature published by *Industrial Marketing*.

> The sales situation at a trade show is the reverse of a field sales call – the prospect comes to you. You have a fraction of the normal time to present your facts. The salesperson has to make more presentations per hour than he or she might make in a day in the field.
>
> Trade show selling is a different sell, and many salespeople simply don't know how to sell in a trade show. They feel like salt water fish that have been placed in a fresh water lake and have difficulty adapting in order to survive.
>
> It's a frightening change. A rapid presentation style has to be adopted. An adjustment must be made to the environmental change. There is seldom the security of an appointment call or sales schedule. A change in priorities must be made. A seasoned salesperson with a good list of steady clients is suddenly faced with a new 'cold call' fear.
>
> Is it any wonder that when the sales rep's regular customer comes into the exhibit, the sales rep may expand the visiting time in order to avoid the unpleas-antness of the trade show's difficult environment?

A piece of research by the American Trade Show Bureau into what visitors want asked the question 'What do you like most in salespeople?' The answers were:

- Professionalism
- Good listeners
- Not too pushy
- Thorough product knowledge
- Enthusiasm
- Caring
- The right product at the right price

Exhibitionitis

This is an illness that everyone visiting an exhibition has had but without realizing that it had a name and was well recognized by exhibition professionals. It not only affects visitors, it can also play havoc with exhibitors.

Simply stated, anyone at an exhibition will, after the first hour or so, begin to feel weary of standing or walking to such an extent that his or her normal business drive will give way to an increasingly urgent desire to sit down.

This is an important threat, and an even more important opportunity. The stand can be designed in such a way that staff members can be seated without appearing to have withdrawn from giving service to customers. Alternatively a roster can be drawn up which allows for periods of relaxation. And then for customers a seating arrangement can be made such that without feeling committed or cornered a visitor can sit and relax while discussing his or her particular interest.

'Are you sitting comfortably?' is a slogan which is well worth considering seriously at any exhibition, large or small.

Budgeting

Arriving at an effective and yet economic budget for an exhibition is both difficult and complex. There are of course some short cuts but these do not necessarily produce the best results. They include:

1. What can we afford?
2. What did we spend last year?
3. How much are our competitors spending?
4. Percentage of anticipated sales.

These and other factors are all worthy of consideration, but perhaps the most logical approach is what is known as the task method of budgeting as described in Chapter 3. Here the 'task' to be achieved is analysed in some detail, ie a listing of specific objectives. Then in conjunction with the stand designer an outline is produced of what is essential for the achievement of those objectives. This outline covers stand location, size of stand, type of construction, style of presentation, special features and any other requirements. This then gives the minimum requirement and provides the basis of competitive quotations for stand construction.

From research conducted on behalf of British Business Press a very interesting breakdown of typical exhibition costs was produced. These are given in Table 6.4.

Table 6.4 Typical exhibition costs. Example 1 is a 30 m² shell-scheme stand, portable exhibits. Example 2 is a 60 m² purpose-built stand, heavy exhibits

	Example 1	Example 2
1. Stand space	3600	6000
2. Stand construction	400	6000
3. Transporting and erecting exhibits	200	1000
4. Stand graphics	800	1500
5. Furniture, flowers, power, telephone, drinks, cleaning, etc.	700	1200
6. Invitations/mailings to prospects	300	500
7. Catalogue and other advertising	1000	2000
8. Leaflets for distribution from stand	500	1500
9. Entertaining costs	500	1000
10. Staff travel subsistence	2000	4000
11. Temporary staff	200	400
12. Unforeseen extras	500	1000
13. Internal meeting hours	1000	2000
Total costs per exhibition	£11,700	£28,100

Memorability

Some very interesting work has been done in the United States on the memorability of an exhibition stand. Its purpose has been to measure just how long an exhibit will remain in the memory of a visitor: also to find what factors affect the degree of memorability.

As can be seen from Figure 6.4, an exhibit is remembered long after the event and indeed it can probably be concluded that exhibitions have a longer retention time than any other medium.

Memorability drops off to around 70 per cent at about five or six weeks but

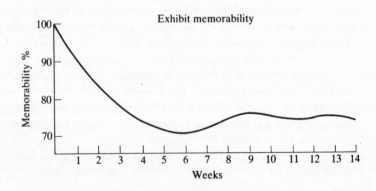

Figure 6.4 Exhibit memorability (USA Trade Show Bureau Report)

then increases to 75 per cent and remains at that level from eight weeks through 14 weeks. Exhibitors probably are following up on their enquiries with literature and personal sales calls which reinforce the exhibit memorability.

Stand staff performance affects memorability the most because the personal contact with visitors creates a strong impact. Stands achieving a high degree of person-to-person contact had higher memorability scores than others. Also the level of awareness of a company was a strong influence on the degree to which visitors remembered visiting an exhibit. In separate analyses of companies considered leaders in their industry or field and companies that spend more money on advertising, their level of memorability was considerably higher than the average.

The type of exhibit approach used is the third major factor affecting memorability. Exhibits using formal or informal product demonstrations generally had higher memorability than static displays.

Perhaps the most important message to come out of this piece of research is that an exhibition investment has a potential value for way outside the duration of the exhibition. The pre-exhibition opportunity to publicize a forthcoming event has always been recognized and exploited to some degree. It may be that exhibitors have not fully capitalized on the favourable opportunity for doing business that exists for many weeks after an exhibition has closed.

The Certificate of Attendance (COA)

The ABC (Audit Bureau of Circulation) has certified exhibition attendances over a period of two decades. Launched in 1993, the COA is a consolidation of two previous ABC audit schemes. The COA has quickly become *the* industry standard for the provision of quantitative and qualitative exhibition attendance data. It provides the *facts* about exhibitions to existing and prospective exhibitors through the provision of detailed visitor data. For organizers it is a cost-effective sales and marketing tool. For exhibition buyers, it is an insurance policy on their buying decisions.

The COA verifies the total attendance of an exhibition and the demographic data held for those attendees.

ATTENDANCE DATA

The attendance list is split into three main categories:

- Registered free: Visitors who attend free of charge via completion of a registration card.
- Registered paid: Visitors who pay an admission charge and complete a registration card.
- Non-registered paid: Visitors who pay an admission charge but do not complete a registration card.

DEMOGRAPHIC DATA

As a minimum, the COA analyses the registered attendance into the following geo-demographic categories:

- Geographical location
- Job title
- Company activity

Any demographic analyses, if auditable, can be included within the COA eg company turnover, number of employees, buying responsibilities, etc.

The certificate identifies the organizer; sponsor (if applicable); the date and venue of the show; the number of stands and stand space occupied; the date and venue of the next show; association membership (if applicable); the target audience and the products/services exhibited.

THE AUDIT SYSTEM

In order to achieve an ABC certificate, organizers must retain detailed auditable records to prove the attendance details and the demographic data for those attendees. The audits are conducted to ABC rules and procedures by ABC's own staff auditors.

ABC's audit is based on a full count of attendees and the associated demographic data. The stringent and comprehensive audit verifies not only the accuracy of the numbers, but the sources from which the data are derived.

WHAT DOES THE AUDIT CHECK?

- *Checks* the attendance list reconciles with the attendance claim.
- *Checks* the attendance list for duplications. A statistically valid duplication test establishes the duplication level, which is then adjusted against the attendance claim.
- *Checks* that the number of registration cards reconciles with the claimed registered attendance.
- *Checks* that the claimed registered attendance actually attended the show by contacting a statistically valid sample of claimed visitors to verify attendance.
- *Checks* that the cash records support the claimed paid attendance.
- *Checks* that the demographic data held on the registration cards have been correctly analysed

Research at exhibitions

Over and above measurement of the specific value of an exhibition, which is dealt with in the next section, there are many opportunities for research work during an exhibition. Quite simply it can be said that within an exhibition hall for a number of days will be a good sample of a particular market or market segment. There is thus an opportunity to ask questions and obtain answers about any aspect of market opinion, behaviour or motivation that one wishes to pursue. And this at relatively low cost and in a very short space of time.

What are the readership habits of this market segment for instance? A well-tried technique is to compile a short-list of the most likely publications and to make up a flip chart with the front covers of each publication on separate sheets. Interviewers can then stop people at random, or talk to visitors to the stand, asking them 'which of the following publications are read regularly?' Within a few days one has a profile of readership which is often quite different from an existing media plan based upon circulation data and/or intuition.

Another particularly useful research project for an exhibition is to market test a new product. Here the product is on the stand, having been well publicized in advance, and visitors are asked to comment on certain pre-determined criteria such as size, shape, weight, colour, speed, cost, accuracy, performance, and application. Product prototypes can obviously be evaluated in this way as indeed can mere ideas or concepts. The opportunity is particularly attractive to manufacturers of specialized products where their potential market is widely spread and could only be otherwise contacted at very considerable cost.

In general it can be said that whatever information is required about a market can be obtained from an appropriate exhibition provided due allowance is made for the sample not necessarily being representative of the total market.

Visitors on the whole do not seem to mind answering a modest number of questions: in fact many seem to enjoy it. It is important however to ensure that the exhibition organizers are kept fully informed of any proposed research work where this is to be conducted in the public gangway.

Exhibition evaluation

The setting of objectives and evaluation go hand in hand. Given an objective of securing 200 sales leads, evaluation at its simplest is to ask whether that number was achieved, and if not why not. It will readily be seen how important it is to quantify objectives from the outset.

It is obviously not possible to write down in detail all the ways in which an exhibition can be evaluated. And in any case this must depend on the objectives which were set for a particular exhibition. What must be said, however, is that having decided to make an investment in the form of an exhibition it would be the height of business folly not to make a determined effort to measure the return on the investment.

The question of evaluation is dealt with in a very useful publication by ISBA called *Guide for Exhibitors*. Their many recommendations include:

1. Boxes for visiting cards.
2. Enquiry pads with room for literature/sample requests (literature must be sent out immediately while visitors' interest is keen and a reply paid card should be included for further information).
3. Visitors' book. Noting of general enquiries – not specifically recorded for follow up purposes. It is advised not to use visitors' books in Eastern European countries.
4. Noting names and number of delegates to lectures and/or film shows at exhibitions. Where one is selling over the counter the total sales less stand/space cost give one the immediate answer.
5. Obtain from the organizers the total number of visitors to the show and compare this with previous years.
6. Note whether your presentation really does stop the crowd.
7. Note the level of activity on your stand compared to others in the near vicinity.

SALES LITERATURE

There are opposing schools of thought on the use of sales literature at exhibitions, some holding that if it is put out, people tend to pick it up indiscriminately, and that if it is not put out people are encouraged to make enquiries; others contend that the more literature distributed the better.

There are good reasons for producing something in the way of an exhibition 'give away' which should be displayed so that people have easy access to it, but which will also include the offer to send on, say, the main catalogue as a means of obtaining future sales leads. Since, however, much of an industrial marketing communications campaign is aimed at getting sales literature into the hands of prospective buyers, it is important that this opportunity be used to the full on a properly planned basis. A jumble of sales leaflets scattered around on a few tables can hardly be said to be maximizing a selling opportunity.

Private exhibitions

An important trend in this field is to mount an exhibition on an individual basis, sometimes to coincide with a public one in the near vicinity, sometimes entirely independently. A further variation is for a number of firms with complementary product ranges to combine and share expenses, a particularly attractive solution where they share common markets.

The reason for the development of private exhibitions lies partly in the spiralling costs of participating in a public exhibition and partly in the degree of attention which can be given to visitors in surroundings which are usually a good deal more comfortable than an exhibition hall, without the distractions of hundreds of other exhibitors, and avoiding the physical and mental exhaustion which most visitors experience at any major show.

Consider for example a medium-sized stand at a national exhibition. The total cost for an area of, say, 100–150 m² may well be of the order of £50,000. Such an event if staged in a nearby hotel may provide three or four times the area for half the cost in a relaxed atmosphere, with far superior reception and entertainment facilities. Moreover, the layout could be such that each visitor is greeted personally, conducted around the entire display, and questioned in depth to find out particular interests and to determine future sales action.

Where a company has a limited market, large numbers of people at a public exhibition looking around for general interest can seriously impair the efficiency of the sales staff on duty. The staff at a private show are able to relax, are more likely to be able to carry out an effective selling job, and can give special attention to major customers and to the press, perhaps in a private suite adjoining the exhibition area. Furthermore, competitors cannot easily intrude to probe for details of new products and new selling approaches.

Partisans of the private exhibition will point to more and more advantages such as not having to contend with the difficulties of restrictive labour practices at exhibition halls, being able to set up a show at a time to suit oneself, not having to pay officials to obtain special services. Certainly there are important advantages.

There is, however, one basic benefit of a trade show that does not apply to a private one, namely that with very little effort on the part of an exhibitor a good proportion of a potential market may have the opportunity of coming face to face with one's products.

It would seem, therefore, that to justify a private exhibition instead of a public one, the potential market will be relatively small, say a few hundred, and certainly no more than a few thousand, with all the purchasing influences within that market well defined. Furthermore, there must be sufficient incentive to persuade buyers to make the effort of a special call, even though the venue is fairly close to the exhibition hall.

If, for example, a new company was launching a range of resistors which had a very wide potential application in the electrical and electronic industries, it would probably benefit by using the established audience of one of the major national or international exhibitions to secure a maximum of sales leads, and indeed to gain valuable market intelligence on the reaction of the new range.

Alternatively if the product was a new piece of equipment for carton manufacturers of whom there were only a few hundred prospects, and these very well defined, a private show might be much the most effective method of exhibiting.

Travelling exhibitions

There may be advantages in moving away from the idea of attaching a private exhibition to a public one, and simply setting up an exhibition in its own right. It might be in one location or, more likely, it would be staged in a number of places near the major potential sources of business. The operation can be efficient since, once the exhibition equipment has been assembled, it is a relatively easy matter to move on to another location. Hotels are generally co-operative in accommodating such ventures and provincial rates can be very competitive. A disadvantage is that a good deal of sales force time, and management, is tied down by these events, and this time must be justified by an adequate level of visitors of worthwhile calibre. Once again it is necessary to set targets, compare costs, and as soon as an operation begins to fail, either take corrective action or put a stop to the project.

Trailers and caravans can provide an alternative or sometimes a supplement to the staging of round-the-country exhibitions. They are also of particular value for export promotions. Indeed there is a good deal of scope for initiative in the field of travelling exhibitions, and the use of railways, barges, ships and aeroplanes has not been anything like exploited to the full. The sheer novelty of such ventures can do much to ensure the success of the operation.

Strengths and weaknesses of exhibitions

Strengths

- Productivity factor of seven over field sales calls
- Best for demonstrations, even over sales calls
- Buyers visit *you* and request information
- Very large number of sales contacts are concentrated into a short space of time
- Contact is made with hitherto unknown members of the decision-making unit
- Very narrow targeting
- Better than other media for enquiries and sales leads
- Quick, thorough, and inexpensive research opportunities into journal readership, new products and new applications/markets
- Opportunity for distributing sales literature and for adding to the database
- Visitors can meet specialists and top management
- Provision for refreshments and entertaining
- Contributes to corporate image
- Ease of evaluation
- Good chances for meeting the press

Weaknesses

- Expensive (but cost per enquiry may be low)
- Sales force away from territories

- Causes administrative chaos before and after the show
- Too many calls for action in too short a time
- Open to competitors (though vice versa)
- Tyre-kickers, ie time-wasters
- Tiring for staff
- Restricted geographical location
- Shows take place only once a year or two years
- Difficulty in getting prospects to attend
- Lack of data – only 10 per cent of UK shows are audited

Checklist

The checklist has been divided into two parts for convenience – pre-exhibition and post-exhibition.

PRE-EXHIBITION

1. Has a proposed exhibition been examined from the point of view of:
   (a) The likely audience to be reached
   (b) The extent of competition
   (c) Location and accessibility of the site
   (d) Promotional activities by the organizers
   (e) Entertainment facilities?
2. Does the exhibition form part of an integrated marketing plan?
3. Has a written objective been produced for the intended exhibition stand?
4. Have all the relevant people been brought into the planning of the exhibition, for instance; sales management, advertising agency, designer, copywriter, R&D and transport department?
5. Has consideration been given to:
   (a) Site, location and size
   (b) Display requirements
   (c) Own entertaining facilities
   (d) Sales literature dispensers
   (e) Exhibits
   (f) Construction
   (g) Stand management
   (h) Staffing
   (i) Planned approach to visitors
   (j) Sales follow-up?
6. Has pre-publicity been organized to ensure a maximum attendance?
7. Has special provision been made for receiving:
   (a) The press
   (b) Overseas visitors?

8. Has a detailed schedule been produced of all activities leading up to the show, including the necessary action for its duration, and termination?
9. In budgeting for an exhibition, have all the costs been included, for example sales staff's time, preparation of exhibits and their transportation?
10. Have you considered how best to exploit photography in:
   (a) Products
   (b) Product applications
   (c) Own factory and processes
   (d) News and events
   (e) People and personalities
   (f) Prestige?
11. Has the use of editorial publicity been established as an integral part of the organizer's press office operation?

POST-EXHIBITION

1. Was the attendance up to target in terms of total numbers, industry category, job status, buying power, etc?
2. What was the cost per 'sales call' or demonstration?
3. Were the numbers entertained satisfactory in quantity and quality?
4. Were any sales objectives met?
5. How many new sales leads were obtained and have these been followed up?
6. How much sales literature was distributed and did this meet the set targets?
7. Did you gain any new contacts regarding decision-makers 'behind the scenes'?
8. What did you learn about your competitors' activities?
9. Was editorial coverage up to target?
10. Were the exhibits delivered, installed and removed on time?
11. Was the stand construction completed on time and did it in every way function to your satisfaction?
12. How did the stand compare with competitors in overall effectiveness, in visitor traffic and in cost?
13. What new market/product knowledge did you gain out of the show?
14. Were you within budget? If not, why not?
15. How did all the above factors compare with the last time you were at this show, and with any other relevant exhibitions?

7.

LITERATURE

It is a common failing that people believe that others outside their company know far more about it and its products than in fact they do. They also expect customers to have a well-balanced and well-informed view of the company's business as a matter of course and to have an intense interest in even the most trivial aspects of a company's operations.

The preparation of a publications or literature strategy can do much to ensure that there is full information about every important aspect of a company's operations and its products or services.

Planning, production and distribution

It is an unfortunate fact that the publication of company literature is often *ad hoc*, unplanned, hurried, ill-conceived and sometimes quite inappropriate. To be effective and efficient, literature must be part of the marketing and corporate strategy. This means quite simply that every single publication must stem from a defined objective which starts with an outline of the audience to be reached, the method of distribution to be employed, and the basic message which it is required to deliver.

It is, however, wrong to suppose that given this start, the production of a well-conceived range of literature will solve the communications problems. It is more than likely that less than 25 per cent of literature, however efficiently distributed, is ever read at all, and certainly page traffic studies of magazines confirm this proportion. With these discouraging statistics, more and more importance centres on what is produced and its quality.

PLANNING

Publications in industry often run late, and even when a production schedule exists it is gradually compressed so that the final printing stage – in a sense the most important of all, and certainly the most expensive – is rushed to the extent that quality suffers and errors creep in. The reason is nearly always bad planning, or at least planning which has lost direction.

The first stage in effective planning is to ensure that the preparation of a piece of literature is carried out in exactly the right sequence. The objectives must be written and agreed before a writer is briefed. A synopsis or outline must be produced before the copy is started and, finally, every single word of copy must be approved before a designer takes over. This is not to say that the designer does not enter the procedure until this stage. The designer should be an integral part of the team from the outset and must work in closest co-operation with writer and executive. But layout, as a general rule, does not start until writing is both complete and fully agreed with everyone who is required to express an opinion.

Presentation of design must vary according to the nature of a job, but it is important in maintaining a time schedule that design work is progressive in the sense that ideas and treatments receive general agreement before the preparation of finished visuals, and policy matters such as style, visual treatment, size, colours, typography and so on are defined to produce work which will meet the specific objectives.

Following this sequence of operations is the type mark-up which must be read as an engineer would read a blueprint before production begins. It is wasteful and unnecessary to wait until proofs are available before deciding that eight point is not really large enough or Times New Roman is too traditional a typeface. The proofs when they come should be an agreeable conclusion to a well-planned exercise. There should be no unpleasant surprises, no radical changes – the job should be exactly what had been envisaged throughout the phases of production.

The second stage in effective planning is to establish from the outset a realistic time schedule and to take steps to enforce it. This is easy to say but sometimes difficult to implement: nevertheless it must be done. If, from past experience, the managing director is likely to require a complete rewrite at a certain stage, the possibility must be included in the schedule, and to do so is probably the surest way of bringing home to him or her just what effect a change of mind can have on a project.

Table 7.1 may serve to underline the value of scheduling. It has been constructed as a typical time-scale for the preparation and production of a 16-page, three-colour brochure. Note that no provision has been made for the commissioning of special photography or technical drawings for instance.

There could well be situations in which a piece of print is required within a week or even less, but to work to high standards it is essential to allow adequate time for a publication which will, after all, last for perhaps a year and sometimes considerably longer.

PREPARATION AND PRODUCTION

The production of good industrial literature is often complex and almost always difficult. The subject-matter is usually of a technical nature, it is

Table 7.1 Print schedule

Produce written objectives and obtain approval	1 week
Brief writer, obtain synopsis and get approval	2 weeks
Write copy	2 weeks
Obtain complete approval	1 week
Visual treatment	2 weeks
Finished visual	2 weeks
Final approval	1 week
Type mark-up and artwork	1 week
Proofs	2 weeks
Printing	3 weeks
Total – 17 weeks	

specialized, and, moreover, must be written with an authority which demonstrates to the reader the expertise of the company issuing it. This maybe indicates that it should be written by an expert but the chances of the writing being interesting and dynamic are then frequently diminished.

Careful choice of the best available writer is therefore of paramount importance. If the technical nature requires that it be written by an engineer, then perhaps it will be necessary for it to be rewritten as a matter of deliberate policy by an expert and stylish writer. Similarly with design, when illustrations are of a highly specialized nature a visualizer will require considerable guidance by experts on precisely which items are of most importance.

In the production of literature there are a large number of variables which perhaps are not encountered with so much force in other media, for instance how many pages, what kind of paper, what size, how many colours, what style of design and typography.

It is reasonable to argue that having hired the best or most appropriate creative people to do the job, they should be left to get on with it. This will only be true if the initial briefing has been full and comprehensive.

Literature must fit into the general company style, shape and size; if not it should be different for a good reason. The creative team must know if cost is the overriding consideration, or if prestige; whether an item is to fit into an existing catalogue, be carried in the pocket, sent through the post or handed out by sales staff. The nature of the audience must be known: different styles will be required for addressing architects and archaeologists, artists and artisans, scientists and directors. Size of typeface and style becomes important depending upon age groups; but a good creative person if equipped with the right background information will be able to produce work which fits a particular audience's frame of reference.

Legibility is of paramount importance, and it is as well to take note of the fact that people over the age of 40 have difficulty with eight point type. Various general rules must be observed: for example, body copy should be in upper and lower case, not capitals. Reversed type is more difficult to read. Leading (space) between the lines, and short measure (width) adds to legibility. Another generalisation is that serif faces are easier to read than sans serif. An interesting piece of research here is one which was conducted among agency art directors as to which of ten typefaces they prefered. The results were as shown in Table 7.2

Table 7.2 Selected type faces for body copy (*Source*: Cahners Research Report, No. 1310.6)

Typefaces	Readers' ranking	Art directors' ranking
Helvetica	1	2
Garamond	2	3
Melior	3	4
Century	4	1
Times Roman	5	6
Univers	6	5
Optima	7	7
Avant Garde	8	8
Caledonia	9	9
Bodoni	10	10

Similarly the most appropriate printing process will tend to come out of the original definition of objectives, or if not here, from the visual treatment. Interdependent with this will be the kind of paper to be used, number of colours, degree of finish and method of presentation.

A more difficult matter is in the choice of a printer. The variations which occur between one supplier and another in quality and delivery make price alone an unsatisfactory and incomplete basis on which to select a printer. The soundest basis is to build up a relationship with a few printers with whom the majority of business is placed, establishing from the outset that certain standards of quality, service and, most important, integrity, must be maintained and that any serious defects will result in a termination of the relationship. Even so, it will be necessary to put an occasional job out to tender in order that cost comparisons can be made.

DISTRIBUTION

Experience shows that much industrial literature is produced at considerable expense, then left substantially unused for a few years before being repulped as wastepaper. This underlines the need for a literature strategy which plans its audiences and methods of distribution.

There will no doubt be a primary audience. For example a leaflet about a new electronic device may be aimed primarily at all design engineers within certain defined industries. Secondary audiences may be the technical buyers and production engineers in the same factories. Other audiences for consideration will be the press, one's own staff, wholesalers and retailers or other end users. A prestige brochure, on the other hand, may be directed towards the senior management of customers and prospects, again to employees, but maybe also to suppliers and to shareholders.

A good general rule is that literature in the store room is wasted though, of course, it is necessary for efficient distribution to maintain adequate stocks to meet demand. Here it is most important to install an effective system of maximum/minimum stock control coupled with a procedure which ensures that before reordering takes places, the full 'pass for press' procedure is used to ensure that the reprint is completely up to date.

Prestige publications

Jargon in marketing has brought down upon itself connotations which are both unfortunate and inaccurate. 'Prestige', for instance, tends to be equated in the minds of many managements with waste of money. If, alternatively, such publications were described as 'image building', the reaction may be even less favourable.

The fact is, however, that when a company name is mentioned to a buyer, if she or he has heard of it at all, a certain image is conjured up. It may be favourable or unfavourable. Indeed it may be highly biased or completely erroneous. Yet it is possible to produce literature which if read will help to create the kind of image that a company hopes to possess. This, of course, presupposes that there exists a plan which defines the company image. Given this objective there are numerous types of publications which can be produced having a sound business basis other than just a general feeling that this is something which ought to be published.

A general company or corporate brochure, for instance, can bring together all the activities of a company expressed in terms which the key audience can recognize as valuable. Such a publication may be preceded by research to establish the level of knowledge about the company and where gaps exist. It is important to avoid being introspective and writing about the company for the sake of it. At the other extreme, if the capability of top management or the existence of modern buildings are outstanding, they are worth publicizing. The first step in such a publication calls for an objective analysis of a company's strengths in relation to competitors and the nature of the audience, and their interest.

A number of companies publish books about their histories, but the important question here seems to be 'who cares?' If the company has had an outstandingly interesting history there may well be justification for such a book. The growth and development may reflect very creditably upon the business as a whole; there may have been outstanding personalities in the business who are characters with an intrinsic interest of their own; there may have been a number of innovations which people in general do not know about – inventions, or new management techniques. On the other hand a company may be in a fast-developing industry where little regard is paid to the past and in which the future – long- and short-term – is all that seems to matter. Perhaps the criterion to be adopted is to demonstrate the need and value of such a publication, and if this cannot be done then not to publish.

Often a company will be in an industry which itself is of wide general interest and can therefore justify a special publication about it. Certain industries producing basic materials such as paper and steel come into this category, along with, for example, textiles, soap, aircraft, electronics, railways and very many others. Sometimes this aspect of literature is covered by an educational programme or classed under the heading of public relations. In the context of this chapter it is enough to apply the question 'will this help to achieve our defined overall objective?' Providing the answer is yes, then the job is worth doing.

It may not be inappropriate at this juncture to emphasize that much industrial purchasing is done on a subjective basis and that attitudes, as well as the placement of orders for capital goods, have an average gestation period of some years. The long-term building of a good reputation is therefore an important activity which is part of the marketing plan. It is no longer inevitable that providing a good product is produced a good reputation will follow without further effort. Customer satisfaction must not only be given, but must be seen to be given.

In much the same way as company publications about an industry can enhance a reputation, so also can literature dealing with other matters which bear on a company's activities. Statistics about an industry as a whole, for example, can prove to be of great value to buyers, suppliers and other interested people. If no other source of such data is readily available many people may take advantage of the statistics and in turn equate the value and reliability of this service with the performance of the company as a whole.

Some marketing principles may be misleading; for instance the proposition that one does not sell product performance, but rather consumer satisfaction, is fine but it can lead to missing quite real selling propositions. The fact is that, no matter how well a customer's identified needs are met by the specification of the product and its performance, there are intangible influences on all human behaviour which will affect decision-making. The task is to uncover these hidden motivations and to take action to satisfy them. Knowledge of the existence of very modern and sophisticated machinery may well be an important factor in a purchasing decision even though it actually makes not the slightest difference to the quality or performance of a product.

Technical publications

In the field of business-to-business marketing communications there almost always exists the need for technical publications which range from specification and data sheets to servicing and operating manuals. To have technical validity and authority these must be written by engineers, technicians or scientists who frequently do not wish to undertake the task and anyway are not able to express themselves clearly.

The result is often a compromise, the outcome of which is that the job is not as good as it might be. There are of course technical writers, but good ones are few and it is not a profession which attracts talented specialists. A solution which is often adopted is to sub-contract the writing to an outside organization which specializes in the production of technical publications. This can be satisfactory, particularly for the smaller firm which may not have a constant demand to maintain a well-balanced workload for its own technical writers. Considerable caution must be exercised in using an outside organization: quality and capability vary considerably, and there is often a high staff turnover which makes continuity of style and quality difficult. One way of getting good technical writing is to sub-contract it to an appropriate technical journalist.

As with many other publicity activities the right solution is perhaps to establish and then pursue exactly those services which are essential. It should then follow that a technical leaflet or a maintenance manual is no more an undesirable but necessary evil than the raw material from which the product is made or the machine that makes it. Thus, if the product warrants first-class materials it also warrants first-class literature and the rate for the job must be paid to the few good technical writers available.

Where a company has a wide range of complementary products it is usually necessary to provide a catalogue, with all the difficulties this involves. Catalogues are expensive to produce, impossible to keep up to date, and never meet the requirements of everyone. Nevertheless, with many technical products they are so essential a part of the marketing operation that they are used by the customer's design department to specify a certain type number, and thus predetermine the brand of product ultimately to be purchased. Interesting catalogue developments are taking place, particularly in the development of microfilm storage units and various other systems of information retrieval, and there is every indication that this technique will continue to develop. In particular, a new generation of publishing techniques must include DTP and – even newer – disks and CD-ROMS. Also to be considered are the use of the Internet and Web sites. Data sheets, for instance, should be designed so that they can be readily faxed. A further but quite different system is one in which a specialist distributor arranges to send out staff to a given market on behalf of a number of clients and actually place into customers' catalogue files the latest material. This scheme is certainly working successfully in some fields, but its application may be limited.

Sales publications

Sales literature represents the opportunity for placing in front of a prospect the complete selling proposition. Even if such material will not always be read, it is nevertheless a good chance to set down in detail a considered view on the merits of the product and the satisfactions it will provide.

A disadvantage is that it is difficult to be specific to an individual's needs in the way in which a salesperson can. A salesperson, however, while having the chance to modify a presentation to suit the circumstances, and to counter objections and doubts by the buyer, does not have unlimited time during a visit and therefore may miss out certain features. Overall, the considered and consolidated argument contained in a piece of sales literature ought to be better than that of any one salesperson.

This is not to suggest the replacement of sales staff by sales literature. Rather it is to emphasize that in technical selling, sales literature has a powerful role to play providing it is carefully produced and used in a planned and purposeful manner.

A sales leaflet or brochure can be regarded as the back-up material to a salesperson's visit during which the buyer will have been taken carefully through each item, relating it to his or her special requirements. Such literature will not be simply an enumeration of product attributes, but a summary of the benefits to the customer. It should probably not be sent out in advance or in lieu of a visit, since it might enable a prospect to conclude that he or she did not require the product, thus creating an unnecessary sales block.

Alternatively, other forms of sales literature, such as direct mailing pieces which are designed simply to create interest but not to call for a yes/no judgement to be made, are an excellent preliminary to a sales call. The contents of a piece of literature or any other item of publicity should not be based solely on what a buyer wants to know. This is only the starting point. The contents must be planned deliberately to provide a prospect with what the selling company wishes him or her to know, no less and no more.

Various other items of print can come under the heading of sales literature. Some of these are covered under direct mail, and others under point of sale. Two that are not used as much as they might be are reprints of advertisements and of editorial mentions or articles. It seems likely that if an advertisement is worth while, it is wasteful to rely simply on its being seen in a magazine. From readership data, it can be reliably forecast that perhaps only a small proportion of a potential market will ever notice it, let alone read it. The exposure must be increased if it is mailed out to the prospect list, and the cost of doing so is very low. A new method of evaluating literature is given in Chapter 12 on 'Media Research'.

House magazines

In this section of the book dealing with marketing communications, consideration is given only to external house magazines (ie for customers and prospects) as opposed to those which are produced primarily for internal circulation to employees. Sometimes one magazine is produced to serve both functions, but it is rare for this to be successful since the interests of the two groups are so different.

External house magazines are certainly a valid means of persuasive communications: their selling role is sometimes rather remote and in fact more nearly related to a long-range image-building operation.

One of the difficulties facing a would-be publisher is that, once started, a house magazine is difficult to stop. As the cost of launching such a venture can be quite high, a major policy decision is required at this stage. Again the solution is to define audiences and objectives and then to produce something which is modest and infrequent but can be strengthened if it succeeds.

The acid test must be whether it can prove to be of sufficient interest to cause recipients to look at it and even read it. Unless continuity of really interesting material can be assured it must become of declining value. It is akin to a new product launch without the possibility of a test marketing operation.

Against the idea of a house magazine is the situation that already too many trade and technical journals are produced commercially and this must restrict the available reading time by prospective buyers. Secondly, it is only natural that the sponsors of a house magazine will view it with a great deal more interest and initial enthusiasm than its potential readership. In the balance against the idea, much more than a printing operation is involved: this is publishing and it includes producing to a deadline and the most difficult matter of distribution – of a growing uncontrollable database which becomes out of date at a rate of at least 10 per cent each year and therefore requires very thorough procedures for maintaining its accuracy. The overall cost of a well-produced house magazine can become very high indeed.

If the advantages predominate, the job must be done well, since this magazine will contribute in very large measure to the image of the company in the minds of the readers.

There are often good reasons for placing the publishing of a magazine in the hands of an outside organization. This is clearly not so if the format is

simply a few duplicated pages of 'company newsheet', but if the work is substantial it is difficult to justify employing a staff with adequate expertise to
produce something which must compete with the best commercial journals.
The very fact of having an independent editor will help to ensure that the
subject matter is written to interest people outside the business, and without
the kind of introverted jargon and detailed trivia which easily creep into an
inside production.

Goals must be set, not only quantitative, but also in terms of reader interest. In Chapter 12 on 'Media Research', page traffic studies are dealt with.
This same technique can be applied to house magazines to establish the percentage interest in each page, and in the magazine as a whole. The objective
should be stated in terms of readership, not circulation. One goal, for example, may be to obtain a readership of, say, 500 hospital engineers within a
year of publication. A formal readership study may subsequently show that
only 10 per cent of the circulation of 1000 is read, the remainder discarded.
In such a clear-cut situation the course of action ought not to be difficult to
determine; for instance, cease publication.

Checklist

1. Have you a long-term plan for literature?
2. Does this plan fit into the company marketing strategy?
3. In the preparation of a new piece of literature
   (a) Has the objective been defined?
   (b) Is the potential audience agreed?
   (c) Has the method of distribution been determined?
   (d) Has a production schedule been produced?
   (e) Does the schedule make provision for
       (i)   briefing?
       (ii)   writing?
       (iii) visual treatment?
       (iv)   quotation?
       (v)   finished visual?
       (vi)   artwork?
       (vii) proofing?
       (viii) revisions?
       (ix)   printing?
4. In briefing a designer has guidance been given on
   (a) Number and size of pages?
   (b) Paper and board?
   (c) Illustrations?
   (d) Style of design?
   (e) Number of colours?

    (f) Typeface and sizes?

    (g) Expense?

    (h) Printing process?

    (i) Quantity?

5. Has provision been made for (a) storage (b) stock control and continuous updating?

8

PHOTOGRAPHY

Still photography is part of the raw material which serves as the basis for promotion and other persuasive communications activities. A good deal of photography is carried out for a specific purpose and is used subsequently for other purposes. Much of the work, however, is done speculatively when the opportunity presents itself in anticipation of future uses.

Subjects

Consideration will be given later to the care which must be exercised in order to match the photographer to the job in hand. Before doing so, it is perhaps useful to examine some of the variety of subjects which can be included in what is part of the promotion programme. This classification of subjects is not exhaustive, but is presented rather to show that a disciplined and analytical approach is possible and indeed necessary even in such a creative area as photography.

PRODUCTS

It goes without saying that there are numerous products which, as such, cannot usefully be photographed – usefully that is in a promotional sense. A management consultancy may be said to fit into this category, and to a lesser extent industrial chemicals, or even for that matter steel strip.

In practice there are many products where illustrations are vital, for instance where appearance counts, as in packaging, and others which cannot be taken to a buyer because of size, as with heavy capital equipment.

Product photographs to a greater or lesser extent form the basis of press advertising, literature, sales aids, press releases, and direct mail, but there can be rather more to product photography than merely presenting a factual static representation of what the product looks like. There is much creative scope for interpretation by the photographer in order that the picture portrays the product benefit rather than only the product itself. Take, for example, a new type of fibreboard box designed to provide extra strength; itself a most mundane subject. Now stand an elephant on it and the picture may

well prove to be of interest to a daily newspaper, and certainly to trade outlets. Another example might be a sheet of cardboard which is particularly
water resistant. Here the product benefit could be demonstrated by con-
structing a boat from it and then photographing it being rowed across the
Thames by an Olympic oarsman.

PRODUCT APPLICATIONS

It follows naturally from the above section that an outstanding way of showing product benefits is to photograph them in use. A radiation monitor
maybe is not much to look at and could well be mistaken for a digital voltmeter or a pH meter, but when put into the radiotherapy unit of a nation-
ally known hospital its use is immediately apparent, as well as the added
value of implied endorsement by the user. An industrial pump designed to
withstand the most rugged of conditions has difficulty in making this point
until it is photographed *in situ* on a massive paper machine with water and
stock jetting all over it.

To ask a photographer to produce a 'dramatic' picture of an industrial
product may be a cliché (a dramatic cucumber was once called for), but a
top-rate photographer with an adequate brief will produce photographs
which sell the goods, sometimes more effectively than written or spoken
words, since here is pictorial evidence of a product providing a service or
satisfaction which is claimed of it. It is a credible demonstration of a manufacturer's claim.

INDUSTRIAL PROCESSES

It has been argued elsewhere in this book that the nature of the manufacturing process can be a powerful support to the selling proposition of a
product. This factor can be utilized by building up a library of the principal
or interesting features of a process.

In photographing the operations of a factory it is necessary in the first
instance to produce a shooting schedule and to confirm this in advance with
everyone likely to be involved. The works manager will be of special importance, since his or her staff will be needed to give maximum co-operation by
repainting machinery, providing clean overalls, pacifying the operatives who
are concerned at losing bonus pay, and providing electricians, labourers and
technical advisers to help the photographer. It is a matter of communicating
to staff that an industrial photograph is a far cry from a seaside snap and is
making an important contribution to the future of the business.

Some photographers on a large assignment prefer to carry out an initial
survey, sometimes with a hand-held camera, to ensure that possible difficulties are anticipated and that any major work the client needs notice of can

be put in hand in good time. A photographer may, for instance, wish to work at night in order to have pure artificial light: this may involve bringing in a special night shift.

Top-class photographers have a creativity and sensitivity which enables them to give life to a piece of plant or machinery. More important even than clever composition and lighting, if the brief requires it, they can illustrate what a machine *does* rather than what it *is*. Furthermore a photographer can build in a feeling of quality and precision which turns a fundamentally passive situation into an active selling picture.

It is not enough to leave things to chance, and hope that the right result will emerge. The briefing for photography must state the specific merits that a series of pictures need to portray: whether it is cleanliness, scale of production, automation, efficiency of factory layout, craftmanship, scientific aids, or quality control.

NEWS PHOTOGRAPHY

This is a separate class of photography and needs certain qualities if it is to be useful – a sense of immediacy, a human interest, an unusual angle.

There is a great danger of producing cliché photography in many news situations – VIP shaking hands with managing director prior to a tour of works; a plaque being unveiled; the mayor shares a joke with one of the workers; or the chairman's wife cuts tape, presses a button or accepts a ceremonial key. These photographs are easy enough to take but are difficult to place with newspapers and tend to be repetitive and uninteresting even for a house magazine.

The best news photographs are probably not planned at all but come out of the persistent trailing of a tour party by a photographer with a news sense. Alternatively news can be created, as for instance when a boat was sawn in half, then stuck together and refloated, to demonstrate the qualities of a new adhesive.

PEOPLE

A basic library of portraits of directors and senior executives is necessary for any firm seriously engaged in marketing communications and public relations activities. This is good reference material and will be used for such events as new appointments and announcements, though such pictures serve little purpose sometimes other than to break up a page of type and provide a sense of satisfaction to the person concerned.

There are opportunities to go further than a straight portrait or a picture of someone sitting at a desk signing a letter or holding a telephone; a happy group of people clutching their cocktail glasses; or those frequently used groups of businessmen with their wives, all in evening dress, standing in the corner of a ballroom looking sometimes self-satisfied, and sometimes embarrassed.

There is now a healthy trend towards photographing people going about their business so as to get across their personalities, functions or features of the products or processes in which they are involved. This is valuable because it is both different and gives the photograph a positive role. It communicates something other than just faces.

PRESTIGE PHOTOGRAPHY

It is not easy to be specific about this since so much depends upon the circumstances. Often it is a matter of looking through photographs which have been taken for other purposes and selecting any which have additional merit. Photographs of industrial processes for instance, apart from showing the equipment and demonstrating its purpose, may be of such a quality in photographic or visual terms that they can be used outside their original intention. Many newspapers and magazines will accept such pictures with a small caption on an exclusive basis.

It is necessary to decide what aspects of a business are likely to be impressive in a general sense. The exterior of a new building, for instance, or an aerial view, a well-equipped surgery, or a fleet of vehicles with a new livery, advanced scientific equipment, or a computer: features of a business which are not directly relevant in a promotional context but tend to be creditable in their own right.

Photographers

Much emphasis has been laid on matching a photograph to its purpose. It follows that the means of achieving such an objective must be to match the photographer to the task. Just as in any other art form, each photographer will have certain strengths and weaknesses, special interests and capabilities. The strength of 'high quality' will probably be matched by the fact that the cost will be high. A photographer who excels at portraiture may be only average at industrial work or news photography.

COMMERCIAL PHOTOGRAPHERS

It is necessary then for a publicity executive to build up a knowledge of sources of supply of various skills and price ranges. Many of the best sources of supply are independent photographers with a small studio and processing unit. Their particular skill is one that is difficult to pass on to an assistant, or to a group of colleagues, and for this reason photographic units tend to be small. The disadvantage is that a one-man or -woman firm suffers from peaks and troughs in demand which will sometimes make it difficult to get a particular photographer on to an assignment at a given time. The sporadic nature of the business may also cause the charges to be high since the photographer must fix fees at a level which will cover the costs on a long term and continuous basis, even when there is little work going through.

A top-flight photographer may command a market price of £1000 a day or more and in the context of the job to be done this may represent good value for money. The provision of a good set of photographs of a new £100 million plant for example is worth every penny of the £5000 a week's assignment might cost.

There is, of course, room for competitive buying in photography. One of the customs of top photographers (and top designers) is that, apart from being able to command relatively high charges by virtue of their excellence, they sometimes base their fees on the use to which a photograph is to be put. Thus a photograph for record purposes may cost, say, £50 while the same photograph for an expensive series of newspaper advertisements may be billed at £500. Advertising agencies, particularly large ones, tend to be at a disadvantage here. A good example was of a photographer on a routine assignment at a fee of £500 a day, who was asked independently by the company's advertising agent to take a particular shot, while he was on the spot, for a press advertisement. He billed the agency £800 for the one shot and the art buyer considered he had obtained good value for money. The client took a different view. No doubt photographers will argue that the marketing executives, for whom they do much of their work, themselves set product prices on what the market will bear and that they should not complain when they are given the same treatment. It is as well, however, to be aware of the situation.

The larger studios employ a number of photographers, perhaps half a dozen, and there are obvious benefits to be derived. The provision of a news service in particular tends to call for a pool of photographers to be able to meet sudden demands. Shared overheads may enable such units to function more economically, and a group of photographers can consist of a number of people who are specialists in their own right. On the other hand it is difficult for a client to build up such a personal relationship as when dealing with an individual and, since changes in personnel occur from time to time, a continuity of style, technique and quality can be difficult to maintain if there are several photographers on call.

STAFF PHOTOGRAPHERS

Bernard Shaw said: 'The golden rule is that there are no golden rules', and this certainly applies to dogmatism about staff photographers or, indeed, any creative staff. The odds are weighted heavily against staff photographers being at the very top of their profession. They cannot hope to be a specialist in all the categories of photography that will be required; moreover their skills will not match those of a £1000-a-day person, or they would themselves be working independently.

Even a very capable staff photographer will tend to get into a rut if he or she always works for one firm, and it is unlikely that there will be the same freedom of creative expression as a freelance has since the work will be controlled by a direct-line boss. The day-to-day operations will be restricted by conventional working hours, by limitations of props and equipment and by general interference, however well-intended.

Nevertheless, for larger companies there is a real value in an internal photographic unit which can cope with the many routine photographic demands which arise. It can supply an essential and very economic service provided its limitations are recognized from the outset.

PROPS AND MODELS

It is so easy, and in industrial publicity so common, to think always in terms of getting work done 'on the cheap'.

If, for example, a home environment is required for a photograph, there is a good chance that someone's actual home will be used rather than a set built at £1000 to match the requirements of the assignment. Similarly, it is much easier to look around for the prettiest secretary to stand in front of the camera rather than pay for an expensive model. For a small firm working on a tight budget these improvizations often make sound common sense, but one gets what one pays for, and there is little doubt that the quality of a photograph can be enhanced radically by the use of professional models and exactly appropriate props.

Expensive photography is not always so expensive as it seems since it rarely needs retouching, often finds many other uses, and projects a quality image which can be of great benefit to both the product and the company.

Processes and production

Some industrial photography is still in black and white, though there is a growing trend towards colour. The nature of the product can be decisive since a carton manufacturer or a printer may well have a very definite need for colour work, but by and large colour is unnecessary and indeed often unsuitable.

Types of cameras can surely be left to the photographer, although it is as well to be aware of the limitations of filmstock as regards size. For some years past there has been a good deal of controversy around the merits of sizes from 35 mm to 5 in × 4 in and even larger. While some industrial photographers still use large film stock, virtually none use 35 mm, and there is a general consensus that 2¼ in^2 is the most suitable. Certainly with fine-grain film and development, very considerable enlargements can be obtained up to 6 × 8 ft without the effect of grain becoming objectionable.

In commissioning photography it is as well to be aware of the importance of lighting, if only to understand and anticipate the needs of the photographer. The hand-held flash unit may be enough for news photography, but for product shots it is frequently necessary to employ a wide variety of sophisticated lighting techniques for the best results. In photographing industrial plant, lighting often becomes the most significant single factor, with high-powered lights located at strategic points often to the inconvenience of the work people. One of the greatest failings among clients is to arrange shooting schedules which do not allow enough time, people, mechanical handling, electricians and power supplies to do justice to the lighting.

SALES AIDS

Obviously black and white prints can be used by sales representatives and sometimes that is all they need. Colour photography here can come into its own since the additional cost may not be great against the realism of the picture.

Consideration should also be given to the use of 35 mm colour film for the provision of slides and film strips and for three-dimensional slides with a special viewer. These visual aids can provide the basis of a very effective sales presentation, sometimes at very low cost, though they have difficulty in competing with multimedia presentations.

Checklist

1. Have you made budgetary provision for photography as a separate promotional element?
2. Have you considered how best to exploit photography in
   (a) Products?
   (b) Product applications?
   (c) Own factory and processes?
   (d) News and events?
   (e) People and personalities?
   (f) Prestige?
3. Have you (a) set up an adequate library of prints, (b) with suitable cross referencing? (c) Are there arrangements for updating this material? (d) And preventing people removing them?

4. In arranging a photographic session, is the photographer aware of the purpose and objectives, both (a) immediate and (b) long-term?
5. With photography inside factories and offices are the necessary line management, staff and works fully informed in order to obtain maximum co-operation?

9.

VIDEO FILMS AND AV

The production of an industrial ciné or video film is sometimes the most expensive single item in a publicity budget and yet, paradoxically, once produced it is often the least used because it has few or no pre-planned objectives. It may indeed prove to be the most expensive white elephant in the promotional field.

As with other media it is necessary to refer again to the marketing and promotional strategies which determine the need for a film or not. It is easy to think of good reasons to justify a film, having already decided to make one, but this sequence of thinking often leads to the film being the end in itself rather than simply the beginning of a promotional process.

'What is the objective?' This is the essential question, and the singular is deliberately used in order to avoid the other common failing in film making, that of trying to satisfy the interests of several different audiences with one and the same film. The result is generally a film of no special interest to anyone.

The objective, for instance, may be to demonstrate to farmers the versatility of a new tractor and its range of attachments, to help a salesperson to put across the selling proposition. From the definition of potential market in the marketing strategy, the precise nature of the audience will be known – say farmers having in excess of a certain acreage – and this will determine the method of film distribution and display.

There is usually a case for examining secondary audiences, but this must not cloud the principal objective. In the above example there may well be an overseas potential; schools, agricultural colleges and young farmers' clubs among others may be interested, but they must be regarded as ancillaries and of secondary importance.

Having set a specific objective, the next step is to restate it in quantitative terms, fixing not only a measurement against which performance can be judged, but also an assessment of value for money before production begins. Suppose the total potential market is 50,000 people, can a realistic target audience be set at 5000 a year? If that seems practicable, having regard to the methods of distribution available and the estimated life of the film, is

the expenditure justified? The answer is often that, given planned distribution, the cost per viewer is very low. In the above example, for instance, a
film costing £30,000 would obtain an exposure in the first year at a cost of £6
per viewer. If distribution continued at the same rate for four or five years,
the cost would come down to around £1 per head. At the other extreme,
there are films which have been so little used that the cost per viewer has
reached hundreds of pounds or even more.

Advantages and disadvantages

In terms of the 'impact diagram' in Chapter 2 (Fig. 2.2), the video or film
can be regarded as one of a number of co-ordinated media which impress a
common message upon the mind of a prospect. It is useful to consider the
merits of a film in relation to other media.

IMPACT

This is clearly of a high order, arguably even higher than a salesperson's
visit, due to the complete absence of distractions. This is not necessarily so,
since there is no opportunity with a film for varying the argument to suit the
circumstances, or to counter an objection. Obviously, however, a film has a
much higher impact than press advertising.

COST

Initial costs very high, maybe between £10,000 and £100,000. A common
ball park figure for a video without location shots is £1000 per minute.
Organizational and distribution costs must be added. Cost per viewer may
be low.

COVERAGE OF POTENTIAL MARKET

Depends very much on how precisely the purchasing influences can be
defined and how willing they are likely to be to view the film. This probably
is the biggest problem and the biggest challenge.

COMPLEXITY OF SALES MESSAGE

In press advertising, for example, the sales message is subject to severe limitation. In a film there is virtually no limit and moreover the sales argument
is presented in two forms – visual and audio – simultaneously and of course
in colour.

SPEED

While films can be produced very quickly, it is usually unwise to do so. Several months may sometimes be needed for production alone. Distribution may have to be spread over a number of years.

INTRUSION

Mention has been made with other media that a buyer may feel a sense of intrusion which can build up a resistance, for example in an intensive direct mail campaign. With a film he or she is likely to have gone to a showing as a matter of choice, and will probably at least start with a positive attitude of mind. Also films have a relaxing 'entertainment' connotation, arising from TV or cinema.

Film-making

The decision to make a film having been reached in principle, there are a number of stages required in logical sequence to ensure an effective result. In the chapter on literature the need for such a procedure was stressed. In film-making it becomes even more important since changes made, particularly towards the end of production, can not only be very expensive, but can lead to the overall quality depreciating with serious results. It is assumed that the objective, audience and distribution procedure will have already been put down in writing and that the budget, type and length of film have been given some consideration.

The following sequence might then be:

1. Outline synopsis
2. Choice of film unit
3. Briefing
4. Treatment
5. Quotation
6. Script and visual interpretation
7. Shooting schedule
8. Internal organization and liaison
9. Rushes
10. Editing
11. Recording
12. Viewing
13. Completion

It follows that plans will be in train concurrently for distribution, and to secure adequate publicity for the film on its initial launching.

OUTLINE SYNOPSIS

It is usually the task of the marketing communications department, or maybe the advertising agency, to set down in more detail the points which need to be made verbally and visually in order to communicate the essential sales message.

It is useful at this stage to consider this not so much from a creative point of view, but rather as a factual outline of events which may or may not be in an acceptable creative sequence. This document will in due course be the basis of the briefing and with this in mind it can well be written while negotiations are proceeding with the film units which have already been short-listed.

From the outset it is essential to secure the active support of top management, and a realization that they will need to devote time at each critical stage to give a considered judgement which is unlikely to be changed. Approval of the outline synopsis is one such critical stage.

CHOICE OF FILM UNIT

Without wide experience in the film business it is wise to have the views and advice of other people who have been concerned in the recent past with the making of a film. A preliminary selection is not difficult as film units will usually have gained a reputation in a particular field of activity, or technique, or price range. It will then be advantageous to see a number of their recent productions and to judge these not only from the standpoint of entertainment, but also as audio/visual interpretations of the client's objectives.

This procedure should lead to the choice of one or two units that appear to meet the requirements. Full discussions must take place to give them the data they require for a quotation and to provide an opportunity of discovery whether a good personal rapport can be established and if they, as a unit, seem capable of understanding and interpreting what is required.

BRIEFING

There are a variety of ways of operating. One satisfactory procedure is to commission the chosen film unit to prepare a treatment and maybe a script for a nominal fee, with a full quotation to follow. The justification for this interim action is that to ask for a quotation before a full treatment has been prepared is rather like asking a printer to quote for a job before it has been designed.

The outline synopsis now becomes the basis of briefing the unit, which must be given every facility to ask questions and examine locations. This degree of co-operation will enable them to make the best possible creative contribution. If the film involves technical subject-matter, a senior technical person must be assigned from the outset. If the factory is to be filmed, the factory manager must be fully involved.

The client company must treat the briefing as a most serious contribution to the subject. Thereafter the matter moves progressively out of its hands.

TREATMENT

This is the document in which the film-maker feeds back his interpretation of the client's briefing. It will be in effect an expanded and detailed synopsis with a written description of both visual and sound effects added. It will enumerate the various locations, the need for music, commentary and direct speech, and animation for instance.

In engineer's terminology this is the film's specification and blueprint combined into one. It should be read and agreed by everyone concerned and care exercised to ensure that the readers are well enough briefed, even with a verbal explanation by the producer, to understand fully the implications of each item.

QUOTATION

A 'treatment' can be costed accurately and, if the above procedure has been followed, the subsequent quotation is not likely to be very different from that which was foreseen. Items which are likely to have a significant effect on costs will have been discussed at an earlier stage, such as the extent and nature of animation sequences, special music to be composed and so on.

The contractual stage of the film and the detailed points in the contract are important to formalize; for instance, progress payments may be required, and provision for contingencies such as bad weather and lack of access to locations due to plant closedown.

SCRIPT

Good writers are not easy to find and it is worth paying for the best. An extensive briefing must be given to the writer and the script must be scrutinized together with the visual and timing schedules so that every single item is seen to fit. Any alteration hereafter can have most undesirable consequences in terms of both cost and quality.

SHOOTING SCHEDULES AND ORGANIZATION

Many people in a client's organization will need to be co-opted in order to ensure the smooth shooting of the film. The importance of management support has been stressed; it is valuable now to line up alongside the film

unit a team of staff with executive authority over the whole internal operation – to plan the organization and liaison in detail and to anticipate difficulties before they arise.

RUSHES

As the shooting of the film progresses, each sequence will become available
for viewing and it is at this stage that the technical advisers should be
brought in to ensure that pictorially there is nothing inaccurate.

EDITING AND RECORDING

There is little that can be contributed by the client at this late stage: in fact
the results will probably be better if the experts are allowed to get on with it.
The client may want to hear the recording to be reassured that the right
emphasis is given to certain passages in the script or that technical words
are pronounced correctly.

VIEWING

The final viewing will be to a mixed audience of all those concerned in the
client's organization, and they must decide that the result is right from their
viewpoint, at least in technical and factual terms. From this stage the film
goes to processing, and production is complete.

Distribution

Just as with press advertising there is an inclination to concentrate the main
effort on the creation and production of an advertisement and to neglect
media selection, so with films there has been a tendency to disregard the
need for a plan of action to make maximum use of them commercially. In
other words, the production of the film becomes almost an end in itself.

There are many channels of distribution available and it is to be hoped
that the distribution plan and budget will have been drawn up and approved
well before the film is completed. Such channels include:

1. Cinema circuits
2. Television
3. Film libraries
4. Trade and other associations
5. Clubs and organizations
6. Customers and prospects
7. Central Office of Information
8. Client-sponsored local film shows

9. Education establishments
10. Part of individual sales presentations
11. Exhibitions and conferences

Re-examination of the target audience will help to determine which methods of distribution are likely to be most effective. From the moment a film is completed it is starting to become out of date; therefore action must be prompt and it must be intensive.

Distribution can be expensive, as well as the maintenance and administration that must accompany it; nothing can be worse than a film arriving late, damaged, or even just not rewound.

In promotional terms, a film represents an opportunity of breaking new ground, influencing new people, and getting across a message often with greater impact than can be achieved with other media. The film, however, must not be expected to do this task alone. It must be supported, perhaps with a brochure highlighting the main features, or with posters and handbills, product displays or instructional charts. A personal introduction or demonstration is also very useful.

A film is only one part of the sales promotion armoury and should be treated as such by being linked with other media. It should be advertised. It will clearly be reviewed in a house magazine. If the subject justifies it, say a steel strip mill, the film may be mailed direct to the top 50 prospects throughout the world. The opportunities are limitless. But with the growing use of videos as opposed to ciné, large numbers can be produced economically for widespread distribution by mail or by the sales force

Pre-distribution publicity

A major event, such as the completion of a new video or photographic film, provides the opportunity for a good deal of pre-distribution publicity, valuable both for general public relations and also to help to stimulate the demand for showings.

A particularly useful way of introducing a film is in a series of previews. The first will usually be for the press and provides the chance for journalists to meet company management as well as the film unit itself. Film reviews in the press can lead to a useful demand and, if the reviews are complimentary, they can be used to form the basis of promotional material.

Following the press reception, there are a number of events which should be considered. Important customers will feature largely when planning such functions, and if staged at a high level in congenial surroundings a good deal of hard business can be generated at them. Particular people will have special interests in a film: suppliers of equipment that was featured, for instance; general suppliers to the company; officials of trade associations; and of course employees, particularly those who have co-operated and appear in the film.

Finally, pre-release publicity can spread across the entire selling function so that for a period the film is being promoted by the sales force, direct mail, inserts in advertisements, through the the house magazine, by envelope stuffers and so on until every prospective viewer is thoroughly informed and interested in seeing it.

Film strips and slides

This chapter would be incomplete without mention of the opportunities provided by film strips and slides, and also the declining use of photographic film.

The oldest technique here is film strips, which go back almost to the beginning of film itself. The process simply involves a series of individual frames, usually on 35 mm stock, each of which portrays part of a story sequence. The setting up of a complex piece of equipment may be the subject, or a comprehensive series of applications in diverse fields. There are also valuable opportunities for a film strip in the educational field and in training for internal staff or for distributors or users. An advantage can be to combine the visual sequence with a taped commentary. This provides a very neat package of a small roll of film plus a cassette which can be used independently of one's own staff, and indeed can be mailed around the world. The cost of a film strip can be held within a few hundred pounds, and additional copies are easy and inexpensive to obtain. Two disadvantages should be considered. The sequence of events is fixed and may not be suitable for every audience. More important, perhaps, is the fact that a special projector is required, and not all audience groups will have ready access to such equipment.

Colour transparencies are the basis of 35 mm slides which can be put together to form a programme in a similar way to a film strip but with the special advantage of flexbility. Slides can be changed, updated, omitted or used in a different sequence to suit the circumstances. With modern projectors, usually widely available, there are few problems likely to be encountered in setting up for a presentation. Specialists in AV programmes have developed techniques involving multi-projector images coupled with integrated soundtracks which provide an impressive show. As with still photography, it is important not to fall into the trap of expecting such a programme to be produced for a few tens of pounds. Top-quality photography is essential and, if sound is to be used, a thoroughly professional recording. Even so, there is no doubt that if the subject is suitable for this form of treatment it can be produced for very considerably less than a film.

Checklist

1. Has the objective been set?
2. Has the target audience been defined?

3. Have the relative merits of video and photographic films been carefully assessed in relation to the objective and audience?
4. Have the methods of (a) distribution and (b) presentation been decided?
5. Has provision been made for checking and maintaining copies?
6. Has the budget been agreed together with the type and length of the film required?
7. Has a comprehensive production schedule been (a) produced, and (b) distributed to every person likely to be affected?
8. Has a date been put on each of the following stages?
   (a) Synopsis
   (b) Choice of film unit
   (c) Briefing
   (d) Treatment
   (e) Quotation
   (f) Signing of contract
   (g) Approval of script and visual interpretation
   (h) Shooting schedule
   (i) View rushes
   (j) Approval of complete film
   (k) Press show and launch
   (l) Publicity
   (m) Distribution
9. Has consideration been given to discs, CD-ROMs, film strips and slides?

10

EDITORIAL PUBLICITY

Here we come to the most neglected channel of all in Business-to-Business Marketing Communications. There is no question but that the power of the trade, technical and business press is supreme. And each journal comprises two parts – the editorial pages, and the advertising. The editorial pages then break down into three main categories – news, features and comment. All the studies that have ever been conducted show that to secure a mention editorially is of far greater value than having the same item covered in an advertisement. The fact is that an item of news, however once covered editorially, will not be repeated, hence the need for advertising as back-up, but this must be as a last resort since it is so wasteful. In examining the budgets for print advertising and what is wrongly called 'PR', it is extraordinary that far more money is spent on advertising. In short, the balance should be reversed.

The value of business publications is well illustrated by a very comprehensive survey conducted by the Periodical Publishers Association (PPA) in 1996. This is representative of over 4000 journals, and showed that one or more magazines are read regularly by at least 95 per cent of business people.

A further question asked for the source rated as most useful, comparing

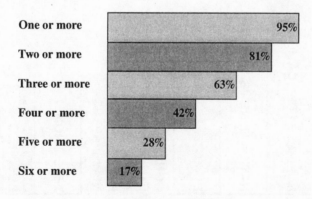

Figure 10.1 Number of business publications read regularly

Staying in touch with what's going on in your sector	Business magazines 79%
	Conferences/exhibitions 6%
Understanding how your sector is changing	Business magazines 78%
	Conferences/exhibitions 6%
Keeping you up to date with news of product launches	Business magazines 70%
	Direct mail 12%
Keeping you up to date with the job market	Business magazines 69%
	Direct mail 13%
Doing your job better	Business magazines 68%
	Direct mail 9%
Selecting new suppliers	Business magazines 58%
	Direct mail 14%

Figure 10.2 Business magazines v. next best source. For a direct comparison with other sources used 'to gain information', business publications again came out well on top.

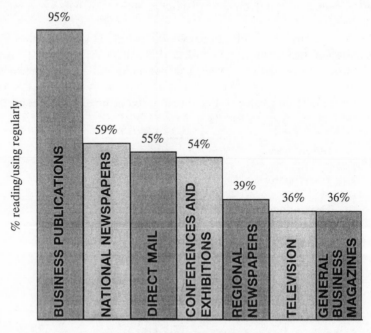

Figure 10.3 Sources regularly used

business magazines with the next best source. For six functions in this particular research, magazines outperformed exhibitions and direct mail.

The above responses did not discriminate between editorial content and advertising, but were viewing business publications as a whole. Taking any one publication, however, and multiplying its circulation by the pass-on readership, there must be a very substantial opportunity to see (OTS) which puts this medium with combined publicity and advertising right at the top of the range of channels of communications.

As a preliminary to this chapter it is necessary to discuss a term in communications which is possibly misunderstood more than any other, namely PR. What does it mean and, arising out of this, just what are the functions of a PRO, a press office and a public relations manager?

The first point is of course that PR can mean either public relations or press relations – two quite different functions. Furthermore, either may or may not be viewed in the context of the marketing function or of the business as a whole.

In this book the term public relations is used in its widest context, that of building and sustaining good relations between an organization and its various publics which include customers and prospects equally with employees and shareholders. The means by which good public relations are maintained include press advertising and direct mail just as much as editorial publicity.

The term press relations is used here to indicate the building up of good relationships between an organization and the various journalists who are likely to be concerned with it in order to secure good editorial publicity about any aspect of a company's operations, whether news about products, or new management techniques or strikes. It should also be noted that 'media relations' is being used increasingly to replace 'press relations'. This is in order that radio and TV shall not be overlooked. Similarly 'news release' may replace 'press release'. On the other hand there continue to be 'press officers' who in turn hold 'press conferences'.

In this chapter the subject of editorial publicity is dealt with only in so far as it contributes to the promotion of sales and is strictly within the confines of marketing activities and objectives.

Of the channels of persuasion which are available to bring to bear a sales message upon the mind of a prospect, the editorial columns of the press, television and radio are powerful media to include and integrate in the overall marketing communications mix. Again, it is important to start with objectives and where possible to quantify these, both in order to determine the amount of effort needed to achieve the target, and as a means of subsequently measuring performance. It is not good enough to aim at 'securing a maximum of editorial coverage about a new type of industrial fire extinguisher'. It is necessary rather to define all the audiences which represent buying influences, to categorize and enumerate them, then specify which should be the target of an editorial message covering the new product. From this point the publications needed to make contact with this audience can be listed and a strategy developed for obtaining editorial coverage.

For example, suppose there are a total of 50 publications reaching the potential market for fire extinguishers of 50,000 people. The duplication of readership can be determined from readership surveys (see Chapter 13) as will be the average page traffic of the types of publication in question. It may be that by a combination of data, experience and judgement, it is concluded that to register with 75 per cent of the total potential market, editorial mention must be secured in 20 of the publications. If the news value is high this may be easy to achieve. If not, then perhaps some special activities will be necessary to create interest amongst the journalists. Alternatively, the answer may be that the objective is not capable of achievement through editorial publicity, in which case other channels of persuasion must be strengthened in order that the total marketing communications impact provides adequate support for the selling effort.

The media, be it national, local, technical or special interest, are concerned primarily with providing information of interest to their readers or audiences, within of course the framework of a given editorial policy. The editor's job is to provide editorial material which will result in the readers' approbation and will influence the prestige of the publication. In due course this will influence its circulation, readership and thus advertising revenue. Editors can select from a wide range of sources: items of news, features, specialized stories, off-beat pieces, illustrations and so on. They must provide a good editorial mix. The function of a publicity executive is to think in terms of the ultimate audience, and to write in a way that will fit in with editorial criteria. To do otherwise is both a waste of time and an insult to the intelligence of an editor. The goal which must be aimed at, then, is to write a story which an editor will regard as a worthwhile item for his publication and which at the same time does a first-class selling job.

Editorial subjects

Approaching the matter with a journalist's eye, there are often too many subjects in industrial publicity: too many for the available staff to write about and, more important, too many for the press (particularly the monthlies) to assimilate. For many companies, having a variety of product lines and markets and applications, it is not difficult to produce, say, one story a week. It is expecting too much of the trade press to hope that all these will be published; even weeklies and dailies have many hundreds or thousands of other sources of news to call upon and regardless of any other consideration they must maintain a good editorial balance.

Thus the release of stories, even very good ones, may have to be rationed and this leads to the discipline (so often missing in press relations activities) of advance planning. It should be possible for the executive concerned to have an outline plan of releases to the press covering at least several months ahead. Obviously unforeseen news stories will emerge, but this does not invalidate the need for planning the basic framework of editorial publicity. Within the marketing communications strategy it is known well in advance which products are to be promoted and when. It follows that editorial stories would be planned to coincide with publicity in other media. A new product, for example, only becomes news when it is released to the outside world. It might have been produced months before and indeed been in service on a restricted basis for weeks, but it is only news as and when a company decides to make it so.

NEW PRODUCTS AND SERVICES

When exactly does a product or service qualify to be called new? It could be argued that for a firm producing plastic bottles or mouldings, every new order is likely to be a new product. But there may be a thousand of these each year. The criterion then should not be, is it new, but does it have news value? A small modification to a well-established moisture meter which results in an improvement of accuracy from ± 5 per cent error to ± 2 per cent has a far greater news value than a new style of lettering on a plastic bottle, even though the moisture meter can hardly claim to be a new product.

The degree of news value must also be assessed, since this will determine the way in which the story is written and presented. For example, the substitution of nylon bearings for metal in industrial castors has news value, though somewhat limited, whereas a process control system to automate a paper mill for the first time in the world is likely to justify major international press coverage.

When integrating editorial publicity with other promotional activities, it is important to emphasize that an item is only news as long as it is not known. Pre-planning must ensure that advertisements do not start appearing before an editor has had the opportunity to publish the contents of a press release.

PRODUCT AND SERVICE APPLICATIONS

Even where a product range is not undergoing a continuous change, a good basis for industrial and business news is the variety and novelty of product applications or new uses for a service. A thickness gauge may be developed and established for use on steel strip. Adaptations may well lead to its application in measuring paper, plastics, rubber, foil and fabric. A radiological dosemeter may seem to lack a very broad audience interest, but applications could well include detecting radioactive minerals in Cornwall, equipping a civil defence force in Sweden, finding a lost isotope through police action, or locating the blockage in a sewer.

The difficulty with application stories is to find them, and there is no easy solution here. The answer lies in the progressive building up among company staff of an awareness of the value of such stories. This is a target at which publicity executives must aim. It can be aided by continually probing and asking questions, by participation in sales conferences, by visiting customers, and by subsequently distributing press cuttings to all concerned. Top management can help by indicating that they regard time identifying and sifting out application stories well spent. This attitude of mind is easier to cultivate if such stories are planned to fit into the overall strategy. The possibility of a substantial financial incentive to employees contributing stories should be considered.

NON-PRODUCT INNOVATION

If a piece of editorial publicity is to contribute directly to the promotion of sales, it follows that it must have a direct reference to whatever is being sold. There are, however, a number of editorial subjects which, while not having a direct selling value, act as a reminder of the company and its products. Many innovations fall into this category, such as the installation of a new type of machine to produce a product not only faster but to closer tolerances, or a more efficient way of storing a product, or a way of processing waste to enable it to be reused. These items do not offer a 'consumer benefit' but they have reminder value coupled with a contribution to the building up of company reputation which is probably one of the set objectives of the public relations campaign.

OTHER NEWS ITEMS

Appointments of new people, staff promotions, new literature, exhibitions, large contracts, new factory openings, visits by VIPs, setting new records (the thousandth order), anniversaries – all these items can be turned with advantage to assist the promotional campaign. Even staff achievements are worth publicizing, like registering patents, lectures, learned papers or even election to the local council.

No listing of news subjects can be comprehensive: rather it is necessary to build up a news awareness throughout the company, a process which is helped a great deal by a perceptive reading of periodicals as well as talking to journalists and continually monitoring their needs. For example, in Chapter 8 we mentioned a very boring but very strong fibreboard box that had been taken into Billy Smart's Circus where an elephant stood on it. The resulting photograph was used not only by the packaging press, but also by the nationals.

FEATURE ARTICLES

Over and above news stories there are many opportunities for having a single subject dealt with in depth, either by offering a journalist exclusive coverage of some item, or by getting a member of staff to write an article dealing with a subject more extensively than is possible in a press release.

Many feature articles which have no direct sales connection fall into the category of public relations but others can be quite deliberately part of the sales plan. For instance, the complexities of the production process, the planning and launching of a product and the marketing research which preceded it.

The big problem is always to find someone with the time and ability to do the writing, maybe one or two thousand words, or even more. For a busy and senior executive to find the time is partly a matter of motivation. Apart from the 'ego trip' it is worth considering actually paying a fee for the job. In addition to this, many publications will also pay a fee for a contributed article, in which case the writer benefits from two sources. Not all people have the ability to write well for the press. In this case the publicity executive may take on the task of editing or rewriting. Alternatively it may be necessary to employ an outside specialist writer; for instance a freelance journalist. Even so the effort and the expense will be well worth the publicity which will be achieved.

Press (or news) releases

THE PRESS LIST

Before beginning to write a press release it is essential to define the audience to whom it is addressed. This may be for instance the decision-makers in a particular market segment plus a number of other categories who are known to have an influence on purchasing decisions. A useful starting point is to compile a list of all publications and other media which can conceivably be interested in news from the company or organization, and use it as the basic checklist for each proposed press release.

Over a period of time the list will be extended by the inclusion of contacts such as freelance journalists, trade organizations, specialist news agencies, house magazine editors, named journalists with a special interest, as well as overseas publishers and agencies. Names will be deleted as publications change or the business is modified.

WRITING THE RELEASE

Editors receive far too many press releases for them to handle or sometimes even read, and few hit the mark. Most often, releases are introspective about 'me' and 'us' and 'how proud we are' rather than about 'you' and 'how your company stands to benefit'. They are acceptable neither to the reader nor to the editor.

It follows that writing a press release is not a job which can be delegated to a junior. Securing adequate editorial publicity is a major part of a publicity programme and needs to be placed in the hands of a specialist. The publicity value of a press release is to be judged on the same terms as an advertisement in the same medium. A release of high interest value may result in an area of editorial space equivalent in impact to several pages of advertisements. The same technique and effort is justified for a press release as for an advertisement.

On the actual writing of the release, the maximum should be, 'If in doubt, leave it out', but generally a story should run to between 100 and 300 words. It should be written in the same style as a journalist would write it, ie giving the news as it will interest the reader. And it should be written in a factual, authoritative manner; it should be lively and interesting, but without the smallest trace of the hard sell.

A good rule to follow is to adopt the style of the inverted triangle with the really important news at the top and the supporting information coming further down. This enables a news editor to sub from the bottom and still leave intact the main thrust of the story.

Structure

As with any piece of writing, it must have a beginning, a middle, and an end.

1. *Headline*   This is vital. It is the signal to the journalists which must at a glance cause them to pause and read on rather than discard the release into the bin. So put in the essential news in three or four words. And play it straight. Other journalists will not use your headline. If they did, they might find some competitive journal doing the same thing to them, so they just won't take the risk.

2. *First paragraph*   The release stands or falls on the first paragraph. It must therefore contain the main news angle written from the reader's point of view, not from yours. The basic marketing concept – identify the consumer benefit.

3. *Second and third paragraphs*   If these are necessary, then they are there to elaborate on the main story already told in the first paragraph. But even so, they must give the highlights only of what you are trying to put across. It is not nearly so interesting to the reader as it is to you.

4. *Fourth paragraph*   Consider putting in a quote from someone in authority, preferably outside the organization and therefore more credible.

5. *Fifth paragraph*   Include facts and data here such as price, delivery, the date an event will happen, and so on.

6. *Further information* Always offer this: give two names to contact, with office and home telephone numbers.

Points to note

1. Keep sentences short; avoid jargon and abbreviations.
2. Have a clear attractive layout, typed double-spaced, on one side only.
3. Send the release only to publications that will really find it of interest.
4. Use a photograph wherever possible and always caption it so that the caption can be seen at the same time as the photograph.
5. Any amplification of the story should be on a separate sheet or accompanying publication which can be used or discarded depending on its relevance to the journalist.
6. Ask journalists to criticize your releases. That's the way to learn.

DISTRIBUTION OF PRESS RELEASES

Press releases should be used as a channel of advance information to a wide range of people over and above the press. These should include:

1. Staff/works notice boards
2. Reception
3. House magazine
4. Salesforce
5. Top management
6. Service engineers
7. Overseas agents
8. Outside services (eg advertising agencies)
9. Distributors
10. Opinion formers (eg local MPs)
11. Trade association
12. Customers (selected releases)
13. Shareholders (selected releases)
14. Solicitors/bank managers/auditors (selected releases)

PHOTOGRAPHS

Most press releases should be accompanied by a photograph. The reasons are varied. A photograph can illustrate special features: it helps to result in an editorial which is different and stands out; it may secure additional column centimetres; lastly it may be published even though the release is ignored.

Something has been said in an earlier chapter on the way in which photography is used in publicity. A paradoxical situation often exists between photography for press advertisements and photography for press releases. In the former the contents and composition are given considerable thought and closely debated by creative people at the agency even before a visual reaches the client who once again examines and scrutinizes the material. A photographer is commissioned, briefed, directed by a visualizer, possibly accompanied by the copywriter or the creative director, and 50 or 60 shots are taken. From these maybe half-a-dozen enlargements are examined until the desired visual solution is found.

Unfortunately the procedure for a press photograph is likely to be very different – a print from the file, or a quick shot by the works photographer with a word from the press officer as a briefing. This makes no sense at all since whether a picture is used by an editor or not will depend in large measure upon its excellence and, after all, the illustrations both for advertisements and editorial are seen by the same audience. Second-rate photographs are a false economy.

TIMING

Editorial publicity must be timed to fit the promotional plan but it must also fit in with the publishers' requirements. Copy dates in industrial publicity range from a few hours for nationals to a month and even more for some periodicals, and this is one of the reasons why it is sometimes necessary to place an embargo on publication. As an example of the need for planning, a press release on one particularly important news event, concerning the opening of a new factory, had to be supplied to a quarterly magazine two months in advance in order that the editorial mention should coincide with the coverage to be given by the dailies.

If the time of appearance of an editorial item is of special importance, a close study is necessary of copy dates of all the major publications involved, perhaps coupled with a personal contact with the editors concerned.

Press receptions

A major piece of business or industrial news will frequently be publicized by holding a press reception, or by taking the press to the factory, or alternatively to see a product being used by a customer. Such an event usually does not involve a very high expense in relation to the overall selling cost, or indeed the value of the resulting publicity.

A press reception enables a subject to be explained in depth and with greater impact than can be achieved by a press release. It enables senior company officials to make personal contact with journalists, to their mutual benefit, and in particular enables an enquiring reporter to get an individual angle on a story which will be much appreciated. Questions are facilitated and these help to avoid misunderstandings, while at the same time a good deal of general company philosophy rubs off on to one of the most influential of a company's publics, the press. Probably most important of all is that for an hour or so, maybe even a day, each journalist is thinking and acting within the company's environment. The company therefore becomes more than a mere name; it assumes an identity, a personality. This is an investment for the future which will have continuing repercussions and almost certainly affect the way in which press releases and other contacts are received subsequently, generally for good.

Journalists, however, do not have unlimited time and cannot be expected to react favourably to devoting hours to a reception where it is dramatically announced that the southern area sales manager has been promoted to national accounts manager. Receptions must be reserved for worthwhile events judged in the terms of editors and their audiences.

Press relations

Key to the securing of good editorial coverage in the technical, or any other, press is to establish strong links with the journalists and editors who are covering the main areas of a company's activities. These people have to cope with large quantities of press releases, many of which are quite irrelevant, and the best way to get noticed is to be known and respected by the editor concerned. Obviously, whether a press release is used or not depends on the level of news interest for the readers, together with how well it is written, but a well-established relationship with the journalist is another factor which must not be ignored. Many people see this task as being one for the PR consultancy; indeed, that is one of the reasons often given for hiring them. This is not always so, however. Journalists want to know, and be known by, the clients, not PR executives, and the more senior the person concerned the better they like it. Good relations also facilitate the development of a programme of feature articles, together with the opportunity to be consulted whenever an industry issue arises.

A typical programme of press relations activities would be to set down, say, the 12 most important publications from the point of view of reaching out to the main target audiences. Next, write against each the name of the editor, or specialist journalist. The programme will comprise writing a personal letter progressively to each person, perhaps one a month, suggesting a meeting in order to explore how best you can supply the kind of information that will be of most use to the journal. A working lunch is ideal. Aim to meet up with all the most relevant journalists within one year, and the foundation is laid for a fruitful and mutually valuable relationship.

An extension to this idea is to host a series of top management lunches in order to strengthen further press relations. The format here is to invite four journalists from non-competing media to meet with the same number of senior managers in order to review and discuss some current or future industry issue. This can be a very rewarding future investment and will benefit both sides. Care must be taken all the time to avoid any suspicion of the 'hard sell'. That can come at some other time. The concern here is simply to build relationships.

Measuring results

Every release to the press must be scrutinized in terms of each and every publication's needs. Therefore, a presupposition in the measurement of results is that most publications receiving a release may be expected to carry the story. It is tempting to send a standard press release to an entire mailing list in the hope that one or two extra mentions might be gained in this way, but this is clearly lazy and expensive and the press quickly learns to ignore the sender. One method of measurement is to determine the percentage of publications using a story, expressed on a base of the total number circularized. One hundred per cent response is sometimes attained but 50 per cent can be regarded as a good achievement. Twenty per cent or lower implies that the release was sent to too many publications or was wrongly written: at any rate it points to the need for enquiry. If a publication consistently fails to use a company's material, there should be an adequate record system to indicate this fact and the editor should be contacted diplomatically to find out why.

Measuring results in terms of sales leads can be misleading. It is well known in technical journalism that reader enquiries can be increased significantly by the simple expedient of missing out certain key data, thus forcing people to write to a company to obtain it. It is true that this provides sales leads and might meet a company's short-term requirements, but reader enquiries will tend to be, say, in tens, whereas readership of an item may well be in thousands, or considerably more. Looking at this particular matter in reverse, if an editor puts himself out to cover a story in depth and publishes a comprehensive feature article, few enquiries may be generated, yet the value of the editorial is many times greater than a short column mention. If response were to be the criterion, the opposite conclusion might be reached.

A technique which is used extensively, but has been subject to a good deal of criticism, is to measure by column centimetres. The disadvantage is that to add the number of centimetres, in, say, the *Financial Times* to that in *Production Equipment Digest* is like trying to add apples and pears. This is certainly a valid limitation. Nevertheless, for a given firm or a particular campaign, the results can be sufficiently homogeneous to be assessed in this way. A refinement which is sometimes adopted is to express column centimetres in terms of equivalent advertising space, and this may well provide useful information on value for money spent.

As a research exercise an investigation of reader impact may be made following a particular piece of editorial publicity. This can hardly be a continuous measure of editorial efficiency since the expense would be too high. Where a certain item of news is restricted to editorial publicity only, the percentage audience reached of a defined potential market can be measured by carrying out a subsequent recall research.

Press cuttings

To carry out an editorial publicity campaign without evaluating the press cuttings is rather like an artillery bombardment without observation of the fall of shot. Not all mentions will be identified, but this can be partly made good by using two cuttings agencies, and by following up publications where no mention is recorded to find out what the reason might be.

Press cuttings can be circulated with effect among top management and sales staff. They are often of great interest to employees in general and can be used in house magazines. They may even form the basis of sales literature. Moreover the widespread circulation of cuttings, apart from improving morale, enables employees to see for themselves the type of story which interests the press and stimulates them to originate ideas for further stories.

Limitations and advantages

While it is by no means true that editorial publicity is free publicity, the fact is that it is not only very good value for money but that it is also in some respect the most effective form of publicity available. Its particular strength derives from the implied endorsement of the publication in which a particular item appears, or, if not endorsement, at least an apparently independent appraisal of a product or service now being offered. As against this, an advertisement for the same product will be seen as partisan and much of its message will be discounted for this reason. And quite apart from credibility it is known from page traffic studies (see Chapter 13) that editorials have far more readers than advertisements: maybe as many as a factor of five. A further benefit to come from editorial publicity is the opportunity for inexpensive reprints, and quotations of extracts.

There are a number of important limitations, the most significant of which is the uncertainty of when a particular piece of news will appear, whether in fact it will ever appear at all, and if so whether it will be an accurate representation of the story. In an extreme case it could well be a negative report and cast doubts upon the value of a product. It is difficult to see editorial publicity as the main component of a promotional campaign since once a story has been reported it cannot be repeated, whereas a requirement of a campaign is likely to be continuity over a protracted period of time, and to satisfy this requirement is going to call for the deployment of a multi-media mix.

Strengths and weaknesses

The first step towards assessing the strengths and weaknesses of editorial publicity is to look at the publication as a whole. The strengths here are that it may well have a sound and well-deserved reputation which can only benefit anything which appears in it, whether editorial or advertisement. It may well be narrowly focused on a specialised target audience, and be one of those media which can be said to penetrate the decision-making unit; that is, it may be read by just about anyone who is anyone, even if people cannot be identified specifically. In terms of general perception, journals are viewed more positively than, say, direct mail shots, which cannot help having commercial connotations, and sometimes an association with 'rubbish mailings' in the consumer field. A final factor is that there is often a large pass-on readership of as many as eight.

When reviewing strengths and weaknesses of publicity, it follows that these will tend to be the opposite of those for press advertising. In summary, the following are worthy of consideration.

Strengths

- Free, or at least cheaper than any other medium
- Higher readership than ads – as much as five times higher
- Wider reach than ads – coverage by more publications than could be afforded with advertising
- Higher impact
- Better coverage of complex stories
- Much higher credibility – implied endorsement
- Can be run on for inexpensive reprints

Weaknesses

- It might never appear
- It certainly will not be repeated
- There may not be any response mechanism
- The journal may get it wrong
- It may even be negative
- No control over when it will appear
- No control over size, location, illustration, colour or, indeed, anything else

Checklist

1. Has the use of editorial publicity been established as an integral part of the marketing communications operation?
2. Is there a plan of action covering the same period of time as the marketing plan?
3. Have quantified objectives been set for editorial publicity?

4. Are the sales staff aware of the value of this form of publicity, and the extent to which they can contribute?

5. Have press lists been drawn up which relate specifically to (a) the company's activities (b) its markets and (c) its products?

6. Has attention been given to the importance of producing press releases which are tailored to the needs of the particular audience and media concerned?

7. Is photography used wherever possible, and is the same attention given to its creative treatment and production as for press advertising?

8. Are press releases timed so as to fit in with (a) editorial press dates and (b) the overall promotional campaign?

9. Have good personal relationships been built up between the relevant journalists and the key company staff?

10. Has provision been made (a) for measuring results and (b) for corrective action to be taken if necessary?

11. Are press cuttings used as a means of evaluation?

12. Are they comprehensive?

13. Are they circulated to personnel who might be interested?

OTHER MEANS OF PROMOTION

In this marketing communications section of the book, the reader has been taken progressively from the initial strategy through each major channel of persuasive communications – press advertising, direct mail, exhibitions, literature, photography, videos and editorial publicity. One of the problems facing publicity executives is that as each of these media is used more widely, its competitive edge is blunted. Maybe this is countered by ingenuity in creative presentation, but nevertheless competition is intense. An advertisement is fighting for attention amidst thousands of others; an exhibition stand may be in a hall amongst hundreds of others, an editorial mention is only a drop in an ocean of words.

The impact of a sales message depends a great deal upon the novelty with which it is presented, but novelty becomes increasingly hard to find as a particular medium is more widely used by industrial advertisers. Each seeks as a result to find more unconventional ways of presenting a message. For instance, the first time a national newspaper was distributed at an exhibition with a special front page entirely devoted to one of the exhibitors it must have created a remarkable effect, as no doubt did the first aerial advertisement to be towed behind an aircraft.

This chapter examines some of the lesser-used industrial marcom techniques as well as some of the peripheral activities which tend to be classed under the publicity function. It cannot hope to be exhaustive, but it will underline the importance of applying creative imagination to new or less used techniques which can give a powerful stimulus to a campaign or even becomes its focal point.

Television advertising

For many years television has been used for industrial advertising, but only for a minority of products. Since it is a mass communications vehicle it follows that it is appropriate only where relatively mass audiences are required. Most industrial campaigns are aimed at audiences of 10,000 or less: television tends to be more suitable for audiences of 100,000 or more. The exception is in the US where the wide variety of channels provides cost-effective advertising opportunities.

There are of course many countries around the world in which television is the major medium but it is largely suitable for consumer products where the target audiences are in the millions. Even so, there are a number of industrial categories where television has proved to be useful, if only sometimes because of its novelty value.

The cost of advertising on commercial television

Because commercial television offers a range of rates dependent upon supply and demand it is difficult to provide exact costs. However, a network 30-second *peaktime* commercial in the UK could cost in the region of £40,000 if that spot got a TVR (television rating – ie percentage of viewers) of 30.

Channel Four allows, on its own, new advertisers with limited budgets to experiment with television advertising. That is not to say that Channel Four is not a medium in its own right. Equally, advertising on ITV 1 need not be a prohibitively expensive exercise. Buying a campaign which does not depend on high-demand peaktime spots may reach exactly the target audience that a business advertiser wishes to reach.

How to advertise on television

Advertisers will obviously consult with an agency initially from a budget point of view. They will then establish the creative approach and the weight of the TV campaign, the latter, of course, being directly related to budget. With the advice of copywriters and the TV production department, a commercial is generally fed out to an independent production house at an agreed cost. Alternatively, if industrial advertisers do not have an agency they may go direct to the television company who will advise and help make the commercial. In this case it is common practice for the advertiser to use a time-buying shop at no extra cost.

THE COST OF MAKING A COMMERCIAL

While a commercial may cost as little as £100 it is likely that larger sums of money will be involved. Below are some ballpark figures on just how much it can cost to advertise on television in the UK.

1. *Five- or ten-second commercials – £200–£2000*   Within this price range, production values will range from the most basic and cheapest slide presentation of a simple message with a station announcer's voice over it, to a multi-slide presentation accompanied by pre-recorded sound on a separate audio cassette. At the upper end of this price bracket, a director and/or producer should also be provided, as well as some editing facilities.

2. *Five or ten second commercials – £2000–£5000* Advertisers requiring high production values can add extra facilities such as special visual effects, or the addition of music, pack-shots of the product; studio use plus colour camera, as well as more of the director's and producer's time.

3. *30-second commercials – £5000–£15,000* Productions within this range will enable the advertiser to be more ambitious in his presentation. A budget at the top end should be adequate to cover a full day's studio use, editing time, special effects, casting, lighting, make-up and art direction, simple set construction and props, and all necessary crewing and transportation and artwork costs and insurances.

4. *30-second commercials and longer from £15,000* Commercials that require location shooting, as well as studio time, synchronized sound, the use of several artists as well as the necessary technical and staffing facilities, can be expected to cost anything from this figure up to £40–50,000. Many factors determine price: the stature of the lead artist or artists; the cost of music; where and if location shooting is required; the complexities of set design; how much editing time is needed – and so on.

5. *Repeat fees and other ancillary costs* In addition to the performance fee paid an artist or artists to appear in a television commercial, 'repeat' fees are due to performers when the commercial is transmitted. The scale of these fees is related to the area(s) in which the commercial is shown, and to the number of times it is repeated.

Radio advertising

Radio is a mass medium in much the same way as television and newspapers. It has a variable audience profile as does television and there will be times when listeners will comprise a higher than usual AB content. Even with this narrow profile, use of radio will be a blunderbuss approach to communicating with businessmen and women, though there are certain time slots in which listeners become highly segmented, for instance during the immediate pre- and post-work driving hours.

The geographical segmentation which can be achieved with local radio stations may be of interest if a firm is setting about a moving sales campaign or road show: it can also help on the rare occasion when test marketing an industrial product. Generally its usefulness is in direct proportion to its number of prospects, ie the total number of companies who may buy a product multiplied by the average number of people in the decision-making units. On a national scale it is probably not worth while for target prospects less than the order of 100,000, though in many other countries radio has for long had an important role to play in what might be regarded broadly as the corporate communications function.

On the credit side, a radio commercial is fast to produce and relatively cheap. Small slots of time can be bought to give tactical support to the sales force. And there are minor spin-offs like reaching out to non-buying audiences (which even so are important in PR terms) such as employees and their families, shareholders, local communities, opinion formers and potential recruits – schools.

A starting point after obtaining audience profiles at various times of day is to conduct a small research amongst existing customers. Get the sales force to ask people they call on for a week if and when they listen to local radio.

Sponsorship

A major new activity in the promotion of companies and products is sponsorship. Simple and effective, this can involve paying for or subsidizing such things as sports, the arts, books, conferences, exhibitions, flower shows, ballroom dances: the list is endless. A clear distinction must be made with patronage which can be applied to any of these activities, but is concerned only with giving support to the event regardless of any possible reward or benefit. Sponsorship on the other hand is the deliberate financial support given to an event in order to achieve a specific commercial objective. Typical objectives might be:

1. To increase brand awareness among customers.
2. To improve perception of company in terms of modernity, warmth, concern, etc.
3. To increase goodwill and understanding among trade customers.
4. To enhance company's image in local community.
5. To raise employees' morale and company loyalty.
6. To create favourable awareness of the company among young potential future consumers.

The staging of numerous 'high visibility' sponsorship schemes by major consumer goods companies tends to imply that there is little going on in the industrial sector. The opposite is probably the case: it is simply that they tend to be specialized, or educational, or at a local level. So their visibility is not very great but in practice they not only do a useful job, but are also very cost effective.

The whole business of sponsorship has been very well summarized by the Incorporated Society of British Advertisers in a booklet which puts up ten points:

1. Sponsorship is a tool of company communication. Its prime purpose is the achievement of favourable publicity for the company or its brands within a relevant target audience by the support of an activity (or some aspect thereof) which is not directly linked to the company's normal business.

2. It should not be confused with patronage, advertising or sales promotion, although they have some elements and objects in common. Sponsorship can prove an important additional ingredient in the marketing communication programme.

3. Sponsorship provides great flexibility – *in the choice of activity sponsored*; the arts, sport, leisure, social or communal activities; *the form the sponsorship may take* – tournaments, events, support of teams or individual competitors; *scale of participation*, from international golf to awards at the local flower show. Terms, conditions and level of financial contributions are invariably open to negotiation.

4. Sponsorship is normally undertaken for one (or more) of the following reasons:
   (a) To enhance the company name/brand image.
   (b) Improve trade relations.
   (c) Foster company's 'good citizen' image.
   (d) Boost employee morale.

5. Sponsorship is unlikely to achieve significant results used on a 'one-off' basis. It should be regarded in the long term, both in setting objectives and budgets. (The possibility of escalating costs should be borne in mind, as should the 'risk' factor in sponsoring a team or individual over a lengthy period.)

6. Setting realistic objectives is imperative; both when deciding the area, nature, level and duration of sponsorhip, and in formulating strategy once participation has been decided upon.

7. Sponsorship is a business deal; a written contract is essential. It is important to establish a good relationship, with mutual recognition of the responsibilities and expectations of both parties.

8. The full benefits of the sponsorship will be achieved only if it is integrated with the company's other publicity activities; eg advertising, PR, sales promotion, staff and customer relations etc.

9. Procedures should be established for the control (including budgetary), monitoring and evaluation of the sponsorship programme.

10. First-time sponsors should consider obtaining advice and guidance – from relevant statutory bodies and/or a specialist consultancy or agency.

Sponsored books

The sponsored book is an excellent method of promotion and, if the editorial theme is carefully devised in association with a publisher, it can prove to be a significant instrument of marketing policy. The book usually relates to subject-matter close to the firm's products or markets and should be practical and authoritative. (*The Industrial Applications of the Diamond* by N. R. Smith, director of the diamond tool specialists, Van Moppes and Sons Ltd, is a good example.) The author is usually a senior member of the firm and his or her name appears on the title page, linked with the name of his/her company. This is the only reference to the firm but all examples, pictures etc. are drawn from the firm's products and customers. The firm underwrites the cost of the book but takes an agreed percentage of revenue from all copies sold. It can thus be a self-liquidating exercise, but if it is not, there is always some financial return as libraries take the book, and the promotional cost is low. It should also be remembered that a published book is the most permanent and deeply penetrating method of communication yet devised.

Telemarketing

A new range of uses for the telephone has grown up over the past few years and looks likely to develop further. Already in the US direct marketing by telephone is said to have exceeded that by mail. In a US survey of industrial companies two-thirds of the respondents said they used the telephone for selling or lead generation, and also for list-building.

In the UK the use of the telephone for selling has been slow to get off the ground due perhaps to the reaction by customers that such calls are intrusive and an unwarranted, and certainly undesirable, invasion of their privacy.

The function of telemarketing has grown in the US into a highly disciplined activity by people having a natural aptitude for telephone conversation. They are well trained and usually work to a structured brief on what to say.

One of the most useful applications of the telephone in marketing is in market research where at least simple answers can be obtained in a very short space of time. There is little doubt however that other business uses of the telephone will arise. Campaign evaluation for example is worth considering as are readership surveys in relation to business people and industrial decision-makers.

Posters

Little use is made of posters in industrial marketing communications, and this may be a good reason for using them. They represent a first-class medium for getting across the basic sales message but the problem is in finding suitable site locations. Some obvious opportunities exist: exhibition halls, conferences, key railway stations, airports and even railway and underground trains. There are the company's own vehicles, sites adjacent to exhibition halls and hotels where visitors are likely to stay, taxis or even sandwich-board men. Posters can be used as direct mail pieces: they even occasionally reach the office wall if the design is outstanding enough.

Point of sale

Many industrial products, especially components, have a retail market and, however small, this is worth supporting. Consideration can therefore be given to showcards, dispensers, display units, give-away leaflets as well as posters. Point of sale material can also be of value in industrial merchandising, for instance, by agricultural merchants, electrical contractors or industrial wholesalers.

Packaging

With very many consumer products, food, toiletries and cigarettes, packaging may lay fair claim to be at least as important as the product itself. Apart from other factors, it preconditions a buyer to adopt a favourable attitude towards the contents: it is a vital part of building up a favourable brand image.

Professional buyers are not immune to subjective forces. A well-packaged or presented product will have the edge on one for which no trouble at all has been taken. It is equally true as with consumer goods that an over-packaged product may set up a resistance.

Most industrial products must be packaged in some way. A wooden crate with wood wool packing can be improved by including around the product a well-fitted polythene bag with a brand name on it. In place of a cardboard box an attractively printed carton can be used. Functional packaging also has a part to play: shrinkwrapping of gear wheels to prevent corrosion; a dust cover for an inspection microscope; expanded plastic case inserts for delicate machinery. A well-produced and appropriate piece of packing confirms the supplier's belief that his product is good enough to be carefully protected.

Gifts

The question of giving business gifts is more likely to set a boardroom alight than the most expensive advertising campaign. Does it establish a dangerous precedent? Will competitors follow suit? Where should the line be drawn and what of those who do not receive a gift or, worse still, get one this year but not next? These questions are answered only by a careful consideration of what to give, how and when to give it, and what repercussions are likely.

There can be few guidelines on gifts since the circumstances vary so much. The criterion is: does the gift make a maximum contribution to the promotion of sales at minimum cost? If to emboss the trade mark will provide additional publicity, for example with an item to stand on a desk or hang on an office wall, then it should be used. If it is likely to be out of place, say on something for the home, then it should not be used. Guidance on what not to give can usually be found in the multitude of business gift catalogues. The items in these are most likely to be what other firms will be choosing and there is a limit to the number of penknives and desk diaries that a buyer can absorb. Choose then something novel, something that sells, is appropriate and in good taste.

Christmas cards

These are included under sales promotion rather than under public relations, because they can be regarded as contributing to the selling effort. Where firms use Christmas cards as another direct mail shot to all and sundry there is a strong case for supposing that they are likely to be either ineffectual or even considered in bad taste and therefore counter-productive.

In industrial selling, however, a close personal relationship is often built up between a buyer and a salesperson – to their mutual advantage – and here an exchange of Christmas cards can surely be regarded as part of the building up of good relationships, and in so far as they contribute to efficient selling, an element of a sales promotional activity.

Brand names

All products, including industrial, must have a name. The buyer, and the user, must identify it and if the selling company does not provide an adequate name or identity, the buyer will invent one.

Furthermore, all products have an image. This may have evolved, or come by chance, or it may have been deliberately planned and promoted. The inescapable fact is that whenever a product is named to a buyer it conjures up a certain image which may be good or bad, cheap or expensive, reliable or unreliable. The brand name itself is not necessarily a significant factor in determining the image of an industrial product. This would be too much to hope for, rather the image will be created by the product itself in the long run. However, it is the case that a product needs a name to identify it and to enable a buyer to recall it when making the purchase. The essential requirement is that it should be memorable, and the simpler the name is the better, both in the number of letters and the ease of pronunciation.

In determining a brand name for an industrial product there would seem to be little point in basing it on, say, the raw materials from which it is made, or the process, or the town, or a nearby forest or river. There may be some advantage in a name which emphasizes the 'customer benefit', but if this leads to a word which is exotic, complex and highly contrived, it is better to abandon it and try for something simple. It is possible to aim for both, but it will be hard to improve on such classics as Oxo or Kodak.

Sales aids

The marketing services or marketing communications department often finds itself closely involved in a number of sales activities such as sales training, sales conferences and sales manuals. This is to be welcomed since it helps to weld the two functions. These, however, are not considered to be a major part of the promotional operation and for this reason are not dealt with in any detail. They are mentioned, however, because it is important that they are not overlooked in the overall marketing mix. Two matters which perhaps can be considered within the marcom framework are sales aids and samples.

Progressive sales managers will devote considerable time in training their sales staff to present the benefits of a product to a buyer, to overcome points of resistance and to close the deal. In this process a variety of aids can be deployed with advantage.

The product itself is the obvious choice together with the facilities to demonstrate it. This may be a demonstration caravan or a well-fitted show case. Where a product is not demonstrable, use can be made of a photograph album, a slide projector, a self-contained video unit or a multi-media presentation. Samples of raw materials, for instance, need to be more than just a handful of pieces of sheet metal; these can be presented in such a way as to project their selling features attractively.

A sales presentation requires the skill of a stage show. The development of the argument needs to be planned, using the salesperson to the full, but support needs to be given with every appropriate visual, audio and three-dimensional aid. Pre-presentation material should be sent in advance to prepare the prospect, and the follow-up should make full use of sales literature, advertisement reprints, press cuttings and any other promotional material.

Whatever material is used, it should be geared to the sales arguments and method of visual presentation being used elsewhere, to achieve maximum integrated impact.

Stickers, stuffers and mailings

Correspondence from a company provides at least three opportunities for introducing, or at least reinforcing, a sales argument.

Suppose, for instance, that a new brand of heat-resisting paint is being launched and that all the conventional media of a major campaign are being brought to bear on the potential market. For a specified period of time and with suitable phasing, the brand name together with the main slogan can be printed on to a mini-leaflet and stuffed into every envelope leaving the company; a small sticker can be affixed to each letter sent out; finally at very low cost all envelopes can be franked with a few key words. In themselves these are small actions, but viewed as a whole they help to give cohesion to a campaign, and have an impressive effect both on potential buyers and one's own staff.

Creative inserts

The following are unusual creative ideas which can be applicable to both advertising and direct mail.

Fragrance Burst

This is a technique for combining little drops of scent with a glue. The glue is then used to gum two pieces of paper together. The scent is released when the two pieces are separated.

Scratch 'N' Sniff

A technique which allows a thin layer of impregnated gum to be selectively placed and then covered with a protective film of ink; when the seal is broken the smell escapes. Used for many products from lemon to leather.

Zippalopes

These are one-piece envelope mailings which are opened by tearing along the perforations on three edges to release the contents. They let you include a whole mailing package of items inside one insert.

Shortfolds

A shortfold makes an insert more intriguing and dramatic by revealing a headline or part of a picture from the next page of an insert.

Microperf

This is the very lightest perforation you can get. It makes removal of a coupon easy, but it is almost invisible and is unlikely to tear during insertion.

Bangtail

This is an envelope with an extended 'lip' which forms the reply coupon. More complicated versions can include a product brochure, a reply device and envelope – all in one piece.

Gatefold and Rollfold

These are two of the most common forms of insert. There are many others but all inserts must have a single leading edge.

(*Source: Farmers Weekly*)

Signboards

Signboards outside a factory are often overlooked, or left to the initiative of an architect or factory manager. A solution is to place the responsibility for company signs firmly on the marketing communications department. These may include large illuminated signs and neon lights, and range down to signposts and notice boards.

Seminars

Although perhaps part of educational public relations, seminars can have a direct selling function. Indeed in some branches of business, such as hi-tech and financial services, they have become a major selling activity. One company took over the Festival Hall to present a technical seminar on a new range of components having certain novel features. Not only did they fill the hall with prospective buyers, they also charged an entrance fee, and made a profit.

Summary

Finally, an interesting though dated indication of the usage of 'miscellaneous promotion items' is given in a publication by Metalworking Production in relation to a segment of the engineering industry (see Table 11.1).

Table 11.1 Expenditure on miscellaneous promotional items

	Percentage
Regular press handouts	54
Christmas gifts	48
Christmas cards	45
Films	34
Calendars	30
Coloured slides and viewers	17
Mobile display vans	8
Diaries	8
Point of sale display panels	6
Press conferences	6
Private film shows/cocktail and theatre parties	4
Technical posters and wall charts	3
Advertising gifts and novelties	3
Works exhibitions and novelties	3

Checklist

1. Are novel means of sales promotion encouraged in order to get the edge on competition?

2. Is 'brainstorming' or other techniques used in which people are able to suggest the most unlikely ideas, without fear of criticism, in order to maximize on creative initiative?
3. Does such creative expression extend past headlines, copy angles, sign-offs, slogans and symbols, to include the medium, eg size and shape, material, colour, texture, feel, smell, wrapping and presentation?
4. Specifically, has consideration been given to:
   (a) TV and radio?
   (b) Sponsorship?
   (c) Telemarketing?
   (d) Seminars and conferences?
   (e) Christmas cards?
   (f) Calendars and diaries?
   (g) Point-of-sale material, posters, or wall charts?
   (h) Sponsored books and pamphlets?
   (i) Outgoing mail, stickers, stuffers, franking?
   (j) Sales aids, manuals, conferences, slides, films?
   (k) Brand-names and symbols?
   (l) Packaging and presentation?

Part 3

RESEARCH

INTRODUCTION

During the past 20 years or so a great deal of progress has been made in applying research techniques to aspects of marketing. Initially this was concentrated in the consumer sector since it was here that the money was most readily available, and in a sense this was an easier area to investigate. The movement into industrial marketing was slow, and often inadequately based because of low budgets, and this in turn resulted in inaccurate results, discouraging further research and leading to yet lower budgets.

Persistence on the part of certain leading companies, publishers, and in particular a few specialist industrial research agencies, has led to a breakthrough to such an extent that sophisticated techniques are nowadays being applied to the marketing of industrial products and services. It may well be that in the future, expenditure on industrial marketing research will exceed that on consumer research.

The distinction should be drawn between market research and marketing research, particularly in the context of this book. Market research is concerned with the investigation of markets, their size, location, purchasing power, growth, capital structure and economics. This is only one aspect of the matter. Marketing research can be regarded as the application of research techniques to any facet of marketing including the market. Thus new product research, concept testing, awareness, attitude and motivation studies, patterns of buying behaviour, structure of decision-making units, are all part of the growing science of marketing research. Into this category fit media research and campaign evaluation, the subjects of the next two chapters.

Research processes are not infallible. The aim of any research activity is to reduce to a minimum the areas of uncertainty surrounding management decisions. The application of research techniques, and the use of scientific disciplines do not of themselves eliminate uncertainty. They merely provide a degree of precision to some of the criteria upon which marketing and other business decisions are based. The tendency in some quarters for marketing research to be regarded as wasteful or misleading is more often due to a blind reliance on, or a misinterpretation of, research data than the data themselves being at fault. The solution lies in using professional expertise not only to conduct the research but also to interpret its significance.

12

MEDIA RESEARCH

Press advertising

Press advertising, together with the accompanying publicity, represents the largest single item in the industrial marketing communications budget.

In Chapter 4 emphasis was laid on the need for accurate media selection and the criteria which should be considered were broken down into fourteen categories. Some of these do not require research to evaluate them, for instance 'frequency' or 'special services from publisher'. Others require accurate data for intelligent decisions to be made.

CIRCULATION

It is necessary to be sceptical when considering media data and to examine closely the basis upon which they have been arrived at. Take for example total circulation. If a figure is quoted by a publisher, but unsupported by membership of the Audit Bureau of Circulation (ABC), an advertiser must draw his own conclusions and at least be doubtful. A good deal of pioneer work has been done by *British Rate and Data* (published by Emap Media Ltd) in insisting on data meeting certain standards before they will publish them.

Given that a total circulation figure is validated either by ABC or by postal certificate or perhaps some other acceptable audit, the question arises 'what precisely does this figure mean?' This at least is an assurance that a certain number of copies went out through the post. But to whom did these copies go? Did they ask for them? And did they pay for them? Suppose in a specialized field there are 4000 separate identifiable purchasing units, and suppose a journal can prove that its specialized circulation is 4000, this is by no means a guarantee that it is addressed to 100 per cent of the market. Where the market for a particular publication is not homogeneous, the variations in coverage between one segment and another can be so great as to make a total circulation figure comparatively useless. A great deal of progress has been made in the UK in providing details of circulation by means of the ABC Standard Certificate. This enables an advertiser to obtain reliable information on methods of circulation (free, subsidized, or full price), circulation to overseas countries and a breakdown under UK geographical regions.

When a breakdown of industries or of occupations is in question, the situation is different. In the first place, such data are not audited and it is an unfortunate fact that from some publishers the figures can be little more than uninformed or approximate head-counting. Even where the job is done thoroughly and professionally by a publisher, there are real difficulties in knowing just how to categorize a given recipient, and in how much detail. Since, however, the usual reason for an analysis being required is to enable comparisons to be made between different, competitive publications it is necessary to note that such data are presented in a form which makes a comparison possible only in very few instances.

ABC STANDARD CERTIFICATE OF CIRCULATION

Each certificate gives an audited breakdown of a number of factors. These include:

- Average net circulation per issue
- Average net newstrade circulation per issue
- Total net circulation
- Newstrade and other single copy issues
- Subscription copies
- Multiple copy sales
- Society/association/institution circulation
- Paid and qualified circulation
- Controlled free circulation
- Non-controlled free circulation
- Exhibition/conference bulk free supply
- Optional geographical analysis

In addition to the Standard Certificate, publishers may opt for a further analysis which takes the form of the ABC Profile. This provides a useful examination of geo-demographic data such as industry and job title breakdown.

It might be thought that no publisher could do without such audited data. Sadly, this is not so, and rather less than half the business publications in the UK are able to provide such authentic information.

One basis which is used by publishers for circulation analysis is the government *Standard Industrial Classification*. This breaks down the whole of British industry with a great deal of detail and provides explanatory notes on what is meant by each sub-classification. This does not enable a conglomerate to be easily classified, but for many requirements it is a valuable starting point.

Finally, it must be appreciated that circulation is continuously changing, with perhaps 20 per cent a year new registrations, offset by 20 per cent lapses. A judgement based on circulation this year, even if it is right, may be wrong after the year has elapsed. It is surprising that to meet the apparent demand of big advertisers, publishers devote their energies increasingly to expanding circulation as an end in itself, when the factor which really has any relevance at all is readership. This, also, should not be regarded as an end in itself since finally it is the impact of an advertisement which really counts, and this will be dealt with in the next chapter on campaign evaluation. In the meantime, there are several techniques which can be employed to measure readership.

TOTAL READERSHIP

Any readership survey is liable to considerable errors from differences in interpretation as to what constitutes 'readership' and how individual respondents react to the term. Accepting an initial margin of error, however, a good deal of progress can be made in measuring the usefulness of a journal in terms of readership as opposed to circulation. The same criticism of total readership applies as with total circulation, namely it tends to be of use only in a homogeneous market, for example hairdressers or market gardeners.

A study of the number of people reading a publication in comparison with its circulation is often most revealing. For instance a magazine distributed only to members of an association or institute may have fewer readers than its circulation because not all members will spend time reading something they receive as a part of their membership. Furthermore they probably do not bother to take it into the office and circulate it. Against this, many publications exist which can fairly claim a readership of eight or more people per copy. Controlled circulation journals probably do not achieve such high reader/copy ratings, partly because they tend to send out individual copies as a matter of policy. Indeed this may be regarded as a strength since, if speed of communication is important, it is not in the best interest of an advertiser to use a publication which takes a month or two to reach out to all its readers.

A research into journals covering the instrumentation and automation industries gave a dramatic example of the differences which can occur between circulation and readership and resulted in quite different assessments in terms of 'cost/1000'. Table 12.1 is an extract from this survey.

As can be seen, journal C was the cheapest based on circulation, and journal E was very poor. In terms of actual usefulness, following a readership survey, journal C was three times more expensive than the best (journal A) and journal E shot up into the top three.

One of the problems facing a researcher into readership by industrial and business personnel is to determine a satisfactory definition of the 'universe' and then to find a reliable method of sampling. Table 12.1 was produced

Table 12.1   Cost per 1000 circulation compared with readership

Journal	Circulation	Estimated readership	Cost/1000 circulation	Cost/1000 readership
C	10,400	9,700	£6	£6.6
A	11,500	42,000	£7	£1.9
D	8,000	28,000	£7.9	£2.2
F	9,200	8,700	£10.7	£11
E	5,000	27,000	£13.4	£2.5
B	16,300	47,000	£16.5	£5.7

from a series of interviews at an exhibition that, because of its size and importance, could be regarded as counting among its visitors a representative cross-section of the whole industry being surveyed. Such an assumption is of course an immediate source of bias and must be considered when assessing the results.

The use of the interview is particularly important in readership surveys since readers are often unable to distinguish between one journal and another without aided recall. The above survey used a flipchart with the front covers of each journal. As can be seen, the ranking order of publications in terms of cost/1000 circulation changes radically compared with cost/1000 readers.

The use of an exhibition is particularly recommended for speed, convenience and simplicity. The procedure is to have questionnaire forms with the list of journals to be researched, and with three columns against each asking 'read regularly, occasionally, or never'. Make provision for 'any other publications', then perhaps job title, buying involvement, and then maybe one or two other interesting questions. In practice it has been found that no more than 100 interviews are necessary, provided it is not intended to subdivide the responses into individual categories, eg male/female. And one person at an exhibition site can complete 100 interviews in one-and-a-half days.

Should an exhibition not be available, the same procedure can be carried out by the sales force, say for every call they make during one week. The telephone is obviously another way, but has the disadvantage that respondents are not able to see the publications, and there is a strong possibility of error. Finally, the research can be carried out by a mailing but here the problem is one of poor response, and even with the simplest of forms, and maybe some incentive to reply, it would be unlikely to achieve a response rate much above 20 per cent.

An early survey into the horticultural field concentrated on two magazines, *Grower* and the *Commercial Grower*. Initially a postal questionnaire was used and a result obtained. The question then arose of possible confusion of names, as a result of which an interview research was conducted that proved that the original results were quite incorrect.

A more recent study, 'Engineering Publications in the UK' by Maclean Hunter, provided a comparison between circulation and readership as shown in Table 12.2.

Without a careful scrutiny of the sample base and the methods involved in obtaining and processing the data, it is not reasonable to take the figures as they stand in Table 12.2 and draw specific conclusions. What can be demonstrated is the extent to which a schedule drawn up on the basis of circulation can be wrong compared with a readership base.

Table 12.2   Readership compared with circulation

	Readership	Circulation	Readers/copy
Engineering	105,000	20,045	5.25
Mechanical Engineering News	89,000	71,767	1.24
The Engineer	87,000	37,964	2.29
Engineers Digest	46,000	15,568	2.95
Engineering Today	44,000	50,932	0.86
Chartered Mechanical Engineer	39,000	47,962	0.81

SEGMENTED READERSHIP

Here the objective is to find the readership habits of a specific group, usually a company's potential market, or a segment of it. Very often a company's own mailing list is not acceptable as being representative of the potential market: it may be for this reason that press advertising is being used to reach purchasing influences which are unknown. Each problem tends to be entirely different, and sampling methods need to be individually planned.

An example of the use of a segmented readership analysis was a survey of buyers of paperboard for carton and box-making. In this case, an examination of the total readership of the packaging press would have been meaningless since the number of converters of cardboard adds up to hundreds, while the number of users of packages as a whole amounts to tens of thousands. The result showed that the most popular and large-circulation journals scored badly, and of course they were expensive whereas certain minor journals did well. The budget was cut by 75 per cent.

DUPLICATION

When compiling a schedule to obtain maximum coverage or 'reach' it is important to examine the overlap of various publications, that is the extent of readership duplication. Researches into this aspect of readership have enabled schedules to be cut significantly, or alternatively for expenditures to be concentrated into significantly fewer publications, achieving much greater impact. A good deal of work on this has been carried out by a leading advertising agency on behalf of its clients. For one product the media department had identified some 100 journals which, at least from the publishers' claims, could be considered as possible advertising media. A survey showed that one journal alone covered 89 per cent of the potential market while the second most important rated 68 per cent. Added together they amounted to 93 per cent, an exceptionally high coverage by any standards and well above the average. It is interesting to note that the sixth journal out of this massive list scored only 26 per cent.

A similar study carried out by an electronics company showed that there was no gain in advertising in more than three journals since the addition of a fourth added so little additional coverage as to be worthless.

A body of evidence begins to appear which leads to the conclusion that the law of diminishing returns applies in media scheduling wherever more than just two or three publications are available to reach a given market. The same results come from research into American business publications and the graph in Figure 12.1 is typical of many such investigations. As can be seen, if duplication of readership is not required there is little point in advertising in more than three publications – in a homogeneous market.

It is interesting, though not surprising, that the law of diminishing returns in cumulative audience coverage also applies to consumer publications. In a survey of United Kingdom newspapers a similar phenomenon was to be found, as shown in Table 12.3. In this example, the addition of *The Times* to

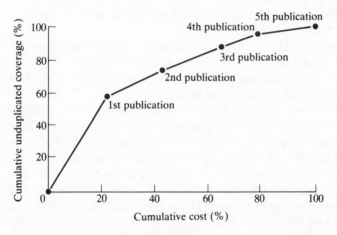

Figure 12.1 Cumulative readership – law of diminishing returns
(*Source:* McGraw-Hill Report 1120.4)

Table 12.3 Cumulative unduplicated readership

Publication	Cumulative unduplicated readership by businessmen (%)
Sunday Times	39
Daily Telegraph	55
Financial Times	60
The Times	62

the schedule would add only 2 per cent to the number of businessmen having the opportunity to see (OTS) a particular advertisement.

EDITORIAL EXCELLENCE

This must be regarded as a highly subjective area and one which must pay regard to the views of experts in the subject-matter of a particular journal. With subscription magazines it might be considered that circulation is some measure of the value readers put on the editorial. This concept is clouded by the variety of circulation techniques used, though readership figures tend to overcome this difficulty.

One interesting research technique, which follows the Starch method in the United States, is the measurement of page traffic, ie the percentage of readers who claim to have read or noted a particular advertisement or editorial item. A few British publishers are using this technique and although the results must be regarded as being approximate, a good measure of consistency has appeared in relating one type of editorial item with another. Making comparisons between journals is a more difficult task but is not impossible.

An extract from a survey of *Business Systems and Equipment* is reproduced in Table 12.4.

Another type of study on editorial excellence was carried out in connection with *Travel Agency*. This showed that respondents spent an average of one hour 12 minutes reading the journal, that 68 per cent claimed to read every issue and 24 per cent most issues.

A further study looked at the place where journals are read and, as seen in Table 12.5, here can be a wide variation between one journal and another. The journals were all connected with civil engineering. The abbreviations are of the names of the journals. In the case of *NCE*, most of the recipients had the journal mailed to them at home which accounts for its high 'at home' rating.

Another hitherto ignored factor about readers is their age. Figure 12.2 comes from Cahners Publishing Co. in the States and portrays a fairly typical spread of ages. It is worth noting that the average age was 45 but that varied from one job category to another. Clearly, this factor is important for copywriters since it will determine the style of writing.

Table 12.4 Editorial page traffic

Editorial item	Interest rating (%)
Comment	60
Planning for decimals	91
Mechanical accounting	
Background to reappraisal	53
Visible record accounting computers	44
Special purpose accounting computers	36
Machine detail chart	26
Business man and machine in the 70s – a two-day seminar	36
Design flow chart	22
Eat, drink and be wary	43
The greatest show on earth	32
Computerscope	
IBM announce magnetic tape keyboard peripherals	19
Insurance moves into real-time	14
A score for Scottish Honeywell	13
Mintech guide to installing a computer	17
The computer bureau scene	
Jobs for the boys	16
Fast start for Inter-Bank	10

Table 12.5 Where journals are read

	NCE	CN	CJ	CE	CP&E	PMJ
At home	78%	32%	22%	9%	18%	14%
At work	25%	63%	72%	75%	76%	83%
When travelling	—	—	1%	—	1%	—
Other	1%	10%	6%	16%	5%	3%

JOURNALS' REPUTATION

Over and above the intrinsic editorial value, a journal acquires a certain reputation which to some extent reflects on advertisements placed in it. It may be claimed for instance that the quality image of *The Times* tends subconsciously to enhance the view a reader takes of a product advertised in it.

There are a variety of techniques which can be used to evaluate 'journal reputation', each depending upon the particular circumstance. An interesting use of a semantic scale has been employed to compare a number of electronic journals. The following is an extract from the questionnaire:

How would you rank the journals listed below for their conciseness, up-to-dateness, etc.?

Here is a set of scales (Figure 12.3). We would like you to mark them as follows: if you find a particular publication eminently concise, just as you would like it in

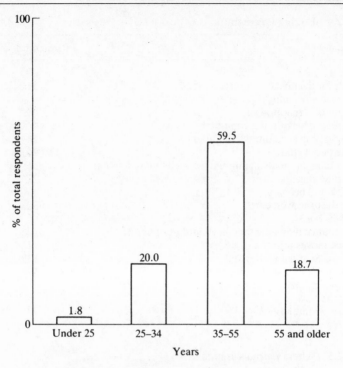

Figure 12.2 Age of recipients of business magazines
(*Source*: Cahners Research No. 536.1)

fact from this point of view, then tick the scale in the space next to the word 'concise'; if you normally find it extremely long-winded, then tick the other end. You may feel, however, that the magazine ranks somewhere between these extremes; if so, then place your tick accordingly.

A survey into the printing industry was conducted in order to establish readership among managing directors of printing houses. Additionally the question

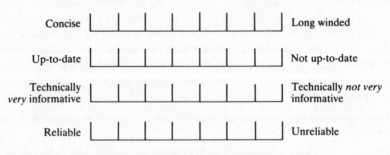

Figure 12.3 Semantic rating scale

was asked 'which single journal do you find most valuable?' The point here is that there will sometimes arise a situation in which two journals score equally well in readership rating and even in segmented cost/1000, but their reputations may be of a different order.

One company asked readers which journal they would look through first if they were looking for a particular component. While the readership figures varied by up to a factor of two or so, the responses to this specific question were quite significant. A selection is reproduced in Table 12.6 to show the effect.

Table 12.6 'Journal preference' for a particular purpose

Publication	Read regularly(%)	Look at first for a particular component (%)
B	59.0	53.9
D	48.4	67.5
A	48.3	8.2
G	41.6	—
E	34.6	18.3
F	29.5	13.9
C	28.9	4.9

FURTHER ADVERTISING RESEARCH

Research activities into business marketing continue to be more advanced in the US than anywhere else in the world. The following summaries come from the Cahners Advertising research reports:

- Advertisements using coupons receive 13 per cent higher 'Remember seeing' scores than advertisements without coupons
- Colour advertisements have a 50 per cent higher noted score than mono
- There is no difference in noting between left- and right-hand pages
- A bleed ad scores 13 per cent higher than non-bleed
- There is no significant difference between advertisements in the first third of a publication, the middle, or the last
- On reputation, the size, colour and frequency of advertising signals to buyers that a firm is a solid, experienced leader in its field

Research into 19 IT journals showed that when the question changes from 'regular readership' to 'most important publication', the ranking order can change dramatically. In the table below, the journal ranked 11 in 'regular readership' shot to the top of the column as the 'most important'. This research, of course, was for one specific market sector, and the ranking order would change for any other segment.

	Regular readership index	Most important index
Computer Weekly	100	100
Computing	89	60
PC User	67	90
Network Week	61	80
National Press	55	—
PC Week	53	40
LAN Magazine	52	50
Personal Computer Magazine	5	10
Network News	50	90
PC Magazine	48	30
PC LAN	42	100
Computer News	30	20
Business & Technology Magazine	22	10
UNIX News	20	10
Communications Week International	19	10
PC Pro	19	—
Infomatics	17	10
Internet Magazine	13	—
Byte	11	20

SPECIAL SERVICES TO PUBLISHERS

Some publishers recognize that it is valuable to assist the industries they cover by providing information which, even if not related specifically to the publications themselves, helps their clients to produce more effective advertising. Such a service is not in itself a reason for placing advertising in a sponsoring magazine, but it is reasonable to assume that publishers who try to meet the needs of their clients with supplementary research data might well concern themselves in a similar way with ensuring that their journals are written and distributed with competence and care. One particular service which has been developed extensively is to access the circulation list for direct-mail purposes. This can be a very valuable supplementary channel of communication.

READERSHIP OF ADVERTORIALS

Advertorials have always been a doubtful way of projecting an advertising message. For the past few years, however, their use in the UK has been growing, largely under the influence of PR consultancies. In spite of this, no one seems to have bothered to do any serious research to measure their value. Rather, the media planners have relied upon a combination of hunch and wishful thinking. The nearest attempt to evaluation has been to measure response, but this is flawed in a number of ways in that response is not always the objective and, even when it is, the number of people seeing and reading an advertorial is going to be substantially more than the enquiries received. For example, with a journal with a circulation of 10,000, the number of enquiries might be 100, whereas the readership is perhaps 40,000.

A new piece of research by Norman Hart Associates shows that in a particular technical magazine the average page traffic of an advertorial (albeit a large one) was 25 per cent, ie a quarter of the readers in the sample recalled having seen it. This figure compared in the same study with an average page traffic for ads of 14 per cent and for editorial pages of 37 per cent. If these data are valid it suggests that serious consideration should be given to replacing conventional display ads with advertorials. The increased 'familiarity' arising from the above could be expected to lead to an increased 'favourability'.

Other results to emerge from the research were:

1. The highest editorial score was 79 per cent (lowest 13 per cent).
2. The highest ad. score was 23 per cent (lowest 3 per cent).
3. Front, back, inside front and inside back covers, when averaged out, scored 8 per cent, ie the very opposite to what is conventionally believed to be the high value of these positions.

Conclusion

The conclusion is that advertorials can be expected to be more cost-effective than display advertising. *Note:* Whilst these results compare well with earlier research, both in the UK and in the US, this particular study was too narrow for any general conclusions to be drawn without further work in particular segments.

Other media

In dealing with each of the major channels of persuasion in previous chapters, emphasis has been laid on the need for measuring results. This is in effect post-research. The object of media research is pre-research or, alternatively, research which, even if after an event, can be applied to future or similar cases.

Attempts have been made to assess the value placed on various media by buyers and it is surprising to find how few people are prepared to admit to being influenced to any degree by advertising, particularly men.

A survey in the *British Printer* asking printers which means of communication they found the most valuable source of information produced the result shown in Table 12.7.

It is interesting to note how the trade press rating changed according to size of company. Indeed the whole mixture changed with company size, which points to another variable in market segmentation and the need to

Table 12.7   Influence of various media on British printing by company size (%)

| | Total | Number of employees | | | | |
		1–24	25–49	50–99	100–199	200+
The trade press	36	28	47	48	50	60
Calls by representatives	40	47	36	31	19	19
Exhibitions and trade fairs	10	8	7	18	25	12
Letters and brochures sent to you through the post	15	19	10	8	9	9

evaluate media against a specific segment whether this be product group, application group, size group, geographical group or whatever.

A similar investigation was included in the *How British Industry Buys* survey from which Table 12.8 was extracted.

Again it is interesting to note the variations which occur between different management functions in a company.

Research carried out in the IT industry concluded that the most important source of information on buying behaviour showed that third party endorsement was way ahead of anything else. After this came editorial

Table 12.8   Influence of various media on different types of personnel in British industry.*

	Board (general management)	Operating management	Prod. engineering	Des. and dev. engineering	Maint. engineering	Research	Buying	Finance	Sales	Other
Catalogues	39	36	45	64	34	64	52	32	44	76
Direct mail	12	9	14	6	31	21	23	14	5	27
Sales engineers' visits	66	61	60	67	78	64	64	60	73	40
Advertisements in trade press	14	32	28	22	21	15	12	23	24	24
Exhibitions	15	17	11	11	47	15	9	19	14	12
Demonstrations by manufacturers	50	41	35	26	37	21	37	38	45	22
Other	6	4		6			5	5	35	

* In industry, personnel with these functions consider, in the percentages shown, these factors to be among the two most important when obtaining information on products. For example: in industry generally board members, who play more than an occasional role in purchasing, in 66 per cent of cases consider sales engineers' visits to be among the two most important methods of obtaining information on products.

publicity, which was considered to be four times more effective than advertisements.

	Index
Recommendation by professionals	100
Recommendation by colleagues	73
Recommendation by consultants	55
Trade press editorials	55
Recommendation by dealers	36
Exhibitions	23
Direct mail	23
Trade press advertisements	14
Buyer's guides	9

EXHIBITIONS

There is considerable scope for the provision of more data on exhibitions, particularly authenticated information which is relevant to an advertiser's needs. Some organizers already record information about visitors as they enter the exhibition hall. This will lead to exhibitions becoming more effective selling functions and in the long term will benefit the whole exhibition industry. Much remains to be investigated: corridor traffic for instance, the value of an island site or one near an entrance, the gallery versus the ground floor, and shell stands as against elaborate tailor-mades.

As has been indicated, research data on exhibitions are hard to come by, and do not yet represent a consolidated body of evidence. An example of useful information comes from a study of the International Electrical Engineers Exhibition. This showed that visitors stopped or talked at an average of 14 stands, and spent an average of 5.3 hours at the exhibition.

A more recent research showed that 61 per cent of visitors attended the International Wire Exhibition in Basle for more than one day as shown in Figure 12.4. The arithmetic average time spent in the exhibition halls was 5

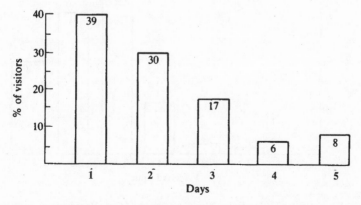

Figure 12.4   Length of stay at exhibition (*Source:* Mack-Brooks Research Report)

hours per day, and the average length of stay for all visitors was 2.2 days. The number of stands visited varied widely between two or three and 30 in any one day: the arithmetic average was 13. The same research investigated the show's value or usefulness. On a scale of 1–7 where 1 represented the lowest perceived value of the exhibition according to the visitor and 7 the highest, the results were shown as in Figure 12.5. Eighty-six per cent rated the exhibition above average and the arithmetic mean was 5.6.

Matching the market

The usefulness of media information – who reads what, who sees what, who is influenced by what – presupposes that a company is able to define its potential market with an adequate degree of accuracy.

A good deal of work has been done in examining who in a firm is responsible for buying decisions and it is evident that there may be up to a dozen people to be reached and sometimes more. An investigation in depth into a large manufacturer established that while a 'yes' decision could be made by four people, a decision not to purchase a given raw material could be made on the basis of a negative report from any one of 23 people. Yet the salesperson concerned saw no more than two people.

A frequently quoted average is eight people per company, and this, when multiplied by the number of manufacturing units in Great Britain (in excess of 50,000), brings the number of people involved in industrial purchasing to nearly half-a-million. And in matching media to market, the industrial press alone consists of over 4000 different publications.

Even so, there is nothing special about the job of matching which cannot

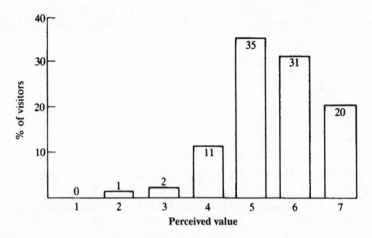

Figure 12.5   Exhibition visitor preference (*Source:* Mack-Brooks Research Report)

be carried out by a normally competent marketing team given adequate support from published and commissioned research and subsequent statistical analysis.

There are two useful reference works which are of particular significance. The first is the *Standard Industrial Classification* which categorizes in some detail every trade and industry, and second the work pioneered by the then Institute of Marketing and Industrial Market Research Ltd, which examined in considerable depth purchasing influence across the whole industrial sector, revealing a number of hitherto unquantified characteristics such as the example shown in Table 12.9.

Table 12.9 Purchasing 'decision-makers' showing who decides which supplier gets an order (%)

	Board (general management)	Operating management	Prod. engineering	Des. and dev. engineering	Maint. engineering	Research	Buying	Finance	Sales	Others in company	Others outside company
Plant equipment	44	28	10	7	3	–	19	1	–	2	–
Materials	17	25	5	6	1	4	52	1	1	1	1
Components	10	25	6	9	4	4	39	1	1	1	–

The extract from the Buckner study given above has been further amplified by a research now published periodically by *The Financial Times*, entitled *How British Industry Buys*.

A further piece of research on decision-makers is to be found in *Modern Purchasing* on the influence of purchasing managers in the procurement of a variety of products and services and this is shown in Table 12.10. As can be seen, the purchasing authority of buyers appears to be very limited.

Evaluating business advertisements

Ever since Lord Leverhulme made his classic remark about half his advertising expenditure being wasted (it is probably nearer to 75 per cent), if only he knew which half, advertising pundits have been vying with one another to find some way of reducing the wastage. Whilst it is true that any pretesting is going to be approximate, the fact is that there are certain criteria which can with confidence be applied in order to achieve the best possible result.

Table 12.10 Purchasing responsibilities of buyers (*Source: Modern Purchasing*)

Product	Actually selects supplier (%)	Has no influence (%)
Computer hardware	8	36
Air freight services	16	50
Vending machines	20	45
Floor cleaning contractors	26	48
Calculators	28	13
Cars	28	29
Fuel oil	44	16
Cartons	63	7
Stationery	74	8
Ball point pens	77	9

After all, it doesn't require a sophisticated and expensive piece of research to find out, for instance, at proof stage that the body copy of an ad is difficult to read simply because it is set solid in a typeface which is too small to read easily, or that the action element has been left out.

The following criteria have been used over a number of years to evaluate industrial or business-to-business ads. The system has met with wide acceptance by the managers using it. It can also be used exactly as it stands to measure direct mail shots. Its rationale is that, over and above that spark of creative genius that can never be satisfactorily measured, there are a number of quite obvious factors which can stop an ad being really effective. Ten such factors are listed below:

1. ATTENTION VALUE (9)

Extensive research in the UK and the US has shown that the majority of industrial or business ads are seen by only a few per cent of the readers of a publication, and read by even fewer. Thus the first requirement of an ad is to have stopping power. Some ads will be passed by simply because the subject matter is not of interest, but even if it is potentially of interest, the ad may not be noticed, for instance, because it is too flat and grey or, at the other extreme, too cluttered. The headline, the body copy, and the picture must all be laid out in such a way as to attract the eye.

2. INSTANT MESSAGE (5)

Providing an ad has attention value, it presents an opportunity to hold a reader's interest for long enough to get across the subject-matter of the ad, which alone will be the incentive to read on. The test here is to hold up the ad for a second and judge whether in that time it communicates a message. Is the headline clear, short, and to the point? Does the illustration show the 'benefit' as opposed to, or at least as well as, the 'product'? Beware the excessively creative headline and illustration which can obscure the essential single selling idea. The vital purpose is first to communicate the chosen message and, secondly, to pull the reader into the ad.

3. IMPACT (2)

It is no use projecting an instant message if it is then instantly forgotten. So will the ad achieve an impact on the mind of the reader such that he or she will retain the message for subsequent action? Is it memorable and is it distinctive? This will be determined partly by its 'attention value' and 'instant message', and also by the overall impression that the ad achieves before the reader moves on to the next page.

4. WRITING STYLE (2)

Whilst business advertising consists of one business communicating with another, in practice it comes down to one person communicating with another person. The style of writing is important, eg always use short and simple words and short sentences, avoiding any advertising clichés and unnecessary jargon. The terminology must be in a form which is familiar to the reader. It must come across as professional within the context. Whilst it must be persuasive, the slick hard sell and hype associated with fmcg (fast moving consumer goods) products is likely to be counter-productive. Familiar copy also extends to familiar illustration: the picture should be in a setting to which the reader can relate.

5. PROMISE A SPECIFIC BENEFIT (4)

A product or service is likely to have a number of 'attributes' which can be expressed in terms of customer 'benefits'. Does the ad clearly get across one specific promise or benefit, or is it a jumble of messages which leave the reader confused as to just what it is getting at? A good rule is to pinpoint the single selling proposition, but ensure that it is presented in such a way as to remain in the mind of the reader after reading it.

6. CREDIBILITY (3)

All the advertising claims are of little avail if they are not believed. So to what extent does an ad ring true? Is there any hard evidence to support the claims, such as a picture of the product in operation, or a case history or, even better, a third party endorsement? Facts are more believable than generalities and exaggerations.

7. LOGICAL PROGRESSION OF THE ARGUMENT (2)

Does the positioning of the components of an ad, and the sequence of the headline, sub-heading and body copy add up to a logical series of statements which together support the basic selling proposition? In short, is the ad easy to understand?

8. LEGIBILITY (8)

It is an extraordinary fact that so many otherwise excellent ads are ruined simply by incompetent typography. Starting with the most dominant features, how readable are the headline and sub-heading? Quite apart from the words themselves and whether they communicate a convincing message, what about the typography: is it simple and clear? Is the combination of typeface, point size, leading, measure and general layout and presentation such that the copy is easy and inviting to read? Basic facts of legibility which will have been taught in the first year at college are continually ignored, maybe in an attempt to be modish or avant garde. For instance, people over the age of 40 have difficulty in reading eight point or smaller. On top of this, leading helps legibility, whereas reverse type reduces it. Capitals make body copy more difficult to read, and serif faces are more legible than sans serif. Leading between the lines helps as does the 'measure' (length of line) and justification. These simple rules can not be ignored.

9. ACTION (7)

All ads have a purpose and, apart from corporate ads, this usually involves the reader taking some action. It surely makes sense then to indicate to the reader what action is intended. The actual offering itself is important since research shows that to offer something tangible will generate a larger response than a vague invitation to 'write for further information'. It needs to be spelt out in such a way that the reader is really motivated to act. And then, visually, the action element must stand out. One of the best devices is the reply coupon – not so much that readers will want to use it, but because of the visual signal that it sends.

10. CORPORATE BENEFIT (8)

It may be that an ad fulfils its primary purpose very well, eg to sell a product or service, or to contribute to brand image, or to generate enquiries. The fact remains, however, that all ads have an opportunity also to influence corporate image or to portray a company's personality – the things that make a company liked, respected and admired. A messy ad tends to indicate a messy company, a small ad, a small one, and a dull ad suggests a company which hasn't much to get excited about. So all ads, both corporate and product, contribute to both corporate image and brand image, whether they are designed to or not.

EVALUATION

To evaluate an advertisement or direct mail shot from the ten rules given above, award a rating against each up to a maximum of the score shown in brackets, eg (8). Award any figure between 0 and, say, 8 depending upon your judgment of how effective it is against that particular point. Then add all the scores together and double the result. This is now the percentage rating of the advertiser. The following groupings give suggested evaluations based upon experience of using this system:

82–100%	Outstanding
72–80%	Very good
62–70%	Acceptable
0–60%	Send it back

TEAM EVALUATION

Having developed a set of rules for advertisement evaluation, these must be applied in such a way as to ensure maximum effectiveness. Some managers are reluctant to make judgements, and tend to defer to their advertising agency who, after all, are specialists. True, they have their part to play, but the people in the best position to make a judgement on how a potential customer will react to such a selling proposition are those who are in contact with customers and prospects as part of their daily lives. So the client must make the decision, and this simply means that every person in the company who needs to have a point of view should be included in the approval team.

In the final analysis, of course, it is the customer who will decide, so it is best to ask a few just to be safe. This requires each advertisement to go through a parallel evaluation with one or more customer panels, or even focus group discussions. Such measures are not statistically sound, but they can be extremely illustrative and contribute substantially to the overall assessment.

Evaluating successful brochures

Following the 'Ten Criteria for a successful business advertisement', a system which has been in place for some years, the same basis can be used for other media, perhaps with a number of modifications. In the case of a sales leaflet or flyer, this can be treated as a direct mail piece, and as such no modification is necessary. With a brochure, however, if the assumption is made that the reader actually requested it, then there must be some changes. The relevant criteria are:

1. RETENTION VALUE (4)

There is no need for 'attention value' if the brochure has been requested: rather, the need is that it will be so attractive and useful that the reader will want to keep it for future reference, ie 'retention value'. It does, however, require some 'attention' element, since it may have to be judged in relation to competitors' literature.

2. PRESENTATION (5)

Whilst a brochure is not required to present an 'instant message', an additional requirement appears to replace it; namely, its general appearance, and in particular the stock upon which it is printed, the number of colours, the quality of the photographs, diagrams, tables, and the number of pages. With regard to the latter, there comes a point at which having too many pages reduces the likelihood of it being read.

3. IMPACT (2)

A brochure has to have impact just as much as an advertisement. One wants the reader to remember it.

4. WRITING STYLE (5)

Even at its simplest, a brochure has more words than an advertisement and thus the style of writing correspondingly becomes more significant.

5. PROMISE SPECIFIC BENEFITS (4)

Whilst with an advertisement the best practice is to decide which 'single selling proposition' is to be the basis of the copy platform, with a brochure it is necessary to put across all of the benefits.

6. CREDIBILITY (5)

It can be argued, perhaps, that it is even more important that a brochure should come across as believable than an advertisement. Hence this criterion has been given a slightly higher weighting.

7. LOGICAL PROGRESSION OF THE ARGUMENT (4)

Again, with more words, greater importance attaches to ensuring that they flow in a logical way. The weighting compared with an advertisement has, accordingly, been increased.

8. LEGIBILITY (8)

This criterion continues to be heavily weighted, since if the copy cannot be read easily, it won't be. There is absolutely no excuse for typesetting which is too small or, indeed, anything other than very easy and inviting to read.

9. ACTION (7)

The action element (ie the response mechanism) is of a more strategic nature than with an advertisement, where a tactical response of a sales lead might be the requirement. But if a brochure is not intended to generate some further activity, what is its purpose? Perhaps the action here is to place an order, or ask for a quotation. But whatever, the question should be asked, 'what action do we want the reader to take?'

10. CORPORATE BENEFIT (8)

Corporate image (or corporate brand) is increasingly recognised as an important factor in the buying process, so the overall impression of the brochure is all the more important.

EVALUATION

The same as for an advertisement. Again, there is no reason to accept second-rate brochures, and to fall below 62 per cent is second-rate.

To evaluate a brochure from the ten rules given above, award a rating against each up to a maximum of the score shown in brackets, eg (8). Award any figure between 0 and, say, 8 depending upon your judgement of how effective the brochure is against that particular point. Then add all the scores together and double the result. This is now the percentage rating of the brochure. The following groupings give suggested evaluations based upon experience of using this system:

82–100%	Outstanding
72–80%	Very good
62–70%	Acceptable
0–60%	Send it back

Evaluating successful exhibition stands

Just as advertisements and brochures can be evaluated, so too can exhibition stands. The criteria are different, but the method is the same.

The procedure should be that each of the criteria given below is considered, and a mark awarded within the weightings given. So, in the case of 'Attention value', a figure between 0 and 4 will be chosen to represent the value attributed to that particular factor. Each of the other criteria will then be assessed in the same way and all ten numbers added together. By doubling the result, the rating can be expressed as a percentage, and this can then be held up against the broad categories already laid down for press advertising.

1. ATTENTION VALUE (4)

Whilst many visitors will decide in advance which stands they intend to visit, others will not. Rather, they will wander around and pay calls on the stands which happen to catch their eye. Even if a plan of action has been decided upon, there will always be odd random calls stimulated initially by an attractive stand design, maybe coupled with some attention-getting activity.

2. INSTANT MESSAGE (4)

A new approach to an exhibition stand is required here. It should be regarded as a three-dimensional advertisement. So, having succeeded in attracting attention, the next step is to get across the key message or messages: at a glance, and in such a way as to make the visitor want to learn more. What is needed, then, is the equivalent of an advertisement headline and sub-headings, all of which can be seen, read and understood at a distance.

3. IMPACT (2)

Simply, 'Is the stand memorable?' The task here is to ensure that after the show, which may comprise hundreds of stands, one's own stand is one of those which springs to mind when further action is contemplated.

4. PROJECTS THE BENEFITS ON OFFER (6)

Whereas with an advertisement the task is to convey the 'single selling proposition', with an exhibition the opportunity exists to communicate all the benefits of a particular product or service since there is more time available.

5. EFFECTIVE DISPLAY PANELS (6)

This is the equivalent to the body copy of an advertisement, and so must be assessed both according to what it says, and how it says it.

One frequently finds that the selling copy is written by an in-company person, such as a sales manager, who would lay no claim to being a creative or persuasive writer and would never dream of being let loose on a piece of advertising copy. As regards legibility, the same rules apply as for an advertisement; namely, it must be both legible and eminently readable. Black lettering on white is more legible than reversed type, serif faces are easier to read than sans serif, and leading between the lines is helpful, as are short measures.

6. ACTION (5)

Some would say that an exhibition provides the greatest opportunity of all media to obtain enquiries and sales leads. But this operation must not be passive – just waiting for prospects to demand attention. A procedure must be in operation, and the sales force must be adequately briefed to obtain names and addresses both for short-term action and for entry on to a database. Obviously, enquiry forms must be available, and must be used for every encounter of any value. Visiting cards must be collected: some stands make profitable use of a 'visiting card competition'. A good way of gaining leads is to have a policy of not having sales literature on the stand. Instead, have a special, well-produced, exhibition leaflet that gives a summary description of all the products on the stand. Each visitor is then offered the opportunity to have the detailed leaflet sent to them that day from head office. This automatically provides names and addresses, but also means that the product leaflet does not have to compete directly with all the other literature collected from competitors at the show. Here, the stand manager has an important disciplinary role to play in ensuring that maximum effort is put into acquiring such leads. Thought must be given to, and procedures laid down for, instant follow-up, since customer interest is at its highest when the enquiry is made and can tail off easily when they get back to their office.

7. LOCATION (8)

Choosing the best location in the exhibition hall can be a critical factor in the overall productivity of the stand. What one is looking for here is a site where there is a 'high corridor traffic'. To some extent this may be obvious simply from looking at the floor plan, but to get a true picture research is required to measure traffic all around the stand, at various times during the day. This doesn't require the services of a market research company: it is simply a matter of counting heads at the previous show, or for that matter at any previous show in the same hall. Coupled with location, there should be some weighting given to the shape of the stand, ie on how many sides it is open.

8. WELCOME (3)

Always assuming that the primary purpose of a stand is to attract people, the design must contribute to that objective. Display units, therefore, should not enclose the stand completely, making it offputting to step on to the plinth, and sales staff must stand well back to encourage the timid visitor who doesn't want to face up to the 'hard sell'. With this in mind, consider placing literature dispensers on the outside of a stand so that people can pick up a leaflet without actually going on to the stand. This might, of course, defeat the objective of collecting names and addresses. Being welcoming is, of course, much more than stand design, and here one comes back again to exhibition training coupled with an active stand manager. The personal welcome involves a fine balancing act between indifference and the 'hard sell'. In particular, there must be a courteous procedure in place for dealing rapidly with 'tyrekickers' and other time-wasters.

9. ENTERTAINING (4)

If providing some kind of entertaining facilities, and talking with visitors in comfort – and maybe in private – is one of your objectives, this must be allowed for. Whether refreshments should be 'soft' or alcoholic is largely a matter of considering the usual practice at this particular show and perhaps the culture of the industry. What will a visitor expect; what is the competition doing; and how can you get the edge on them?

10. CORPORATE BENEFIT (8)

Amongst the strengths of exhibitions as a medium is that they can be used to put across a powerful message about the company in addition to carrying out a selling function. To what extent does a stand contribute to the corporate image? Information about the company's history, production processes, awards, achievements and so on will help a prospect to decide that a company is one worth doing business with.

All the above criteria apply to an open trade show as opposed to a private exhibition, where different factors and weightings should be used. The evaluation is essentially a procedure to be used before stand construction is given the go-ahead. Since an exhibition also involves people (as opposed to advertisements and direct mail which don't) it is also useful to apply the same tests during and after the show. A final point about all promotional assessments is that the criteria should always form part of the brief to the service provider.

Research techniques

The techniques for media assessment are not excessively complex, difficult or expensive: nor are the results any more or less approximate than those from other types of research. It is perhaps surprising that this sector of marketing research has not expanded more rapidly, since the savings which can be achieved are both immediate and large. Given the lack of suitable information on all types of media it must follow that any promotional budget which does not make provision for some form of readership or comparative research is not likely to be utilizing its expenditure to the full.

Commenting on the opportunities in assessing advertising effectiveness, Aubrey Wilson, a pioneer in this field, had this to say:

> Advertising results, even the most enthusiastic supporters concede, are still largely unpredictable. Thus advertising poses one of the most difficult areas for management decisions and, therefore, one in which the accumulation of any knowledge is disproportionately valuable. Mistakes in advertising strategy and technique are costly and difficult, if not impossible, to rectify and expenditure is almost invariably irrecoverable. A misplaced purchase of a machine tool or vehicle will, at worst, yield the second-hand value of the product. Not only can nothing be saved from unsuccessful advertising but often additional monies will be needed to correct the errors made. For these and other reasons advertising research is taking on a new importance as industrial advertising begins to take an increasing part in industrial marketing operations.

Checklist

1. Are your target audiences defined in sufficient detail to enable media readership to be compared with them?
2. Have you made an assessment of each proposed publication in terms of
   (a) Circulation – total and segmented?
   (b) Readership – total and segmented?
   (c) Cost per reader?
   (d) Rates – possible reductions?
   (e) Authenticity of any research data?
   (f) Editorial quality?
   (g) Journal's reputation?
   (h) Method of circulation?
   (i) Frequency of publication?
   (j) Readership duplication?
3. Have you set aside a budget for media research to supplement the available information?

4. Is there evidence to justify using more than three publications to reach a particular audience?
5. Are the publishers you are patronizing prepared to co-operate by way of (a) page traffic studies, (b) split-runs and (c) mailing list?
6. Have you established the relative importance of each channel of communication with your particular potential customers?

13

CAMPAIGN EVALUATION

Campaign evaluation can be difficult and expensive, but this is by no means inevitable. It is true that some campaigns cannot be measured in total, but this does not mean that measurements cannot be made of some of the component parts, which will result in an improvement in cost-effectiveness.

The position has been well stated by L W Rodger, whose comments on advertising could be taken to apply to the whole range of promotional activities.

> The advertising budget probably represents the largest amount of money disbursed by manufacturers with no precise measure of what it can be expected to achieve. The spending of large sums of money on advertising without some system of accountability can be compared to conducting a business without a bookkeeping or accounting department. Advertising accountability has lagged far behind general management accountability in that the latter is held responsible for accomplishing certain specific and, usually, measurable results in relation to money spent. Sound business operation demands that expenditure and results be related. The idea of holding advertising accountable for accomplishing certain sales results is certainly not new. But there is now a growing body of expert opinion that the sales criterion, as applied to advertising in isolation, is based on a fundamental misconception.

Rodger goes on to develop his theme on the criteria for evaluating a campaign in terms which are relevant to the media and also capable of implementation:

> Advertising is a means of communication. Its results can only be measured in terms of communication goals, in terms of the cost per advertising message delivered per customer for a given result. In other words, according to Colley, 'an advertising goal is a specific communication task, to be accomplished among a defined audience to a given degree in a given period of time'.

Lack of progress in the development of campaign evaluation is generally to be put down to the lack of defined specific goals, or alternatively to the setting of goals that are invalid.

It is not only the number of individuals in a company who contribute to a purchasing decision who must be considered, but also the many factors which are likely to influence each person's judgement on where an order should be placed. Typical influences give an idea of the complexity of the operation:

1. Used it in my previous firm.
2. Saw it at an exhibition.
3. Salesman convinced me of its quality.
4. I'd heard of the company's name.
5. Read about it in the press.
6. My MD knows the supplier's MD.
7. Swiss machines are always more reliable.
8. This firm was the only one to supply enough technical data.
9. I always get a bottle of Scotch from this firm.
10. All our other machines are this make.
11. Recommended by a friend.

The list is endless and highly subjective, notwithstanding the usual test of 'price-delivery-quality-service' which so many buyers like to believe is the sole basis for decision-making.

To take expenditure on advertising, or sales promotion, or even on the overall marketing function, and expect to be able to relate it precisely to sales (that is purchasing) is clearly unrealistic. It is made more complicated by the fact that for many industrial products, the gestation period between the original enquiry and an order is often more than a year. One authority has estimated an average time lag, depending on the product, of between one and four years.

Component research

If all influences cannot be researched in total, it is necessary to examine each 'component' of purchasing influence and decide whether it is amenable to scientific evaluation. From the various 'channels of persuasive communications' many criteria, some more detailed than others, can be tested. Copy-testing an advertisement, measurement of product awareness, brand-name research, product–company association, attitude studies, and finally, measurement of communications goals are some examples which can be examined here.

An examination of the sales communication process in Figure 13.1 well illustrates how very simple it is to consider each stage from advertisements to repeat business. Clearly, each block is amenable to some form of evaluation and a relationship can be established with the next in the process. But equally it can be seen how easy it is for extraneous factors to invalidate conclusions based solely upon such a simplistic flow diagram. If the product performance is unsatisfactory, or the price or delivery, then the conversion factor between quotation and first order will be affected. If competition

Figure 13.1 Sales schematic diagram

suddenly becomes fierce, conversion from enquiry to sales call may change. There are, then, factors quite outside the marketing communications area which prevent a valid relationship between advertising and sales being established as a basis of campaign evaluation.

An analysis of the communications process can be taken further and broken down into more components in order to make monitoring more effective and accurate. Figure 13.2 as a model is perhaps a somewhat academic approach and has been devised quite deliberately in this way so as to allow readers to adopt a system of their own in more practical terms.

In Figure 13.2, known as Sequential Advertising Measurement, the starting point is with the product and its performance attributes. These must now be expressed in terms of customer benefits which lead to the 'message' (selling proposition). This is then formulated into a 'creative expression' (eg advertisement), which appears in a 'medium' (journal) and achieves 'attention' (page traffic noting) and 'impact' (recall). This then changes the 'attitude' of a prospect which arguably changes his or her 'behavioural intent' (what is to be purchased) and ultimately leads to a certain 'behaviour' (the order). Fulfilment of the order leads to 'contentment' as a result of acquiring the 'product' which has a 'performance', representing to the customer a 'benefit' which is the basis of the selling proposition, ie the 'message'. And so the circuit is complete.

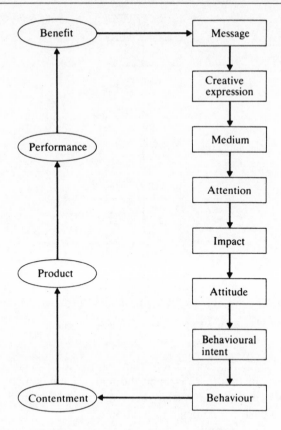

Figure 13.2   Communications model

Now the proposition is that each block can be taken in turn, objectives set, quantified, measured and adjusted. The diagram has been converted into a table referred to as an Ad Evaluator Checklist, and showing nine discrete stages together with suggested sources of data.

From Table 13.2 a somewhat alarming calculation can be made of communications efficiency. Suppose each of the stages is 80 per cent efficient, and this is surely unlikely, then the cumulative efficiency of this particular communications system would be 17 per cent. This compares interestingly with a classical work on this subject in which messages from top management to shop-floor operatives were received by only 7 per cent. This was referred to as a 'somewhat opaque situation'. Maybe advertising executives would do well to face up to the opaque screen which screens their products, their messages and their company.

Table 13.1 Seventeen possible sources of data for the evaluation of advertising within a sales context

Communication component	Data source
1. Customer benefit/message	1.1 Customer needs and wants – group discussion 1.2 Syndicated research
2. Creative expression/advertisement	2.1 Ad pretest – group discussion 2.2 Brand name pre-test
3. Transmission/medium	3.1 Readership research
4. Attention/interest	4.1 Page traffic 4.2 Read-most rating
5. Impact/action	5.1 Enquiries 5.2 Recall 5.3 Brand awareness
6. Attitude	6.1 Company/brand reputation
7. Behavioural intent/procurement motivation	7.1 Brand preference 7.2 Test market
8. Behaviour/1st order	8.1 Sales statistics 8.2 Competitor research
9. Satisfaction/repeat purchase	9.1 Sales statistics 9.2 Sales reports

Advertising testing

There are a number of techniques in common usage:

PAGE TRAFFIC

A first requirement of any advertisement is that it should be seen or 'noted'. In the United States it is not uncommon to use Starch ratings obtained by questioning readers by personal interview, on which advertisements they can remember (by 'aided recall'). In the United Kingdom the same idea has been tried by a number of publishers, but usually using a postal questionnaire.

The technique is to send out a second copy of a particular issue, say two weeks after a monthly publication, asking a sample readership to cross through any advertisement which they recall having noted in the original issue. An alternative approach is to ask respondents to indicate which advertisements they found of interest.

Such a technique may appear to be subjective and approximate, but a high enough degree of consistency is obtained to enable an advertiser to draw the conclusion that a particular advertisement is not performing as well as is required. Table 13.2, extracted from an interest rating survey by *Modern Purchasing*, indicates the kind of results that can be obtained.

Table 13.2   Advertisement page-traffic

Product type	Advertisement size	Interest rating (percentage of respondents finding an advertisement of interest)
Raw material	1 page black and white	20.3
Raw material	1 page black and white	5.9
Raw material	¼ page black and white	12.7
Raw material	2 pages black and white	12.7
Electrical goods	1 page 2 colours	3.4
Industrial fasteners	½ page black and white	14.4
Industrial fasteners	1 page 2 colours	6.8
Machinery	2 pages black and white	8.5
Tools	¼ page black and white	16.9
Exhibition	Inset black and white	17.8

In the issue in question, the highest rated advertisement was for storage equipment, a single page which scored 33.1 per cent. It is, however, by no means unknown from other researches for advertisements to score zero, but this does not necessarily mean that the advertisement itself is useless. It may only be in the wrong publication. But it does mean that it is not doing its job.

It is interesting to compare such ratings with those obtained from editorial items. Referring again to the *Modern Purchasing* survey, the average score for recall of advertisements was 9.9 per cent whereas for editorial items a figure of 41.4 per cent was obtained.

From data made available by publishers, some interesting facts emerge. For instance in Figure 13.3, the percentage of readers showing an interest in a particular ad can be compared with the interest ratings for editorials. The interest profile for ads peaks at around 7 per cent, while editorials cover a very wide span, from 10 to 90 per cent, and peak at 35 per cent.

These data come from an examination of seven different researches covering three particular non-competing business publications and encompass an evaluation of 484 ads. This number is regarded as sufficiently large for further analysis which at least can be said to be indicative of trends.

Take as an example the widely-held assumption that an advertisement will do better if it is positioned facing editorial instead of being drowned in a sea of other ads. In terms of interest created, there was no significant difference between the 250 ads involved in this study.

Another commonly held view is that the addition of a second colour will

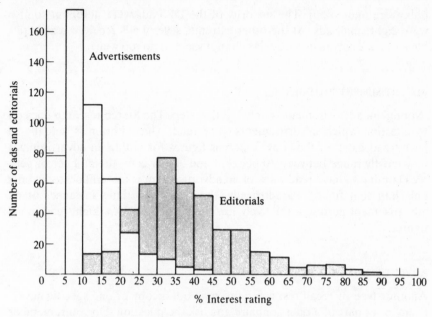

Figure 13.3 Advertisement ratings compared with editorials

increase the effectiveness of an advertisement. To throw some light on this factor, the ads in the above survey were further analysed and while a few two-colour ads achieved the highest individual scores, the overall effect was of no difference.

This of course does not reflect the attitude or image created, but merely the interest. Even here, the scope of the survey is not sufficiently broad to enable firm conclusions to be drawn. It does, however, call into question the blind acceptance that a second colour must produce better results.

Even when small advertisement spaces are used, it seems that some good performances can be obtained. There is a similarity between interest ratings for quarter pages as against half-page ads. From this it would seem that providing the subject is right, and creatively expressed, the size of the ad does not make too much difference.

There must come a stage at which the dominance of an ad is determined by size. Evidence of this comes from a comparison of the average score for two-page and larger ads with the average figure for all ads. The larger ads achieved something like twice the effect of the average.

In order to draw some conclusions about those advertisements with the highest scores, a detailed examination was made of the top 67 ads – scoring 20 per cent and over. The two highest (over 40 per cent scores) were both two-page black and white, but more than half were single page, of which the bulk were one-colour. The majority of the DPS ads were here, but so also were eight small ads. At the other extreme, several ads received a zero rating and back covers in particular did not seem to do too well.

ADVERTISEMENT READERSHIP

'Noting' an advertisement is only the first step. The Starch research goes on to question which advertisements were read. The criterion is actually to have 'read most' of the copy. Whereas figures for noting an advertisement may mostly range between 10 per cent and 30 per cent, the number of people claiming to have read most of an advertisement is more likely to be only only half that figure. Paradoxically, there are sometimes instances of an advertisement getting a relatively low 'noted' score, but a high 'read most' figure.

ADVERTISEMENT RECALL

Another type of recall test can be to mail out a copy of one specific advertisement as part of a questionnaire and ask the question 'Do you remember seeing the enclosed advertisement?' This has the merit of assessing the overall effectiveness of the advertisement, having regard to all the publications where it appeared. For example, a research in connection with printing machinery determined that 30.1 per cent of respondents remembered seeing the advertisement and 69.9 per cent did not. A similar investigation for computer equipment obtained a recall of 34.6 per cent and a negative response of 65.4 per cent. From such tests, over a period it is possible to determine the effectiveness of one advertisement against another, and the degree of penetration being achieved.

An alternative technique is to telephone a sample of readers and ask questions about a particular advertisement. One such research for a dictating machine produced recalls over a period of time ranging from 40 to 60 per cent.

ADVERTISEMENT ENQUIRIES

In Chapter 4 on 'Press Advertising' the use of enquiries or sales leads was discussed as a means of advertisement evaluation. This can be a valid criterion and indeed it may be argued that it matters little what 'attention' an advertisement scores; what really matters is what action follows. If action in the form of enquiries is what is required of an advertisement, then this is a reasonable argument, provided the quality of the enquiries can be measured.

ENQUIRIES RELATED TO SIZE

A little publicized but immensely important piece of research was conducted by Cahners Publishing Co. in America. The first, No. 250.1, produced the information shown in Figure 13.4. The data came from an analysis of 500,000 enquiries and can therefore claim a reasonable measure of statistical reliability. They show that size of advertisement has surprisingly little effect on the number of enquiries generated, and certainly nothing like a linear relationship.

The next step is to plot these data against cost per enquiry (see Figure 13.5) whereupon it is shown that enquiries from whole page ads cost more than double those from small sizes.

Other Cahners research shows that:

1. Advertising readership (as against enquiries) is not influenced by the use of coupons (Cahners 114.1).
2. Copy set in reverse (white upon black) is read at a 10 per cent slower rate than black on white (Cahners 1310.1).
3. Type set in lower case is read 13 per cent faster than that set in all capitals (Cahners 1310.4).

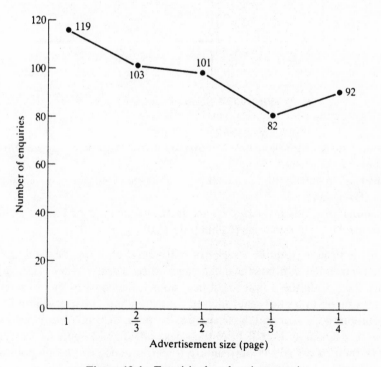

Figure 13.4   Enquiries by advertisement size

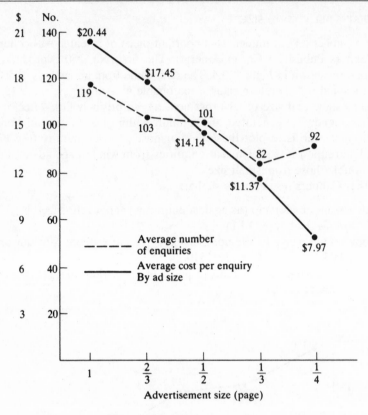

Figure 13.5   Cost per enquiry

4. From a survey of 35 journals the average readership per copy was three (Cahners 412.0).
5. Cover ads receive a higher recall by an average of 40 per cent (Cahners 116.1B).
6. Readership of ads increases as size increases in spite of figures shown earlier relating to enquiries (Cahners 110.1B).

With some product groups, a series of marketing ratios can be established which, if constant, can enable a campaign to be assessed very effectively. For instance, given the average cost per enquiry, the conversion into a sales lead, moving on to a sales visit followed by a quotation, the average number of quotations per order and the average value per order, an advertising budget can be calculated directly from the sales budget and targets set for each stage in the process so that any failure in performance can be pinpointed, and corrective action taken. However, few product groups are so simply constituted as to enable this procedure to be implemented with any degree of certainty.

Product awareness

How aware is a potential market of a product's existence? A conventional questionnaire can ask respondents to list the 'top three industrial floor cleaners'. Such an open question will enable a manufacturer to determine whether his product is top of the list, rates number three, or perhaps does not appear at all.

A campaign may very well have as an objective to raise the level of awareness from sixth position to being among the top three. The plan of action will estimate the cost of achieving this result and will indicate the time-scale. By monitoring progress, it can be determined to what extent a campaign is achieving its objective. This procedure is particularly useful for a new product launch since at the outset product awareness will be zero, and by progressive researches the real value for money derived from promotional activities can be gauged with accuracy.

This is still of course 'component research' since a product can be pushed up to the top of the awareness charts and still not sell, but at least one factor has been identified. The market knows about the product and further investigation must now be made to establish why sales are not being achieved.

An example of product awareness, and indeed company awareness, comes from an American study of a campaign for Sta-flow, a plastic produced by Air Products. Table 13.3 shows how after an advertising campaign product awareness increased from 0 to 23.8 per cent and in Table 13.4 company awareness increased from 4.8 per cent to 64.3 per cent.

Table 13.3   Product awareness

	Pre-ad mentions (%)	*Post-ad mentions (%)*
Lexan	85.6	88.1
Noryl	80.8	52.4
Cyclolac	77.9	81.0
Tenite	53.8	90.5
Sta-flow	0	23.8

Attitude studies

A natural sequence is to determine the attitude of the buying public to a product. This may come from questionnaire research – 'which is the most reliable voltmeter?', 'which is the least reliable?', 'which is the best value for

Table 13.4 Company awareness

	Pre-ad mentions (%)	Post-ad mentions (%)
GE	79.8	85.7
Eastman	74.0	90.5
Borg-Warner	62.5	73.8
Mobay	53.8	76.2
Air Products	4.8	64.3

money?' – and so on. A technique often used in the consumer field for motivation research is focused group discussion. This can be applied to industrial matters by getting together a group of buyers without disclosing the precise nature of the question to be answered, or indeed the name of the company concerned, and starting discussion of the subject in general with a group leader guiding the conversation towards the topics being researched.

Such a study was conducted to determine the attitude of packaging buyers to *solid* fibreboard cases and why it was they preferred to buy *corrugated* fibreboard cases. The fact emerged that tne buyers did not know the difference between the two products and as far as they were concerned simply bought fibreboard cases. This led to a campaign to identify solid cases as a specific product with certain outstanding qualities. Research was undertaken before and after the campaign to measure the level of knowledge which buyers had of the benefits associated with solid cases.

Product–company association

The question of which supplier comes first to mind when a buyer is seeking a given product can be explored by postal research. A question such as 'which first three company names come to mind when considering the purchase of...' generally produces an answer. This kind of research is especially useful since not only does it enable a company to determine its own position in the market, but also shows up the relative position of its competitors.

Thus in a campaign to promote a new quality of raw material a company was able to see its product–name association creep up from 3 per cent to 18 per cent in a year, while its principal competitor dropped from 16 per cent to 8 per cent. Clearly the campaign was achieving a tangible effect.

A problem related to product-company association is brand name–company association. It is not uncommon in industrial marketing to come across a 'Hoover situation' in which a brand name becomes generic applicable in a buyer's mind to any one of a number of suppliers. If this happens unknown to the company it will in the long run nullify the value of the brand name.

Brand name research

A campaign may be required to establish a new brand name, or to reinforce an existing one. In the first instance, research techniques can be applied to the selection of a new brand name.

If a brand name is designed to conjure up a certain image, a number of possible names can be put to a sample of respondents to comment on what connotation they would associate with each name.

It is useful to make such an investigation a personal one, and invite people to speak each name. This will produce another valuable indicator, whether or not each word is easily readable, and if so whether it is pronounced as intended.

The memorability of a brand name is particularly important, and this again can be measured. An example was a new material for which a shortlist of three names was produced. These were each printed on a card, and 100 people interviewed. The procedure was to ask each person to look at each name in turn, while it was exposed for a standard time. No reason was given for the request. One week later each individual was re-interviewed and asked to write down the three names. The results were that one name had a much higher recall factor than the other two, and over one-third of the respondents could recall the name exactly as it was shown to them.

The next step with the brand name adopted was to launch a campaign to establish it. At the outset, the level of knowledge in the potential market was zero, but research was conducted to discover which was the leading brand name for that particular product group. After an extensive campaign of six months, further research showed that the new name had already secured top place in the ratings. It is significant that the sales of the new product, a basic raw material, were at that time not more than a few per cent of the market whereas the brand name preference had a rating which made it market leader in perceptual terms of several tens per cent. This is to be expected with such a product where long-term contracts inhibit a rapid change in the purchasing pattern. The campaign was in fact a success measured in communications terms: had sales in the short term been used as the criterion, if would have been regarded as a failure.

Image research

A less tangible objective is the establishment of the right image for a company or brand. It is doubtful whether many companies have defined formally and in exact terms the precise image they wish to project and yet they will have an image, whether they like it or not, and moreover will not infrequently spend a good deal of money to enhance what has been referred to as their prestige.

The fact that all organizations have an image is indicated by a panel research which asked buyers to discuss certain companies and how they viewed them in terms of price, quality, delivery and so on. The research company inserted a 'control' name, that is of a company which did not exist. Many of the discussion group were found to have decided views on its image, even though the majority registered that they had never heard of it.

An example of formal research into the public's attitude towards a company was exemplified by one very large manufacturing group which was number two in size in its particular industry. It was a public company and was beginning to realize that apart from the effect on sales, there were such matters as raising loans, and the value of shares to be considered in connection with the expense of promoting a company name. Initially research showed that it was hardly known at all to the publics the company considered to be important. The company agreed to spend a large sum of money on prestige advertising, but in order to obtain tangible value for money, it set the objective 'to be listed among the top three' in response to the question 'name the leading company in the industry'. Two years later the objective was achieved.

The test in any campaign is whether or not value was obtained for the money spent – whether the objectives were achieved, and if not why not. For an organization not to bother to measure the result of its expenditure on advertising and promotion is simply neglect of managerial responsibility.

Public relations evaluation

For years it has been argued, by none more than by PR professionals, that the success of public relations is difficult, if not impossible, to measure. And client companies, not wishing to appear ignorant, have accepted this, believing that such people really should know what they are talking about. However, as PR budgets have climbed upwards the demand for some measurement system has grown, and out of this have emerged a number of organisations claiming to offer PR measurement. Sadly, what they mostly provide is a method of counting and measuring press cuttings, albeit rather more sophisticated than hitherto. Nothing wrong with that, of course, but it is not PR – and anyway, it is only addressing 'transmission', not reception or anything which follows.

Measurement of public relations, like measurement of anything else, is simply a matter of setting quantified objectives, checking to see if the objectives have been achieved and, if not, looking at why not and what should be taken in the way of further action, if any. In the case of public relations, as has been indicated, the principal objectives are likely to be to achieve a certain level of awareness of an organization, followed by a positive perception, ie corporate image, or reputation. Some may argue that there are four outcomes to be looked for in any public relations campaign; namely, awareness, perception, behavioural intent and behaviour. Supposing this to be so, then what measures need to be in place to form a reliable assessment?

AWARENESS

Nothing could be simpler. A particular, homogeneous, group of people who are to be influenced, for example a market segment, will be defined under 'Objectives'. Messages about the organization will be directed at such people for a planned period, after which there will be a measurement of what increase in awareness has occurred compared with the original benchmark over the planned period of time. Take, for instance, an hotel setting out to become better known by a certain group of people. For defining the benchmark, carrying out any tracking, and the final evaluation there will be two types of question asked, one unprompted, and the other one prompted. So if the target group were to be local inhabitants, people would be stopped, perhaps at random, and asked to name all the hotels they could think of in the area. Was the target hotel mentioned and if so, by what percentage of respondents? Did this meet the objective? The second question would be prompted; namely, to ask the respondent to look at a list of all the local hotels, and say which ones he had previously heard of.

PERCEPTION

It may be that an organization is very well known, but is it perceived in a favourable light? In the case of a local hotel, responses to the question could be such as to make for a league table. Here the question could ask which local hotel was the best in terms of whatever criteria were being evaluated. This might be luxury, value for money, or any other factor. To probe the matter in greater depth and, indeed, to find out which were the main criteria to be tested, would be the task of one or more focus group discussions. In other words, qualitative research followed by quantitative.

BEHAVIOURAL INTENT

This is a matter of how people intend to behave when an issue next arises. This is easy enough to measure but is likely to be flawed either because people don't know or because they respond with an answer which is untrue. For whatever reason, such researches are often substantially wrong. Parliamentary election forecasts are a good example. Nevertheless, the qualitative/quantitative formula can be useful. After all, it is only a matter of the degree of error, and the benchmark may well have suffered in the same way so that the comparisons in fact turn out to be valid. When applying such procedures within the marketing area, the behavioural intent factor is influenced by other considerations such as financial limitations. So a person may have heard of Rolls-Royce (awareness) and consider the company to be first class (perception) but have no intention of taking any action (behavioural intent) because they cannot afford to.

BEHAVIOUR

Behaviour brings us back to reality. Did the target audience take whatever action the campaign was designed to prompt? So in the case of a charity, did people actually make a contribution? Again, as with awareness, this is a yes or no question, but here the figures are accurate and require nothing in the way of interpretation.

The fact that public relations should be measured in terms of outcomes doesn't mean that transmissions should be ignored. These fall into the category mentioned in the marcom plan as secondary objectives. So targets must be set for all the channels of communication and prominent here will be press or media coverage, not because this is PR – it isn't – but because it is the most cost-effective medium bar none, and must be exploited fully to achieve PR objectives just as much as to achieve marketing objectives.

EDITORIAL PUBLICITY

The first measure is the number of publications covered by a press release where news is concerned. A critical initial factor, ignored by many, is the conversion rate; that is, the number or percentage of publications actually running the story. This is a factor in evaluating the accuracy of the media database used, and the content and presentation of the release itself. Maybe 50 per cent should be aimed for – and it certainly shouldn't fall below 40 per cent. Next, of course, comes the most popular measure; namely, press cuttings. So, how many mentions were achieved against the target set? This is followed by the number of column centimetres or inches, and at this stage the results must be categorized into positive/negative and accurate/inaccurate. Some attempt is now being made by an increasing number of consultancies to classify publicity according to whether or not a key message is getting through, though this is still transmission rather than reception. Also, such results are increasingly being produced on a computer printout, perhaps in an attempt to give them some extra implied authority. In fact, there is absolutely no difference between this and what has been done by any competent manager in the past. Another measure which is often presented to demonstrate the press coverage achieved is the opportunity to see (OTS). The value of this in organizational marketing is that for most publications readership figures are not available. In their absence, circulation figures are used quite incorrectly. In any case, most circulation figures are not audited and thus must be regarded as dubious. In the most favourable circumstances, where genuine readership figures are available, the procedure is to say that if an editorial mention was achieved in a journal having a readership of, say, 40,000, then there was an OTS of 40,000. Taking, then, all the publications in which mentions have been secured, it might then be said that a particular editorial campaign achieved an overall OTS of 250,000. This is, of course, important information, but what is actually needed is some measure of what size audience actually saw, let alone read, a particular piece of news. In other words, the only completely valid criterion is page traffic. From OTS, the next stage is to determine the Advertising Equivalent Value. This, again, is measuring transmission, but at least it gives proper weighting to each individual cutting. In this way, a mention in the *Financial Times* can be reasonably added to one in *PR Week*, though even here one must exercise judgement since it may well be that for a particular story *PR Week* is actually more important than the FT. A particular criticism is that one would never have allocated such sums of money to advertising anyway. This may be true, but in view of the much greater value of editorial publicity, it usually does not represent a exaggeration. The final system of measurement has to be enquiries, and this will take in reader response cards, letters, telephone calls and, increasingly, faxes and e-mail.

How to measure other PR media? In the first place, against the quantified primary objectives like awareness, no matter what media are used; and then against secondary objectives relating to the specific medium itself.

ADVERTISING

With many PR budgets, advertising is the largest single item of expenditure; with TV commercials for banks and petrol for instance. There are a range of what might be said to be tactical outcomes starting off with pre-testing and going on to post-testing – say, recall and, increasingly, response. Focus group discussions play a major part, especially in formulating relevant messages, as does consultation with customer panels.

EVENTS

Whatever the event, there will be an objective, a reason for holding it. This is what will be measured. Maybe it is to get a given number of a certain type of person to attend. In that case, the measure will be to see how many people actually attended. A further built-in objective is sometimes to achieve a certain amount of press coverage, in which case you might measure the number of journalists attending, and then the number of press cuttings, etc, for pre-show, show, and post-show. These should all be set against the target for the event. The quantifying of any such activities might be felt to be just too difficult. Upon what basis should a number be chosen? When targeting for the first time it is often little more than a well-thought-out guess, which will probably turn out to be wrong. But with each and every subsequent activity, the quantifying of objectives will become increasingly accurate as experience is gained. In this way, budgets become more and more precise and less money is wasted.

COMPETITIONS

Just as for events, consider how many entrants you are aiming to attract, and what about any supplementary press coverage? Were the objectives achieved? If not, by how much did they fail, and what should be done next time? And results don't always fall short of targets – they sometimes go way over the top, and that can be a serious embarrassment.

ROAD SHOWS

See 'Events'.

DIRECT MAIL

What was the reach achieved, were there any adverse comments – or positive ones – what were the number of mailing returns and, most important, how many responses compared with the target?

EXHIBITIONS

How many visitors walked past the stand, how many walked on to the stand, how long did they stay, how many enquiries were received, how many leaflets were taken, how many drinks dispensed...? All these and more will add to the evaluation by company staff and, indeed, customers.

SEMINARS

Seminars, conferences and private exhibitions are being used increasingly to differentiate both companies and products. Again, you should aim to use quantitative measurements coupled with qualitative which, in this case, can be based on delegate assessment forms: 'How useful did you find this seminar on a scale of 0 to 5?'

VIDEOS

Long before a video is ever commissioned there should be a comprehensive distribution and viewing plan stating what is regarded as the optimum number of showings coupled with the optimum size of the target audiences. Measurement is thus facilitated. How many people falling into the prescribed target audience category have viewed it, and what did they think of it?

What it amounts to is that just about every PR activity can be measured to some extent, and the more measurement that is undertaken, the more accurate it will become, thus reducing budgetary wastage, and making the whole operation more efficient. It will never be totally precise, and will certainly not eliminate the need for brilliant creativity and mature judgement, but that is no reason for abrogating the responsibility for having the most cost-effective procedures.

Customer panels

A number of references have been made throughout this book to research activities, with the suggestion that maybe 10 per cent of the budget should be allowed for measuring that the remaining 90 per cent is being spent wisely. Some such work is best put out to professional researchers who, for the most part, are very competent, if rather expensive. It is perfectly possible for in-house people to undertake a good deal of the work themselves, for instance readership habits of visitors to exhibitions, internal image audit, etc. The single most important research activity in terms of communications, and which can easily be set up by one's own staff, is the customer panel.

All organizations, commercial or non-commercial, should have one or more customer panels. They will comprise some eight people having a variety of characteristics such as small/large customers, old/new customers, male/female, north/south and, of course, representing a variety of market segments. They might meet once a quarter and will act as a sounding board for all manner of topics, past, present and future. What do they regard as the single selling proposition for a particular product; what are its other benefits/satisfactions; how can customer satisfaction be improved; what is their assessment of a proposed new brochure; how about this business gift? For every single item in the marketing communications armoury, one's own staff are making judgements based upon their own personal views. A customer panel overlays such judgements with the most important opinion of all – that of the customer.

As to the cost, there isn't any. In most cases the customers feel flattered to be asked to be a member of an advisory team and welcome the chance to influence a company. It may even be to their benefit. Obviously, expenses should be offered, and it may be that a bottle of something is handed out at the end of such a meeting, but otherwise no expenditure is necessary. The ideal format is to meet over a working lunch, and this need not be anything lavish or expensive. For next-to-nothing, a procedure can be set up to give continuous feedback on all marcom activities. This can easily be extended to overseas markets.

Customer panels do no more than provide qualitative data and clearly cannot be relied upon to have any statistical validity. Indeed, they may form the basis of a subsequent piece of quantitative research. This may not be necessary. If, for instance, the feedback from one or two customer panels on the most significant benefit for a direct mail campaign agrees entirely with what the company staff have already decided, this is just the reassurance needed before putting the campaign into practice. But suppose there is unanimous disagreement with a proposition – then, clearly, there is a need for second thoughts. In conducting an image audit, by all means consider contributions from internal staff – but it would be unwise not to consult with the outside world at some point.

Checklist

1. Does your promotional budget include a sum for campaign evaluation?
2. Has each of your campaigns a specific objective which is capable of being measured?
3. Has provision been made for continuous checks to be made to ensure that results are being obtained?
4. Is there a system for feedback of results to enable changes to be made to a campaign in sufficient time to achieve the final objective?

Part 4

PUBLIC RELATIONS

14

PUBLIC RELATIONS

The fundamental difference between public relations and press relations (or editorial publicity) is that editorial publicity is a medium just as much as press advertising and exhibitions, while public relations is a strategic function running parallel with marketing and dealing with all the many publics which can be involved in influencing the operation of a business from whatever point of view, sales or otherwise. It includes customers and prospects, but here the concern is not so much to be directly involved in selling, but rather to project the corporate image, and create a climate in which the selling operation can be conducted with greater efficiency.

In broad terms the public relations function is to establish and maintain a mutual understanding between an organization and its publics, to communicate a company's views, objectives and purposes, while at the same time monitoring, feeding back and correcting the publics' attitudes and reactions.

Planning for public relations

The need for a planned programme of public relations stems not from some new management concept but from the fact that organizations are finding, somewhat to their dismay, the need for a formalized corporate strategy. This need is being interpreted in a number of ways, but simply stated is that it is no longer good enough to take random actions for long-term effect: rather, it is necessary to give mature consideration to future objectives and the means of achieving them. Such objectives will incorporate financial investment, labour force and staffing, marketing aspects, production, research and development, and of course profit. This is no more than a move from past practices in which future events were just allowed to take their natural course, to a position in which a company sets out deliberately to move to a predetermined position. The weakness of any attempt at corporate planning is that unforeseeable events are bound to cause the objectives to be changed, but this is no reason for not taking action to influence the course of events so as to hit the desired target as closely as possible. Public relations are but one of the management functions which can be used to help achieve this goal.

The need for corporate goals and for a strategy to achieve them stems from a growing number of influences, external and internal, which if ignored may well undermine the profitable development of a company and indeed threaten its very existence. The increasing tendency by governments to impose controls is a major factor as are international regulations at one extreme and a vigorous consumerist movement at the other. Thus trade barriers and constraints, scarcity of raw materials, inflation, high taxation, are factors which play a larger part in the development of business. Equally the growing interest by employees and trade unions with their sometimes massive influence must be taken into consideration in any future planning.

In this section an examination is made of public relations from the point of view of *what* they are, *why* they are necessary, to *whom* they should be addressed, *when*, and *how*. Finally, the all important question of the results that might reasonably be expected of such an activity.

First *what*. This term is used to signify the deliberate attempts by an organization to maintain the best possible relations with each and every identifiable group of people whose interests and activities may be supposed to have an effect, for good or ill, on the prosperity and progress of the business. Such an operation is intrinsically linked with communications in both directions since without communications of some kind it is difficult to see how any change or impact can be obtained. It is important at the outset to realize two things. First, that no matter how efficient any corporate communications system may be, it will be of no avail unless the object of the communication is sound. In just the same way, no amount of advertising will ever sell an unsatisfactory product. The second point to be made is that every single means of communication must be considered for possible use, not just the classical PR media such as press releases, factory visits, booklets and special events. Public relations then are the building up of a good *reputation* with a company's many and varied publics. An old-fashioned term sums it up very well – *goodwill*.

Clearly the kind of activity being described is going to cost money. Hence the need to ask *why?* The plain fact is that all companies have an image whether they like it or not, or even if they are totally unaware of it. That is to say that a company is perceived by people in a variety of ways, depending upon the messages, conscious or unconscious, they have received about it. And the perception varies from one public to another. Customers may view a supplier as a thoroughly reliable and trustworthy organization with which to do business, whereas its employees may take the very opposite view.

The reason *why* corporate relations are important is that it is only when relationships are positive and sound that the most effective and efficient business can be conducted. For example is it reasonable to expect the best possible applicants for a job with a company which has a very poor reputation as an employer? It may be argued that in such a case the simple solution is in changing the conditions of employment so that they are really attractive, but this is overlooking the essential ingredient of corporate communications, for if people are unaware of a situation they cannot react to it. And if, as often happens, they are misinformed about it the opposite result to what was intended may be the outcome. The reason why corporate communications are important is that in one direction a company is receiving messages about itself from all the interested publics, and on the other hand it is sending out messages to those same people to ensure that they are fully informed, that they understand and that they are convinced. The reason *why*, thus, is in order to establish and maintain a series of relationships in which business can be conducted most efficiently.

The *when* of public relations can be dealt with simply. A reputation is with a company all its life. It's no use having a public relations function, and a corporate communication programme for a couple of years and then closing it down. People's memories and attitudes are dynamic and will change over time. A company must decide whether or not it is really serious in the matter of building its reputation, and if it is, and it wishes to maintain it, this can be achieved in one way only, and that is by a continuous programme of activities. It should also be borne in mind that the time-scale to achieve any major change is likely to be of the order of years rather than months, so advance planning is required as well as continuity.

Turning now to *how* corporate relations are to be achieved, this of course is where the difficulties arise and where the answers tend to become diffuse, uncertain and even contradictory. In outline it can be said that the starting point is to draw up plans, both strategic and tactical, to set objectives, to measure results, to co-ordinate all related and parallel activities, and to ensure that an adequate administrative and professional facility exists to guarantee proper execution.

STRATEGIC PLANNING

The key to successful strategic planning for good public relations is in the setting of comprehensive objectives. Two examples have been chosen to illustrate this point. First, a major multinational corporation which listed five aims:

1. To increase the share of people's minds available to the company.
2. To engender favourable attention and acceptability from its diverse publics.
3. To explain the realities of the company's social and economic contributions to the countries where it did business.
4. To state the case for business in general and MNCs in particular.
5. To correct some of the myths and refute irresponsible allegations.

The programme which evolved consisted of a package of five interdependent activities, each mutually supporting, making its own unique contribution, but working to the same plan and objectives. The elements of the package were an advertising campaign, a public information brochure, an external house magazine, a press relations programme and the establishment of a speakers' panel, and the complete programme was based on a publicly stated philosophy of openness, frankness and fact.

The second example is for a well-known company in the high technology business. The programme had five objectives:

1. To extend the company's corporate identity and to enhance/improve attitudes held towards the company among the defined target audiences.
2. To establish and promote the company as a leader and innovator in advanced technology.
3. To promote the company's capabilities and achievements in selected areas of advanced technology.
4. To create a high level of awareness and knowledge among target groups in prospective market areas for the technological excellence of its products.
5. To create a favourable attitude among target groups so that divisional marketing activities for particular products or systems could be carried out more effectively.

The main thrust of the campaign to achieve these aims was a most adventurous press campaign of very large advertisements in the colour supplements, backed by supportive advertising in 'management newspapers' and the specialist press.

TACTICAL PLANNING

It is not sufficient to produce one major homogeneous campaign and leave it at that. It is vital to examine each and every other sector of communications with its own specialized objectives, audiences, messages and media in order to ensure that these contribute also to the common objective of the company's reputation. In this way marketing communications, employee communications, a safety campaign, city and financial news, and all the rest add together to make up a synergistic whole. It can be seen that organizationally there is a need for the provision of top management direction to ensure the proper orchestration of all the many parts which are being conducted on a day-to-day basis.

The second part of tactical operations relates to what might be termed 'reactive activities'. This is where over and above the carefully constructed proactive ongoing campaign there arise events which, if not handled properly, can work against the corporate objectives or alternatively fail to give the potential support that may otherwise be achieved. Examples may be in an industrial dispute where bad handling can undo much of the goodwill which might have been built up over a period of years. It is necessary then to develop a programme for crisis management in which plans are laid down for handling any particular contingency that may arise. Equally, but in the opposite direction, failure to exploit fully the securing of a major overseas contract is a loss in terms of the very favourable light in which such an achievement can be shown to the target groups that together make up the corporate public.

Such contingencies cannot by their very nature be incorporated in any plan, but the organization must be sufficiently flexible to be able to react fast to each of these as they occur and to have in mind not just the event itself and how to solve or exploit it, but also the overall objectives.

The most important factor here is to be proactive rather than reactive.

CORPORATE RESEARCH

Early in the growth of the marketing concept and of corporate planning, communications activities were characterized by 'prestige advertising' and by a narrow form of public relations which relied mainly on what was loosely termed 'press relations'. It was unusual to have specific goals, and large sums of money were invested to transmit self-congratulatory messages about oneself without much regard to the interest of the audiences or indeed what the effect on them might be. Companies indulging in these activities became sceptical of their value and as economic conditions became tougher any attempt to buy prestige declined.

The growth of corporate affairs as a function, and public relations as an activity, has been accompanied by the precise setting of objectives in quantified form, and by a programme of research to ensure that any investment will achieve tangible results. Business people have begun to demand that expenditure in this area should be accountable and the effects measurable.

The starting point of any properly constructed programme of corporate communications is to make bench-mark measurements against which progress can be compared as the campaign proceeds. It is no use making such measurements at the end of a campaign as by that time it is too late to take any corrective action. A company may decide that it wishes to increase the level of awareness among certain discrete publics and at the same time gain an improved attitude towards itself and its products. Sample groups from each segment must be chosen and an assessment made of their current level of awareness and the nature of their attitudes. Only with this information can an effective plan be drawn up. From this a budget is set with the task to move from a current level A to a targeted level B in a given period of time. Using the same audience segments, methods of sampling and questioning techniques, research must be planned at intermediate stages in order to find out whether the results are on schedule, in advance of it or behind it. Variations can be made at this stage in order to bring the campaign back on to course and the changes may be simply in the direction of the campaign, or it may be necessary to increase expenditure, or for that matter cut it back. So the operation breaks down into four stages – set objectives, quantify, research, verify. The ten-point marcom plan can be used here – as a public relations plan.

BENEFITS

A well-constructed and properly funded public relations programme can lead to many benefits of which the following are but a few of the more obvious examples.

1. Increased market reputation and market share
2. Happier and more satisfied employees
3. Rise in share prices
4. Greater productivity
5. Favourable government support
6. Better quality applicants for jobs
7. Improved treatment from suppliers
8. Better understanding by, and less criticism from, outside pressure groups

While benefits will accrue to any company the chances are that the larger the organization, the greater the need for a formalized corporate communication policy. This applies with even greater effect where the products concerned fall into the category known as 'undifferentiated'. With little to choose between one brand and another – for example with petrol, oil, banks, cigarettes, detergents – what are the real determinants of a purchasing decision? There is a good deal of evidence to suggest that the customer will go for the brand or name he or she knows best and for which he or she has the greatest regard. Where products are intrinsically the same, the most important factor must become that indefinable property which lies behind the product – its reputation. And this applies with equal force to industrial products and services as to consumer ones.

It is now well established that there is a correlation between 'familiarity' and 'favourability' ie the better known an organisation the more likely it is that people will wish to do business with it – to buy its products, work for it, or become shareholders. This relationship is well illustrated by Figure 14.1.

From all this discussion there are two laws which can be propounded:

The corporate image law

The stronger the corporate image, the higher the price the customer is

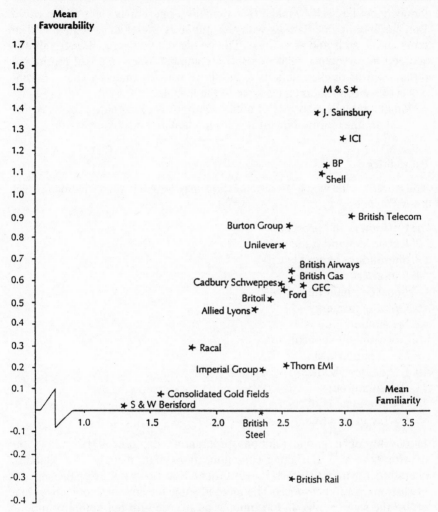

Figure 14.1 Familiarity and Favourability

prepared to pay and the greater the effort he is prepared to make to acquire the product.

Law of favourability

The stronger the familiarity with a brand or company, the greater the inclination to make a purchase or do business.

It is important to stress that the greatest single factor in a business is the people who work for it. It is true that sophisticated communications techniques must be used to make the company's operations clear to the world. But paramount in relations with the public is the chief executive and an enthusiastic staff and workforce. The public relations practitioner will only succeed in projecting what exists. If a company deserves a bad reputation, no amount of public relations expenditure will eliminate it. The only remedy is to concentrate on the source of the trouble.

Finally, the ultimate goal of public relations is to increase profit. As such it is just another form of investment as in plant and machinery.

PR publics

The publics with which an organization may be concerned include the following:

1. Customers and prospects
2. Employees and trade unions
3. Shareholders and 'the City'
4. Suppliers
5. Local communities
6. Opinion formers
7. Specialized groups
8. Government departments
9. Local authorities
10. Educational bodies
11. Pressure groups
12. International bodies
13. People in general.

In developing a public relations programme the procedure follows the development of a marketing communications plan, namely to produce an overall plan with written objectives broken down now under publics instead of customers and prospects. The methods of achieving these objectives may utilize the same media and techniques as are used for marketing communications. Press advertising, direct mail, photographs, editorial publicity all have contributions to make to the public relations programme but there are a number of differences in detail and a number of techniques not usually dealt with under marketing communication.

Having widened the scope of public relations beyond its more common 'press officer' context, to be effective the executive responsible for it needs to be an experienced communications person rather than the conventional ex-journalist. His or her place in the management structure needs to be examined in this new light, and this is dealt with under 'Publicity Organizations', Chapter 15.

Public relations activities need creativity. Frequently, to secure the greatest impact, the techniques require novelty and need to be adapted to the particular audience, the subject and the existing climate of opinion. There will therefore only be general guidelines and examples here.

PR activities are broken down under the key publics to whom they most often refer, though any one activity may influence more than one public or indeed all of them.

Customers and prospects

In considering public relations activities aimed at influencing customers and prospects, it is inevitable that there will be an overlap into what may be considered the marketing communications area. For instance, is prestige advertising PR or marketing communications? This question also applies to editorial publicity about new appointments, technological advances, large contracts. Indeed the closeness of these facets of publicity would tend to indicate the need for some form of central control.

Overall, one may say that public relations is concerned with creating a favourable image, or, to use a less emotive word, a favourable reputation. Evidence of the value within a marketing context is provided by Dr Theodore Levitt in his study *Industrial Buying Behaviour* for the Harvard Graduate Business School:

> One of the venerable questions in marketing, and particularly the marketing of industrial products, is whether a company's generalised reputation affects its ability to sell its products. With the great flood of new products in recent years, the question has been focused more sharply around the extent to which a company's generalised reputation affects its ability to launch new products. While nobody claims that a good reputation is an adequate substitute for a good product supported by a good sales effort, the question remains as to what contribution a good reputation can make to a good selling effort. Thus, all other things being equal, does a relatively well-known company... have a real edge over a relatively obscure company? Would it pay for a relatively obscure company to spend more money to advertise and promote its name and general competence or to spend more on training its salesmen?

Following this question, the study goes on to identify sixteen areas in which a good reputation can be shown to have a positive benefit. It concludes: 'Having a good reputation is always better than being a less well-known or completely anonymous company.'

The emergence of reputation as a factor in the marketing mix leads on to the extension of the classical Four Ps into Five. The third P of promotion (which more properly anyway should be 'perception') now has to be considered as those activities which are involved with the product (brand image) and those concerned with the company (corporate image). It can be said then that whether or not a product is purchased is dependent on five factors – the product, its price, its availability, the brand image and the corporate image. Each one of these variables can act in a positive or negative way but the nett effect must obviously be positive for a purchase to take place. Thus a product might be very good (positive) but the price rather high (negative) and not too readily available (negative). The brand name might be unknown (negative) but the manufacturer highly regarded (positive). The product benefits and corporate image in this case must clearly be strong enough to overcome the 'price', 'place' and 'brand image' barriers.

The attractiveness of the total product offering is diagrammatically illustrated by the example below which demonstrates both the polarity of each factor (positive or negative) and the intensity of each. A series of such diagrams facilitates the comparison of all competitive products in a segment, and highlights their strengths and weaknesses.

Such an analysis enables a strategy to be selected for increasing market share of one's own product simply by considering which one (or more) of the five factors is likely to be the most cost-effective in beating the competitors.

Alternatively one can look at a constant market share but a trade off of one factor against another one, eg price could be increased but corporate image strengthened without loss of sales. In so far as PR is the function which builds reputation or corporate image it can be seen then to have a direct correlation to sales and hence to profit.

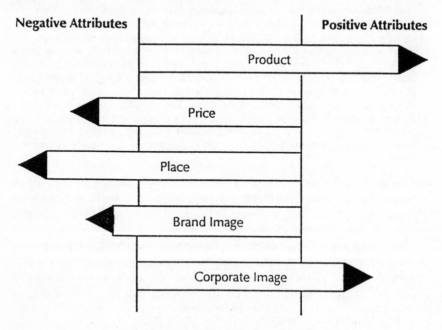

Figure 14.2   Five Marketing Variables

THE MARKETING FUNCTION AND PUBLIC RELATIONS

The following diagram illustrates the principal marketing functions, all aimed primarily at customers and prospects. The non-face-to-face elements are shown as breaking down into the various channels of communications, such as advertising, publicity (editorials), direct mail, exhibitions, and so on. There is a comprehensive, and hopefully synergistic, marketing communications plan which, together with a similar sales plan, goes to make up the Promotion element of the Four Ps. Note that public relations does not come into this since it is, by definition, concerned with the reputation or image of the organization behind the product.

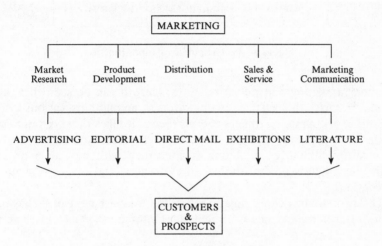

Figure 14.3   The marketing function

THE PUBLIC RELATIONS FUNCTION

The diagram below can be seen to bear a remarkable resemblance to the previous one, except that the number of target audiences has been increased to cover, in effect, all the 'stakeholders' of a business. Thus, the appropriate messages are sent out to employees, shareholders, pressure groups, and so on, but using precisely the same channels of communication as in the case of marketing. Certainly, editorial publicity figures high on the list but, equally, consideration must be given to advertising where publicity alone cannot achieve the public relations objectives.

RELATIONSHIP BETWEEN MARKETING AND PUBLIC RELATIONS

A block schematic diagram, as shown below, indicates the relationship

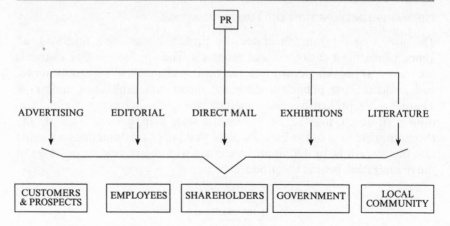

Figure 14.4   The public relations function

between marketing and public relations. Here it can be seen that public relations starts with a state of unawareness amongst its various publics including, of course, customers and prospects. It takes them through being aware of a company and on to perception which, of course, needs to be positive. Similarly, marketing is concerned with moving a prospect from unawareness of the product to awareness, and on to a favourable perception.

The two streams come together with the establishment of 'behavioural intent'. But here, and in subsequent stages, three other factors come into

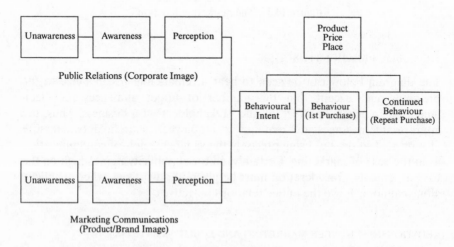

Figure 14.5   The relationship between public relations and marketing

play which might render all the communications in the world useless in terms of subsequent sales. These are the remaining three Ps, product, price and place. If the price is too high, for example, then the product will not be purchased (behaviour), or even considered (behavioural intent), let alone continue to be purchased.

CONCLUSION

Public relations throughout the world is beginning to be recognized as a new and independent management function, quite separate to marketing. It is essentially strategic, and contributes to the overall business objective by providing effective communications channels to assist all the other management functions.

Its relevance to marketing in particular, however, is well illustrated by a piece of American research, as illustrated below.

Some of the special PR opportunities which can be used for public relations purposes with particular relevance to influencing customers and prospects are discussed below.

FACTORY OPENINGS

The building of a new factory or a major extension provides the opportunity

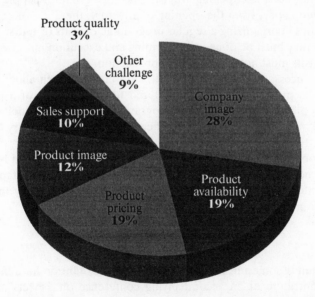

Figure 14.6 Biggest challenge in converting prospects into buyers
(*Source*: IntelliQuest Inc., Austin, Texas)

to generate enthusiasm and goodwill as well as publicity in the press and on radio and television.

For any large-scale operation it is essential to produce comprehensive plans well in advance, and six months is not an over-estimate, particularly if there is a VIP opener.

Arrangements in a large factory are complex and involve a great number of people whose co-operation is essential. It is important to include on the planning board of a factory opening the most senior executives of the company. Personal responsibility is essential for the efficient running of the operation: key executives must be allocated to such matters as transport, security, catering, cleaning and painting, press, unveiling, public address system, signboards, first aid, publications, gifts or mementoes, special treatment for VIPs, protocol and precedence, trades union relations, technical explanations, tour parties and even lavatories!

The rehearsal is particularly important and must simulate as realistically as possible the conditions which will apply on the day. The results of factory openings are hard to measure but clearly the fact that a hundred or so of a company's most important customers and outside contacts should think and talk about a company for a whole day has very great value.

FACTORY TOURS

One does not need an 'opening' to justify taking a group of people around a factory. Quite apart from the opening of a factory, there are often valuable opportunities in organizing a regular programme of visits or tours.

If done they must be done well: planning and execution must be immaculate, and visits must not interfere with production.

Care is necessary to ensure that tours are not too much about the company and its processes but rather tailored to the interests of a particular group. People are impressed by a programme which avoids delays or too much walking: also an adequate number of guides are necessary to ensure personal attention.

For important groups a great deal of benefit can be obtained by arranging for some unusual feature, such as a special train or chartered aircraft. People visiting a factory must be made to feel they are really important, which of course they are.

CONFERENCES

An opportunity sometimes occurs during a trade exhibition for a member of staff to contribute at an accompanying conference on aspects of a company's activities. Even if there is not an official conference it may be useful, while customers are concentrated in one place, to stage a conference either concerned solely with company interests, or perhaps sponsored by the company. A variation on a conference is a seminar which can deal in depth with some aspect of a company's activities, maybe from a more academic point of view.

Again, if a number of customers and prospects are known to be spending some time, maybe overnight, in a city, this is an opportunity to offer some completely social function, the contacts from which will pay off handsomely in terms of strengthening personal relationships.

The cost of such functions may seem high but this is often apparently so of other public relations operations as well as exhibitions and advertising, but if an investment is needed in order to develop a business then the investment should be made. Investment in PR may be intangible, but so is the investment in machinery which will stand idle if the orders are not forthcoming. It must be clearly understood that PR is not free or cheap publicity. It can be very expensive; it can also be very worth while.

Employees and trade unions

While the task of dealing with employees falls to line management, public relations executives should occupy a primary role in the means of communicating with workers and staff and also in anticipating and interpreting their reactions.

INFORMATION

Notice boards are the traditional medium for communicating with employees. They are often poorly designed, badly sited, inadequately lit, and frequently contain a hotchpotch of out-of-date, poorly duplicated notices in language which is difficult to understand.

It is surprising that since so much industrial unrest is due to misunderstanding, greater attention has not been given to communicating information accurately, effectively and speedily. One reason is that line managers regard themselves as the proper channel for communications and are sceptical of the value of PR here. Certainly they must not be short-circuited, but their efforts can benefit substantially from support from other channels of communication.

Notice boards have a part to play, but responsibility for their presentation and maintenance should rest with the public relations department.

Other methods of communicating with employees do not differ fundamentally from those used to influence customers. Direct mail can be used, literature suitably written and designed, stuffers in wage packets, posters, display units and exhibitions, open days, receptions and lunches. The formula is similar since the objective is the same: to influence people and to inform them with impact of the facts. The difference is often that customer information tends to be handled by professionals, and employee information by people whose skills lie in other parts of the business.

A particularly interesting comment on employee communications came from a UK survey by *International Management* magazine. This concluded that: 'Audio visual aids are an effective way for a company to communicate with its employees. Yet this is the method least used.' The survey measured the cost-effectiveness of different methods of communications. It found that although slide presentations, overhead projectors, films, and video tapes are all highly effective ways of passing information to workers, these methods are rarely used. Notice boards are widely used, it said, but are generally ineffective.

More than half of the companies surveyed communicated corporate policy and objectives to employees through the annual report or a popular version of it. These methods scored low in effectiveness.

The survey also found that employment policies and procedures seldom are passed along to workers during induction programmes.

The report suggested that companies publish more frequent and relevant news sheets for individual plants or units, rather than company-wide magazines.

HOUSE MAGAZINES

These are essentially part of the process of feeding information to employees, though in fact they can achieve much more by building up a corporate spirit and a feeling of unity.

A firm employing one or two hundred people does not need a house magazine, though an occasional newsheet from the CEO is often appreciated. With larger organizations a magazine of some sort is a useful vehicle for providing information and building up goodwill amongst employees. No doubt there are publications which are welcomed, and secure a fairly high readership rating. The editing of these publications is not the job for a part-time amateur; nor should it result in a highly polished magazine which sets out to compete with professional glossy monthlies. It should have written objectives, a carefully planned editorial and a presentation style which is compatible with the audience it is addressing. Readership research can be applied here with considerable effectiveness.

PRODUCTIVITY AND SAFETY

Effective communications are necessary to get across to employees ideas on safety, productivity, cleanliness, tidiness, good attendance, personnel lateness and, indeed, many aspects of management. Line or staff specialists, maybe the safety officer or the company doctor, will provide the ammunition, but the firing of the bullets can only properly be the function of the public relations department who will call upon conventional publicity media to achieve the result. A works or a shop seminar on safety, or a specially designed campaign incorporating leaflets, films, posters and displays, are as valid on the shop floor as the market-place.

INDUSTRIAL DISPUTES

There are occasions in a company when an industrial dispute arises, and when there is a need for swift and decisive action not only in negotiations, but in communications.

It is all too common that the press is able to get hold of a story from the employees' side so much more easily and quickly than from the management. This is understandable, since an employee has to refer to no one in expressing a point of view, whereas a company official has to exercise great care to ensure that he or she is putting across company policy and is doing it in a way that cannot be misinterpreted.

Though situations are diverse it is possible to lay down general procedures which provide machinery for handling the press during a dispute.

The press officer must be fully informed of a dispute as soon as it arises, or even if it is anticipated, so that he or she has the opportunity to gather the necessary facts and to advise on a plan of action. Whether to say nothing, a little or a lot; whether to be conciliatory or vigorous – these are matters which cannot be left to develop at random during a press interview.

If the press and the public (including shareholders, customers and employees) are to get a balanced view, it follows that an authoritative statement by the management is necessary. Such a statement can be prepared in advance and issued to the press, preferably in writing. Where supplementary questions are asked, these should be noted, and answers written down, considered, and then read back to the press. In practice an experienced press officer can write out likely questions and produce in advance answers which are unambiguous and in accordance with company policy.

The use of a public relations executive in this way calls for a person of ability and seniority coupled with a close involvement in top management thinking.

Shareholders and 'the City'

Public companies need to pay high regard to the way in which any story about their activities is likely to cause repercussions on the stock market.

Financial PR is not random action to keep bad news from the press and inflate good news. It calls for careful planning and involves a range of activities, including press advertising, literature, financial and policy statements, shareholders' meetings and the annual report. Advance planning will ensure that each opportunity is exploited to the full.

The overlap with other key publics should not be forgotten. Employees read annual reports, and take pride in the company they work for. Customers and suppliers have an interest in such information.

Share values and the response to an issue depend largely on financial criteria, but a company's reputation can have a significant bearing on the matter. Press releases dealing, for example, with winning important contracts will be designed initially to influence potential customers, but they also contribute to the building up of a firm's image with investors, stock brokers and bankers.

Economic and industrial journalists probably have most influence in interpreting a company and its policies to the public, and relationships of mutual understanding must be cultivated. Journalists can, after all, only report on events in the light of their own personal knowledge and experience. A very useful operation in this respect is to arrange for groups of journalists to meet informally from time to time with members of a company's top management. Such functions should not be centred around a particular news item, but be planned deliberately to exchange views and impart information of a general nature. It does no harm, either, for top management to understand and respect the requirements of journalists.

Suppliers

Suppliers make up one of a company's key publics. The building of a good business relationship depends in part on an understanding of one another, and the respect of suppliers for their customers can be valuable. Suppliers, after all, have preferences among their customers and these can well lead to benefits in terms of service, delivery and even price.

A further factor is that suppliers have many contacts within their trade and their views often reach a wide variety of influential people. Their recommendations count in building up a company's reputation.

Local communities

Much of the strength of a company lies in the quality and attitudes of the people it employs. Local communities are a major source of recruitment at all levels, and local public relations activities can be a source of encouragement to potential employees. Existing employees, too, like to feel that the firm they work for has a favourable reputation in the locality, is known to have enlightened management policies, and is providing a useful service to the community.

A company also depends a great deal on the local authority, on councillors and permanent officials, especially when acquiring new premises or expanding its operations. It needs good relations with public utilities, with the police, educationalists, local organizations, and other businesses in the area whose co-operation is sometimes of considerable value in matters of common interest whether rateable values, rates of pay or the sharing of a common bus service.

A firm which sets out to play a part in the life of a local community has much to gain for little investment, though its obligations cannot be satisfied simply by sponsoring a football match or contributing to a charity or two. Senior people from the company must take a genuine interest in local affairs and be seen to be doing so.

Opinion formers

This is one of the 'jargon terms' of public relations practitioners. The thought behind the term is that within a community there are certain people who by reason of their function or position are likely to be able to exert a special influence on public opinion. The contention is that general opinions are formed or changed by people whose views are respected. A teacher or a youth leader for example may have a specially high influence on young people, while other typical opinion-formers include members of parliament, academics, top business men, clergymen, local community leaders and lawyers.

Having defined what amounts in selling terms to the potential market, it remains to plan the action necessary to direct an adequate level of persuasive communications at them in order to achieve the desired effect.

It is true that such an operation can be expensive and also that the results may be difficult to measure. More than usual judgement must be exercised in order to equate the investment to the likely return in terms of impact upon sales, finance, recruitment and all the many activities which contribute to a company's profitable existence.

Specialized groups

In most organizations a situation arises which requires a special group of people to be informed or persuaded in order to understand fully a company's point of view.

This was the case when radioactive isotopes were first introduced into industry for measurement and control. There was concern about radiation hazards among safety officers, trade unionists, government departments and members of parliament. In particular there was the suspicion that material passing in front of an isotope could itself become radioactive. This was scientifically unfounded but nonetheless had to be treated as a serious potential point of sales resistance. A good deal of scientific publicity and official backing was required at a number of levels in order to overcome what were quite genuine and serious fears.

Another interesting problem confronted a certain manufacturer who relied on large quantities of waste paper as a basic raw material. One major source of supply, the housewife via refuse collection, began to decline. There were a number of specialized groups to be informed of the importance of saving paper, and of its value to the economy. The housewife was the primary source, but her co-operation was of no avail unless the dustman kept paper separate from other refuse. Here it was necessary to influence the public cleansing officer who controlled the dustmen, the local authority committee and even the mayor. Other sources of supply were youth organizations, who could raise funds by collecting waste paper, and industrial concerns like printers who as a matter of course were large producers of waste.

A solution to the shortage of waste paper could have been to increase the price paid for it until supply caught up with demand, but the cost would have been very great and in turn would have been passed on to the consumer. In the event a major public relations campaign was mounted to reach all the interested groups. For housewives, conventional consumer media were used such as television, radio, posters, door-to-door circulars and talks to women's groups. The annual conference of public cleansing officers included in their programme a visit to a factory to see waste paper being used. The Lord Mayor of London held a reception, which every London mayor attended, and heard of the national need for waste paper. A novel feature which caught the imagination of journalists was an exhibition of waste paper which involved dumping several tons of it in the middle of the Savoy Hotel. A pop song was written and recorded, a film made, schoolchildren were informed, and the network of publicity spread to the key publics likely to affect the situation.

When a company decides to move from one location to another, a very well-planned public relations campaign is required not just to employees, but more important to their families. In setting up a new factory there are often local community interests that must be considered. Largely it is a matter of informing people well in advance and of giving them an opportunity to express their views. They will want to know how it will affect them personally, for instance will there be opportunities for employment? Will there be undue smell or noise, or an increase in traffic? Will it disturb a local bird sanctuary? And so on.

A feature of public relations in connection with specialized groups is the tendency to wait for a situation to arise before taking action. This is sometimes inevitable, but a plan to maintain good relations and provide an adequate flow of information to such people on a continuous basis can function even if at a relatively low intensity. Indeed, such a procedure will do much to avoid crises arising which require crash action, usually expensive, and sometimes too late.

People in general

'How do we want people to see us?' This is a question that a company should ask itself periodically, and work out an answer in some detail and in writing. This will then become the foundation of public relations policy.

Consider how an impression of an organization is formed. Is it through a salesperson, or a buyer? Perhaps it is through the receptionist or a van driver? Maybe it is the letter heading or the exterior of a building: perhaps what appears in the press as editorial or advertising. Whatever the medium and whatever its primary purpose, it also has a public relations connotation.

An important factor is 'house styling'. The process begins with the name of the company and its subsidiaries. The name should be simple, appropriate, easy to pronounce, memorable and, of course, registerable. Is a trade mark or symbol necessary? If there is a house colour, is it useful and is it the most effective colour?

If a 'style' is to be established to what should it apply? A designer must know this before starting work, and the items may include letter headings, invoices, order forms, visiting cards, vehicles, notice boards, advertising, products, company ties and even security police cap badges. There can be many complications and arguments for deviation from the standard specification, and much expense in implementation, but in practice the introduction of a new house style can lead to considerable economies. Standardization of paper sizes and of forms can save hundreds of pounds. A change from embossed letterheads to litho printing, a reduction in the number of colours on vehicles, the elimination of copperplate visiting cards, provide opportunities for savings, especially where a company has grown up over a number of years and each element of the business has been developed on an individual basis.

Message sources – the internal image audit

THE CORPORATE PERSONALITY

The essential preamble to any study of corporate image is to be absolutely clear as to what image it is required to project. This might come out of the mission statement. Simply expressed, it can be regarded as the corporate personality. It is the impression which should come to mind whenever the company name is mentioned. It is not simply a question of having a good or bad image. It must be refined in order to project the nature of the business. Other terms which are loosely regarded as synonymous are corporate image, corporate reputation, corporate goodwill and corporate perception. A few examples will serve to indicate the attributes which may be associated with a company name:

1. Innovative, proactive, creative
2. Market leader, profitable
3. Well-managed, reliable, safe, responsible
4. International, British, Japanese – or any other nationality
5. Diversified, specialist
6. Authoritative, technical leader, expert
7. Honest, decent, truthful
8. High quality, value for money
9. Friendly, responsive, caring
10. Excellence in pre- and post-sales service

The above qualities can well be illustrated graphically by means of a chart showing their respect intensities. Such a chart (see Figure 14.7) can then be overlaid with similar charts of competitors to show where the differences occur.

THE IMAGE AUDIT

Over the past few years, a new way of examining an organization's image has been developed, based on a rather broader view of the many factors which go into the creation of an image.

The starting point is obviously to appraise all deliberate and active sources of publicity such as advertising, direct mail, exhibitions and so on. An advertisement, for instance, will have a specific purpose – maybe to generate enquiries for a particular product or service. Whether it is successful or not might be said to depend on the number of enquiries produced compared with the objective. This, however, is to overlook another important role which is performed by any advertisement, and that is the impression that it creates of the organization behind it. A small advertisement tucked away at the back of a publication might pull in enquiries but give an impression of being a minor business by comparison with its competitors. Equally, a large and lavish advertisement might give the impression of a business which is not too careful with its money – which has more money than sense. So, every 'active message source' should be evaluated in terms of the impression it will create.

In the field of marketing there are many other message sources, some of which are far more important. The single most influential factor on whether someone buys a product is what might be termed third party endorsement, ie recommendation by a buyer or user of the product. This introduces a whole group of influencers, which can be pulled together under the heading 'outside message sources'.

But it is not just people outside the organization who affect what people think of it; it is the people inside it, the employees. What impression is given, for instance, when the chief executive makes a speech? Good or bad? And what about the telephonist, or a secretary, or the sales force? Specific groups of people should be identified and evaluated so as to see where changes could be made in order to improve the impressions being created.

A final round-up brings in what are referred to as 'passive message sources'. These comprise any single factor which in any way contributes to public perception. The appearance of the offices and reception for instance, coupled with the way in which visitors are greeted. The tidiness of the office desks, people's job titles, the style of letter headings, the type and condition of vehicles: the list is endless.

One of the great attractions of conducting such a comprehensive review of message sources is that in many instances changes can take place quickly and without any great expense.

The starting point is to produce a checklist of message sources which will be used for the audit. Then a small project team of three senior people needs to be assembled in order reach a consensus on whether any given message source is creating an impression which is favourable, neutral, or unfavourable. The objective is to end up with a list of all those message sources which are obviously in the unfavourable category, with a view to setting in motion an action programme. Stage two is to examine the neutral

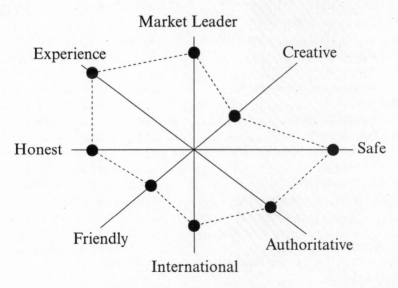

Figure 14.7 Corporate personality

message sources, while the final stage is to assess whether those which are already favourable can be made even more favourable.

The following schedule lists 100 fairly common message sources which are found to exist in any commercial organization. To these, of course, there will be many which any individual business will have uniquely to itself.

ACTIVE MESSAGE SOURCES (PROMOTIONAL)

1. Press advertising
2. TV
3. Radio
4. Outdoor
5. Public exhibitions
6. Private exhibitions
7. Films, video and AV
8. Demonstrations and visits
9. Sponsorship
10. Telemarketing
11. Sales leaflets and brochures
12. Business gifts
13. Directories and yearbooks
14. Educational packs
15. Sales calls
16. Merchandising
17. Point of sale
18. Sales promotion
19. Envelope franking, letter stuffers and stickers, etc
20. Sales aids
21. Direct mail
22. Seminars and conferences
23. Press releases
24. Press receptions
25. Press visits
26. Parliamentary and other lobbies
27. Charity support
28. Feature articles

OUTSIDE MESSAGE SOURCES

29. Agents and distributors
30. Customers – specifiers, authorizers, purchasers
31. Users
32. Media/journalists

33. Trade associations
34. Consultants
35. Local community
36. Competitors
37. Suppliers

PEOPLE MESSAGE SOURCES

38. Company VIPs
39. Sales force
40. Service engineers
41. Telephonist
42. Receptionist
43. Employees in general
44. Spouses and friends
45. Shareholders
46. Applications for jobs
47. Handling complaints
48. Membership of trade associations
49. Membership of learned institutes
50. Attendance at conferences
51. Chairing committees
52. Public speaking
53. Local community activities
54. Social activities

PASSIVE MESSAGE SOURCES

55. Annual report
56. Sales letters
57. Company name
58. House magazine/newsletters
59. Sales office back-up
60. House style
61. Packaging
62. Labels
63. Telephone contact
64. Business cards
65. Specification sheets
66. Test certificates
67. Instruction manuals
68. Service manuals
69. Delivery notes and invoices

70. Cars, delivery vehicles
71. Price list/credit facilities
72. Pre-sales service
73. Christmas cards
74. Telex
75. Facsimile messages
76. Telephone directory entries
77. Trade mark
78. Calendars
79. Diaries
80. Wall charts
81. Photographs
82. Showrooms
83. Appearance of factory
84. Location
85. Ties and emblems
86. Brand names
87. Logotypes
88. Royal Warrant
89. Queen's Award to Industry
90. Reception area
91. Notice boards
92. The product – quality, appearance, etc
93. Delivery promises – reliability
94. Group name
95. Nationality
96. Range of product/application
97. Guarantee cards/trading terms
98. Samples
99. Job titles
100. Visitors/entertaining

CHARACTERISTICS THAT MAKE A COMPANY A KEY PLAYER

The positioning of a company in relation to its competitors depends on the business it is in. One particular study in the field of information technology showed the characteristics that go to make a company a key player as:

	Index
Reliable products	100
After-sales service	81
Value for money	79
Leading-edge technology	75
Financial stability	75
Range of products	70

	Index
Good distributor support	61
Large market share	60
Supplier understands issues	60
Well-known name	60
International coverage	50
Good sales force	31
Advertising	16

The following is an example of an image audit put into practice.

	Favourable	Neutral	Unfavourable
Active message sources			
Advertising		■	
Exhibitions		■	
Demonstrations & visits		■	
Sponsorship		■	
Telemarketing	■		
Sales literature		■	
Educational packs			■
Sales calls		■	
Merchandising		■	
Point of sale			■
Sales promotion			■
Envelope franking, etc		■	
Sales aids			■
Press releases			■
Press visits		■	
Charity support		■	
Feature articles		■	
Passive message sources			
Desks			■
Canteens			■
Toilets			■
Car parks			■
Language		■	
Accents			■
Smoking	■		
Outbound faxes			■
Reception			■
Telephone contact			■
Communications			■
Hospitality		■	
Signage			■
Annual report		■	
Sales letters			■
Company name	■		

continued overleaf

	Favourable	Neutral	Unfavourable
Passive message sources *(continued)*			
Sales office back-up	■		
House style	■		
Packaging	■		
Labels		■	
Business cards		■	
Delivery notes/invoices		■	
Cars		■	
Price list			■
Pre-sales service			■
Showroom			■
Appearance of factory			■
Location		■	
Brand name	■		
Royal Warrant	■		
Notice boards			■
Product quality appearance	■		
Delivery promises reliability			■
Group name			■
Nationality	■		
Range of products	■		
Trading terms/guarantees			■
Samples		■	
Job titles			
Outside message sources			
Agents & distributors			■
Customers			■
Users	■		
Non-customers			
Trade associations		■	
Consultants	■		
Local community		■	
Competitors		■	
Suppliers		■	
Key influences		■	
Press		■	
Banks			■
Police			■
People message sources			
Company VIPs		■	
Sales force/complaint handling		■	
Receptionist/telephonist			
Employees in general			■
Spouses & friends		■	
Shareholders			■
Applications for jobs		■	
Local community activities		■	

Checklist

1. Has the difference between public relations and press relations been established? Do top management understand this?
2. Has a plan of action been drawn up to influence the following audiences?
   - (a) Customers and prospects
   - (b) Employees and trade unions
   - (c) Shareholders and investors
   - (d) Suppliers
   - (e) Local communities
   - (f) Opinion formers
   - (g) Government departments
   - (h) Local authorities
   - (i) Educational bodies
   - (j) Specialized groups
   - (k) Pressure groups
   - (l) International bodies
   - (m) General public
3. In drawing up such a forward plan, has each medium been considered, i.e. in addition to editorial publicity – press advertising, direct mail, exhibitions, literature, films and so on?
4. In addition to conventional media have opportunities under the following headings been examined?
   - (a) Factory openings and tours
   - (b) Conferences and seminars
   - (c) Speakers panel
   - (d) Notice boards
   - (e) Closed-circuit television
   - (f) House magazine
   - (g) Factory signs
   - (h) Employees' clothing, overalls, uniforms, badges
   - (i) Meetings between journalists and top management
   - (j) Sponsored events – local, national and international
   - (k) Involvement in local community activities
   - (l) Demonstrations
   - (m) House styling

Part 5

PUBLICITY ORGANIZATIONS

15.

MARKETING ORGANIZATIONS

There has been considerable change in the past decade in the position of the marketing communications function in relation to the top management structure of a company. The most significant development was that publicity in the industrial field achieved recognition as a serious and valuable operation, albeit as a part of the selling activity. A typical company organization chart (Figure 15.1) in the classic tradition was:

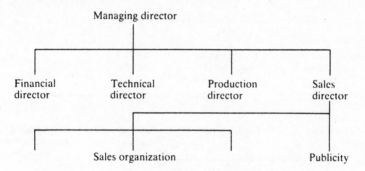

Figure 15.1 Company organization chart 1 (sales orientation)

This scheme was usual whether the company was large or small, and would range from large publicity departments with managers responsible to sales directors, to small operations in which the chief sales executives handled the publicity themselves.

In changing from a sales- to a marketing-orientated organization there have been, and still are, a number of interim stages in which for instance the publicity manager reports to the managing director who (unknowingly) thus assumes the function of part-time marketing director. Sometimes a marketing director was appointed, but placed alongside a sales director, with the inevitable clash of interests. This is not to say that a company cannot operate efficiently and effectively without conforming to some theoretical ideal structure. Each situation requires its own solution having regard to variables such as the size of the company, the nature of its products and market, and inevitably the capabilities and personalities of the people it employs.

Figures 15.2, 15.3 and 15.4 represent typical organizational structures for industrial companies which are marketing oriented, have 'own products' but vary considerably in size. Such a company, as in Figure 15.2, may employ a few hundred people and have a turnover of £10 million. Here the sales manager is very much out in the field with accounts of his or her own. The marketing communications manager would in some cases have no more than a good secretary as an assistant, and would not only handle advertising and public relations, but also arrange whatever marketing research was required. Marketing planning would be the job of the marketing director who, as the company developed in size, might add a marketing executive as an assistant but in a staff rather than line capacity. Much of the publicity work would be bought in, and in a small company this is far better than employing a number of specialists with a corresponding increase in semi-fixed overheads.

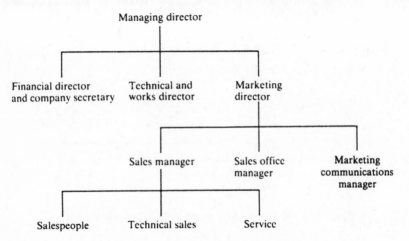

Figure 15.2   Small company organization

Figure 15.3 represents a company with a turnover of, say, £50 million and employing a thousand or more people. A new title has been introduced, 'marketing services manager' as an alternative to marketing communications manager, a function designed to supply every service required by the marketing operation. There is still no separate marketing planning function, but this takes place within the marketing services department under the direction of the marketing director. No independent provision is made for product development, but depending on the nature of the business the function is shared between the technical department and the marketing services department.

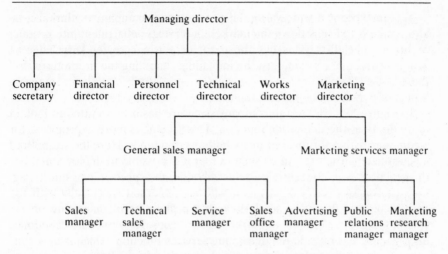

Figure 15.3 Medium-sized company organization

The three functions under the marketing services (or marketing communications) manager then break down as follows:

1. *Advertising*
   (a) Press advertising
   (b) Exhibitions
   (c) Direct mail
   (d) Literature
2. *Public relations*
   (a) Public relations
   (b) Press relations
   (c) House magazines
   (d) Videos
   (e) Photography
3. *Marketing research*
   (a) Market research
   (b) Product research
   (c) Product testing
   (d) Attitude research
   (e) Campaign evaluation

Whether to put videos under public relations is simply a matter of which category films most often tend to fit in a particular company. As the company develops within this structure, the number of specialists can be increased so that there will be an exhibitions manager, a press officer or a photographer under public relations, and a statistician or economist under marketing research.

Where there is a wide variety of products in a company of this size, an alternative is to break down the marketing services department into product or brand specialists. This has the merit of getting greater knowledge of products and markets amongst the individuals handling the promotions, but these same people now need to have a very broad experience of every aspect of persuasive communications.

In Figure 15.4 the overall company structure has been omitted to look in more detail at the marketing function. This scheme is more appropriate for a company with a turnover of many millions of pounds. Here the strength of a centralized structure can be seen in that it is possible to deploy a number of specialists who concentrate exclusively on one aspect only of marketing. One person or even a department will be concerned specifically with the search for new products: similarly with the planning of marketing operations and the development of marketing strategies. Research and economics have been taken outside the marketing services function, which is now concerned principally with making a direct contribution to short- and medium-term marketing operations. The 'brand manager' concept is introduced in the form of product group executives and they, in turn, can call upon specialists in particular media to contribute to their operations.

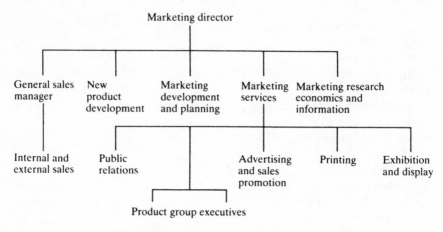

Figure 15.4   Large company organization

It is arguable whether public relations should be allowed to go so far down the line as shown in this structure. An alternative is to make this directly responsible to the marketing director, and with a connecting link to the managing director. Indeed, these days it is more and more common for the PR executive to report directly to the CEO, and possibly even to sit on the board.

It may be necessary to have a number of sales managers reporting to the marketing director. When the span of control begins to become too great a marketing manager can be introduced to administer the other marketing functions. No provision has been made in any of the structures described for the 'creative' function. It has been assumed that outside agencies will be used and that the need for visualizers and copywriters will not arise. This will be discussed in the next part of the chapter.

A matter of continual debate in larger companies is whether to centralize marketing communications or to split it up amongst the operating divisions, each with its own marcom department. It is probably not important, providing those operating the business believe strongly and enthusiastically in the system they are using. This is often borne out by the changes recommended by management consultants. Frequently if marketing communications is centralized, consultants recommend decentralization and vice versa. Both systems work. If anything the balance must be slightly in favour of central control since the increasing use of sophisticated marketing techniques calls for specialists who cannot be justified, or indeed fully utilized, by a small organization.

A final point to be made emerges from research by the author and that is the significant replacement of sales directors by marketing directors. It is also noticeable that increasingly advertising and PR functions are being merged under the umbrella of someone at board level with a title like Corporate Communications Director. Where this happens the responsibility and authority for advertising and related functions rests with just this one person – which is a good reason for having him or her. In the majority of cases, however, the advertising manager, or equivalent, has the responsibility but not the authority. Research has shown that only 37 per cent of marketing communications managers can approve an advertisement and only 12 per cent a campaign. In 75 per cent of the cases authority for approving an advertisement had to come from at least one director.

In-house services

It is now necessary to consider briefly each of the marketing communications functions and how, if at all, a department should set itself up to handle them. An examination of such departments shows a wide diversity of views, with some industrial companies making do with a very modest staff, and others employing tens and sometimes hundreds of people.

A good basic rule for the creation and development of a marcom department is to keep it as small as possible. The reason for this is twofold. Specialist services are almost always available from outside agencies and they are often of better quality than an internal department can provide. Secondly, if a company goes through a difficult financial period it is sometimes forced to make drastic cutbacks in current expenditure, and such economies are inevitably made in activities which will have the least deleterious effect *in the short term*.

These are generally marcom, training and R&D, often with results which are later regretted. The comments which follow are of a general nature and it is to be expected that there will be exceptions which work extremely well.

PRESS ADVERTISING

Few firms produce their own press advertising, and thus there is rarely a case for a company to employ its own advertisement visualizers, typographers and artists. Far better ones are available outside, and certainly no top-grade creative person will stay for long with an industrial company. Even if that person is brilliant to start with, this will soon wear off without the variety, challenge and stimulus of an agency or studio atmosphere.

With technical copywriting there is a strong body of opinion that an agency cannot produce adequate copy, and that it takes longer to produce the brief than to write the copy oneself. This is not only untrue: it is nonsense. Writing is a highly skilled and creative function, which requires a top-rate craftsman. Few advertising managers (or sales managers) would claim to have this facility. It is true that most advertising agencies find technical copywriting difficult, and that many are incapable of doing it. The solution is not to do it oneself, but to change the agency.

The production side of press advertising, voucher checking and so on is usually handled well by an agency, and there can be little justification for a marketing communications department being involved in this.

MEDIA PLANNING

Agencies are in a difficult position on press media planning. They cannot obtain adequate data from publishers, and clients as a rule are unwilling or unable to allocate adequate funds for a thorough investigation to be undertaken. Some agencies are breaking new ground in this respect and much progress will be made over the next ten years but, in the meantime, the solution seems to be to encourage the agency media department in every possible way, but for the marketing communications department to retain a strong measure of control and scrutiny.

As regards the media mix outside press advertising, most of the 750 or so agencies in the United Kingdom have good experience of press media, and some of literature and exhibitions, but for other media few have strong enough all-round experience to compete with a company's own department, particularly in the specialized industry and product groups in which a firm is operating.

DIRECT MAIL

This is usually most efficiently directed and executed within the marcom department. Partly the reason is that many agencies are not set up to process this medium; partly because the maintenance of lists can usually best be handled at the client end; partly because action is usually required at a moment's notice; partly because this is very much a personal means of contact from supplier to customer.

A sales letter, for instance, is usually something which a sales manager or an advertising manager can do better than a copywriter. This is not to contradict the argument in favour of professional writers for press advertising: it is a matter of horses for courses, and the professional in sales letters is, or should be, a sales manager.

Direct mail is, of course, not confined to writing a letter, and there is a good deal of outside creative expertise from advertising agencies, art studios, freelancers or direct mail houses, which can be used with considerable advantage.

The lead and initiative should, however, rest with the marketing communications department.

EXHIBITIONS

These must be a co-operative effort. Only rarely can an outside consultant or agency know enough about a company to be able to handle the whole process from the initial briefing to the final opening. This is particularly true in view of the company changes in policy and personnel which may take place over the period of planning an exhibition. Moreover a stand is a highly complex publicity medium and should be produced as an environment where company personnel will be required to sell actively and efficiently.

It is equally rare that a company employs people on its staff who have adequate knowledge of design, writing, architecture, décor and construction to be able to do the job independently.

The answer is to organize a joint effort, but to do this formally with each element of the job analysed, isolated and planned so that the appropriate specialist is used for the appropriate job, and then integrated into the whole. Figure 15.5 is a simple diagram that can be used as a starting point for a more detailed network which will incorporate a time-scale.

LITERATURE

Organizing literature usually involves another compromise. Few marketing communications departments can carry out the visualizing, and few agencies or outside consultants are capable of writing the text. The final difficulty is that very few marketing communications departments are able to write the text either, unless they are large enough to justify the employment of specialist writers.

There are agencies who employ writers able to do the complete assignment, and there are freelance writers who can sometimes be used. Technical

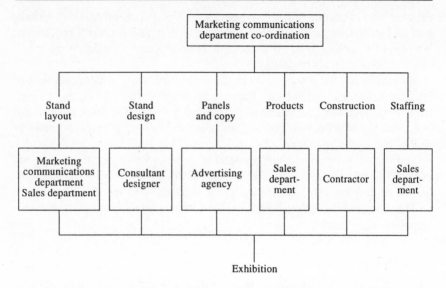

Figure 15.5   Planning for an exhibition

journalists can be hired on a freelance basis and generally produce good work. Alternatively, someone inside the company may write the basic text to be passed on to a professional writer for finishing.

On the production side there is not much to choose between using an agency or having a specialist on the staff of the marketing communications department. If the workload is steady and sufficiently great, it pays to employ a full-time executive: if not, an agency will probably do a first-class job, but will charge anything between 15 per cent and 25 per cent of the total print bill for the service. For the smaller company, many printers have their own designers, or maintain a close contact with a design unit. This can be satisfactory, especially if the work is not too detailed or specialized, but the disadvantage is that it lengthens the chain of communication.

For house magazines, the solution is to appoint a professional editor. Whether that editor should be on the company's staff is immaterial provided he or she is capable and is given a wide degree of freedom to implement editorial policy within the budget.

PHOTOGRAPHY

To have a staff photographer is a decided advantage providing this does not mean that every photographic job must be handled by him or her. Some photographers specialize in creative work, others in industrial work, portraiture, news, landscape, advertising, and it is too much to expect to find all these skills in one person employed as a member of staff. Alternatively, much company photography required quickly, or for record purposes, or at little expense can best be done by a staff photographer.

PRINTING

No matter how many, or how sophisticated, the offset litho machines a company installs, they cannot replace outside printers. With a larger firm, a print department can make great savings on forms and routine internal jobs. Even some external work is acceptable for certain purposes – a news-sheet, manuals or an exhibition handout for example. Outside this, however, for sales literature, it is unusual for a company to be able to produce work of acceptable quality or even at competitive cost.

FILMS AND VIDEOS

Hardly a firm in the country is equipped with its own film unit. A video-camera has some use for sales and the management training, and perhaps for other internal communications, but not much else. If films or videos form a large part of a company's publicity programme it is essential to have an executive on the staff with specialist experience or alternatively to take counsel with experts at the advertising agency.

The essential function for the company is to make active provision for the promotion and distribution of films. This cannot be farmed out, notwithstanding the existence of one or two distribution libraries. These provide a good physical distribution service, but films are made to be shown actively to specific audiences, and this will not happen unless a company plans for it and sets up the necessary organization.

With the emergence of video recording there has been a swing back to using in-house facilities which with care can result in very competently produced programmes. This however is more in a technical sense than creative, where the services of an outside specialist are vital.

EDITORIAL PUBLICITY

It is difficult to justify employing an agency for editorial publicity as distinct from public relations. The preparation of press releases and of press conferences calls for a professional executive, but the degree of in-company knowledge, contacts and accessibility required favours the employment of a staff person. Furthermore, the press tend to prefer to deal direct with a company since they need answers with both speed and authority. An agency or a consultant is at an inherent disadvantage in this respect.

An outside PR organization has contacts as part of its stock in trade of course, but these can be matched in time by most companies themselves and with greater effect.

PUBLIC RELATIONS

Even the best of public relations practitioners, after immersion in a company environment for a few years, begin to acquire a biased point of view. They are, after all, subordinate to the management they are advising and must exercise a certain caution in giving advice which in turn is not always regarded as highly as that from an outside source.

There is much to be said for retaining a public relations consultancy to give top-level advice, to work in conjunction with a company's own PR staff and to be available to provide assistance for special events which are outside the scope, capacity or experience of staff executives.

The staff person has an important function and, as already indicated, should have direct access to the chief executive. The range of public relations activities, however, is so broad that an agency can usually bring to bear a good deal more experience on a problem than a staff executive who, as time goes on, becomes more and more specialized, and operates within a restricted environment.

MISCELLANEOUS PUBLICITY ACTIVITIES

All manner of miscellaneous activities fall to a marketing communications department, and rightly. The marcom staff are the company's experts in communications whether internal or external, and should be used as such. Sales conferences, gifts, Christmas cards, samples, factory signs, notice boards – all these and more fall to the department to organize. Some limits may be necessary, particularly as when the department is asked to produce raffle tickets for the sports club dinner, and the procedure here is to require that some estimate should be produced of how much it costs to use an in-house service for some of the smaller items which could just as easily and effectively be produced elsewhere.

PLANNING AND BUDGETING

This task cannot be delegated. It is in fact the single most important job of a marketing communications department, and the only one which emphatically cannot be 'put out'.

The one key function of a company's marketing communications department is to operate within the framework of the marketing strategy, to plan, budget, administer, monitor and to assess the overall range of marcom activities.

16.

PUBLISHERS

Publishers of periodicals merit special attention since they play such a significant role in business-to-business marketing communications. The United Kingdom is unique in this respect, both in the number of publications (4500 trade and technical), and in the share of budgets allocated to press advertising (about 40 per cent). Even if the average circulation for a journal is taken at a modest 5000, with 4000 publications this would amount to 20 million copies per month (or whatever period) and multiplied by the 'pass-on' circulation, perhaps five per copy, this results in a total potential readership of 100 million. Clearly, there is much duplication in the figure of 100 million.

Quantity, however, is not necessarily a sign of strength: indeed the number of periodicals currently being circulated is likely to prove to be the weakness of the publishing industry, in that there is a limit to the amount of reading time that any one person has. Nevertheless, considerable sums of money are invested in press advertising; one estimate puts it at well in excess of £1000 million a year, and this is adequate justification for a detailed examination of publishing.

Development of the press

There have been three distinct phases of development that have taken place over the past decade or so, and these are very akin to the changes that were earlier outlined for products in relation to marketing development, ie product orientation followed by sales orientation and marketing orientation. In the publishing world it is possible to restate these developments as journal orientation, circulation orientation and audience (or readership) orientation. It is necessary to look into each of these phases since many publishers are still heavily entrenched in the first two stages.

Each stage of development tends to be characterized by the nature or function of the person at the head of a publication. In the first phase it is the editor who is primarily responsible for laying down policy. In the second phase the advertisement manager emerges as the principal executive. Finally, and some companies have moved well into this position, the senior executive is a general manager or publisher who can call upon all the modern marketing services to assist in the promotion of his or her product.

This leads to an alternative method of identifying the phase of development reached, by asking 'what is the product that a publisher is marketing?' In the first phase the answer is a journal: in the second, it is circulation that is being sold. In the third phase the product being marketed is an audience or a readership – vastly different from circulation. Apply the classical question 'what business are we in?' The answer is surely not writing (phase 1), or publishing (phase 2) but communications. It is only by accepting this concept that periodicals can maintain their predominant position in the marketing communications mix.

Publishing organizations

A good deal of change has taken place, not only in the emergence of a marketing concept, but in rationalizations and amalgamations which have facilitated the implementation of a marketing approach. The three organization charts (Figures 16.1, 16.2 and 16.3) represent the three phases of development, and while it may appear that they cover respectively small, medium and large operations, there are examples of the smallest of publishers being completely marketing-orientated and the largest still operating around the journal-production concept.

Many publications exist today which fit into the pattern outlined in Figure 16.1. Some are extremely successful in financial terms: others may even be satisfactory communicators. The basis of operation is that the editor intuitively produces an editorial mix which he or she has found over a period of time to be successful in terms of paid-for circulation. Advertisers, if they have liked the appearance and contents of a publication, have been welcome to participate providing they did not get in the way of the editorial. It was commonplace, and is still not unknown, for publishers in phase one of development to be unwilling to disclose even their total circulation let alone other data. The product is the journal.

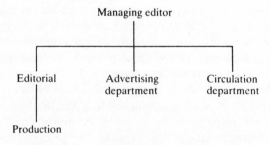

Figure 16.1   Publishing organization – phase 1

The editorial department here decides on editorial content regardless of any other considerations. It will usually control layout and presentation, production and sometimes circulation and distribution. The advertisement department is concerned with selling space, and indeed in the absence of adequate information to reinforce a sales argument, many space representatives are, through no fault of their own, little more than collectors of orders for space. At best they are salesmen of the old school whose success depends upon their personality and their ability to capture the confidence of a prospect – but in themselves rather than their product.

This over-simplification does not imply that a given management structure automatically places a publisher among the has-beens, nor that a managing editor is incapable of comprehending and implementing the marketing concept. There are exceptions as always with general rules and procedures.

The organization in Figure 16.2 may not appear much different from that of phase 1, but there is a higher degree of specialization, and the addition of some central services.

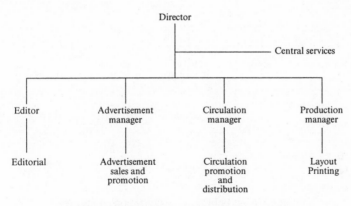

Figure 16.2   Publishing organization – phase 2

The differences lie not so much in the organization chart as in the significance of each of the functions in the business operation. A director at the head is to signify that it is an all-round business executive who lays down policy and makes decisions, and that these are on a commercial basis. The editor is rated level with the other departmental heads, and the advertisement manager, for instance, can expect to have as much influence on the make-up and presentation as the editor. Significantly, circulation is treated as a separate and important function with paid-for circulation giving way to free distribution if this is considered necessary to secure business.

Central services are an indication of the growth of publishers into larger units which can provide specialized facilities such as an art department and marketing communications. Further developments of central services take over responsibility for printing, sometimes distribution and even production and circulation.

Adopting the phase 3 concept of the 'product' being an audience and the 'benefit' exposure or access to that audience, it follows that the product development function in publishing is concerned with maintaining the right readership to meet the advertisers' needs (see Figure 16.3). While many products in industry remain static, at least for a short period of time, and therefore may not require development, in publishing the audience is in a continual state of change. As new readers register, and people move jobs, the audience mix will become unbalanced and therefore in effect a different product which may not be wanted by advertisers.

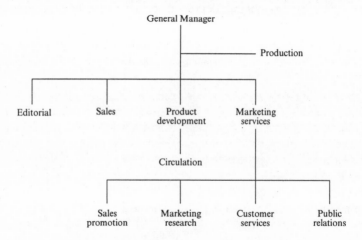

Figure 16.3　Publishing organization – phase 3

The 'market' is of course the potential advertisers, and so the starting point in the development of a product in publishing is to assess the market's needs, what audience does it wish to reach. This requires to be broken down into segments which will relate to, for example, industrial classification, job category, geographical location and size of firm. From this point it is necessary for the editorial team to devise an editorial mix that will appeal to the audience which emerges, and for a method of circulation to be set up which will reach it.

In marketing services, the research people will be monitoring the success of circulation, and the interest of readers in the editorial. They will study the impact of advertisements, the number of 'pass-on' readers and various other factors of importance to advertisers such as the value of different positions in a journal, the influence of colour, bleed and so on. These data will provide the ammunition which will be fired first by the sales promotion department and then by the sales force. Public relations will take as its task the building of good relations and a good understanding with all the publics of a journal including readers, advertisers, distributors, contributors, trade associations, suppliers and shareholders.

Customer services is a function which is not yet fully established in publishing. Each journal has certain strengths which derive from being in its particular business. Some of these strengths can be marketed in one form or another to existing and prospective customers. For example, a journal's circulation list can be hired out as the basis of a direct mail operation. The editorial team have technical knowledge which can be applied to the staging of seminars and conferences. The editors are writers, and some of this talent can be expanded into writing house magazines, leaflets for clients or film scripts. Publishers are also in a good position to sponsor exhibitions. 'Customer services' will also include carrying out specific assignments for customers, such as working with them to measure the total effectiveness of a campaign. Split runs for instance are easy to arrange, but few technical publishers offer this facility, let alone promote it as a sales feature.

Production is shown as a central service. So probably should be marketing services unless the idea of product groups is adopted. In this case, a number of complementary journals are marketed within one product group. The editorial teams need to be separate, but the sales force and all the other functions can be operated to serve all the publications in a group. This method of operation is particularly suited to larger organizations: indeed with large numbers of publications, it becomes necessary in order to maintain a workable span of management control.

Departmental functions

EDITORIAL

It has been said earlier that press advertising is 'too cheap'. This is evidenced throughout all departments in a publishing organization, but no more so than in the editorial department. Considering the national importance of technical journals in disseminating information on new developments in industry and commerce, it is disconcerting to find the conditions under which the editorial side is often forced to work because of the limited finance available to it. An editorial team often consists of little more than an editor and an assistant, and sometimes works under conditions of employment which are not attractive to specialists of stature and calibre. A comparison with the situation in the United States where there are relatively fewer publications, shows that an editorial team may be made up of a dozen or so specialists, each a respected authority in his or her own right.

Inadequate staffing leads to a high proportion of technical journals which are produced largely from press releases selected almost at random and mixed in with contributed articles from sources that may or may not be authoritative, dealing with subject-matter that tends to be determined by the contributors rather than defined as part of a planned editorial programme.

There is also a lack of research data to assist editors who therefore do not accurately know for whom they are writing: nor are they accustomed to having a feedback on which items are of interest to readers and which are not. Editors of most journals have to operate largely on the basis of experience and intuition.

ADVERTISING

Many publications function with only an advertisement manager and a secretary to sell their advertising space. Others have one or two space representatives. A commission system is usually built into the salary structure so that when a journal does well (often a matter of chance) high incomes can be obtained, and when it does badly the advertisement staff are underpaid. Opportunities for promotion have tended to be few, though this is changing as publishing groups grow and encourage interchanges between publications.

Publishers have difficulty in recruiting sales staff of high quality, and it is argued by many space buyers that representatives have little or no influence on the choice of media in an advertising schedule. The lack of media data is obviously a contributory factor here.

CIRCULATION

The traditional circulation manager on a subscription magazine may be little more than a senior clerk, sending out occasional mailing shots to prospective subscribers, attending trade exhibitions and dealing with renewals and the paper work involved in handling thousands of low value accounts. It is not generally realized that the cost of securing renewals is usually as high as the total net income from subscriptions; that is to say, it makes no difference financially to a publisher whether it sells a publication or gives it away.

Circulation departments are changing and some of the more advanced publishers are utilizing the most sophisticated equipment and techniques to secure at least the right circulation mixture, if not the right readership.

PROMOTIONS

In general, little effort is put into the promotion of either advertisement sales or circulation. This is rather strange when it is considered that the publishing industry represents the largest single item of promotional expenditure among its clients. Very few magazines use any form of advertising themselves, neither for that matter do they invest in any of the other channels of persuasion to any marked degree.

Lack of promotional activity is often an indicator of lack of anything to promote. Where this is not the case, an increase in sales promotion would help the publishers by making their marketing operations more efficient, and it would help the advertisers by providing them with more information.

PRODUCTION

Few publishers are themselves involved in the business of printing. Their production side then comprises one or two people concerned with bringing manuscripts to the repro stage, and pasting these up with illustrations according to a laid down design formula for the make-up of the journal including the disposition of the advertisements.

Methods of circulation

There are a number of basic methods of circulation, each with variations and each having advantages and disadvantages. Broadly it can be said that methods fall into two categories, paid-for and free.

PAID-FOR CIRCULATION

It may then be supposed that a paid-for readership is by definition an interested one, and indeed this is still arguable. There are two factors which operate against it from an advertiser's point of view. Firstly, many readers receive their publications from within their company, and therefore to them they are free. Secondly, a company tends to have an internal distribution list which often means that some readers receive a magazine weeks or months after publication, by which time it may not be of any great interest. Publishers of subscription journals will argue that the in-company distribution of their publications represents a strength in that it results in a readership many times greater than circulation. It could, however, be a weakness.

A special category of paid-for circulation is when a subscriber receives a copy of a publication as a result of being a member of an institute or association. Here there is often no pass-on readership: indeed it is not unknown for real readership to be somewhat lower than total circulation.

The problem with subscription journals is that since anyone can buy them, the publisher cannot, or does not, control who receives them, and therefore is not able to direct the circulation into those areas which are wanted by the advertisers. The circulation therefore is random, often highly fragmented and as a result sometimes not commercial. There are also real difficulties about determining where copies go, particularly if they are obtained through newsagents or bookstalls.

FREE CIRCULATION

The first journal in the UK to receive popular acclaim in the field of free circulation was *Industrial Equipment News*. Nowadays a good proportion of trade and technical publications are distributed free of charge either in part or in entirety.

The term 'controlled circulation' needs to be examined since the degree of control is entirely at the discretion of a publisher. The result is that in some instances it is applied only in a very loose sense and is often under the jurisdiction of a relatively junior employee. The fault lies as much with the advertisers, as with publishers, for not taking a stronger line and applying a greater degree of scrutiny.

At the lowest level there are journals which are simply sent out to a mailing list, with no requirement for readers to register or to qualify. Publishers may argue that such circulation is controlled since they control who they send it to. For instance, they may take the published list of members of an association and mail personal copies to each member. A refinement could be to eliminate people working for companies employing less than 100. Mailing lists can be purchased from specialist sources – some advertisers are willing to make their lists accessible, for instance, but it is important to realize that such mailing lists for a free circulation journal are never likely to be as good as those which a firm can produce for itself. Special caution should be applied to journals which overnight increase their circulation by a significant number, for instance, from 5000 to 7000. This can be, and is, done quite simply by finding some additional source of names and adding it to the existing list. Alternatively, by sending to the same companies on the lists, but instead of addressing one copy to the buyer, to address two copies, one for the buyer, one for the works manager. There is maybe a case for doing this, but the advertiser is well advised to scrutinize the details of the circulation methods adopted.

A number of free circulation journals require a reader to register and to be in one of a number of defined categories, for example to exercise a purchasing influence. Such registration ensures a measure of interest in a journal but if copies are sent only to those taking the trouble to register, the coverage of any one market is no longer 100 per cent. A further problem with registered readers is that they seldom cancel or transfer their application when they change jobs or retire. This leads to publishers inadvertently sending sizeable proportions of their circulation to dead-end addresses or recipients who no longer have any interest or importance. Moreover, there is no practical way in which an applicant's form can be authenticated by a publisher, and so the validity of a circulation even of 'applied-for' journals depends upon the validity of the data supplied by the readers, who tend to inflate the importance of their position as a means of obtaining a personal and free copy of a journal.

A method known as rotating circulation is a lesser used practice but poorly regarded. The technique is to build up a list of, for example, 50,000 firms, then send each consecutive issue to a different 10,000 until after five monthly issues all the mailing list has been covered. This tends to bring high enquiry response rates initially and enables a publisher to make claims about his circulation which may be misleading.

In general the concept of free circulation publications is based upon the sound marketing philosophy of defining a market then going all out to achieve a maximum share of it. Many magazines in this category have achieved outstanding success and are firmly entrenched as valuable advertising media. Readership researches confirm that they are hitting the target. While they do not get the same pass-on readership as subscription journals, they have the merit of going directly to the person most concerned who is able to give his immediate attention to it.

The editorial format which has become associated with free-circulation journals is perhaps unfortunate in that the concentration on new products, sometimes to the exclusion of features, confuses the issue and has led to the assumption that maximum reader response comes from free journals and that serious articles in depth are published only in subscription journals. This is not inevitably so: either editorial treatment or a mixture is suitable for either type of circulation.

HYBRIDS

Almost all circulations are hybrid in the sense that there are a proportion of copies which are free and a proportion which are charged at a lower rate than usual. Perhaps what is not realized is that many formerly paid-for journals have been forced by competition to inflate their circulation, and that this has been done by giving away copies. It is not unknown for a journal to have as many free copies as paid-for, but to trade under the heading of a subscription publication.

Authentic data

Publishing has been described as 'the last refuge for a gentleman', but this is not always true. Advertisers have been misled deliberately by some publishers who have blatantly said one thing and done another. This situation is changing fast under the influence of various organizations, notably the Audit Bureau of Circulation, but there are still many publications which are not prepared to submit their circulations to the independent audit which an industrial advertiser requires.

The ABC Certificate (see Chapter 12) represents a valuable step forward and its continued development will do much to increase the efficiency of media selection and thus advertising efficiency. In the meantime the growing demand from advertisers for data has led to a variety of publishers' information being supplied, and experience has shown that some of this is irrelevant, inaccurate or misleading. Circulations are known to have been quoted well in excess of the total market, and in excess of the print order. Circulation breakdowns by category have been known to be closer to wishful thinking than the actual facts of the case.

As always, the buyer would do well to exercise considerable caution, and adopt a tough line with suppliers who will not supply the service that is required.

17

ADVERTISING AGENCIES

Advertising agencies still suffer from their origin as agents for publications, selling advertising space to 'clients' in consideration of a commission from the media owners. From that point the situation developed to where agencies competed with each other by offering free services, primarily the creation of advertisements for their clients who not unnaturally accepted the services and asked for more. Gradually agencies identified themselves with clients rather than the media they represented until they cut adrift completely from individual publications and set up exclusive relationships with their clients, the advertisers. It was, and still is, difficult for them to be completely independent and objective in their relations with the media since the press (and TV) continued to pay a commission whereas certain other media, for example exhibitions, did not. Thus many supplementary services were provided for clients but were paid for out of commission from press advertising. The merits or demerits of this situation are examined later, but it explains why many agencies are still oriented around 'above the line' advertising, while their clients are often heavily involved in other forms of persuasive communications.

Agency organization

There are over 1000 advertising agencies in the United Kingdom split in numbers about evenly between London and the provinces. Since the largest agencies are almost exclusively in London this is where the greater majority of advertising agency activity is concentrated, but recent years have seen a significant growth in regional agencies.

Agencies vary from those consisting of one or two people, with a turnover of a few hundreds of thousands of pounds, to very large businesses employing hundreds and sometimes a thousand or more people and having turnovers of many millions. In comparing such turnovers with other businesses it should be remembered that profit margins are of a relatively low order, usually little over 1 per cent. It is true of any business that its strength lies first in the calibre of the people it employs, and this is especially so in agencies since that is all they have to offer – there is no plant and equipment to make good the deficiencies of human beings and relatively little in the way of scientific research, quality control and inspection to safeguard the quality of their output.

The organization of agencies is extremely varied in detail. There are some structural characteristics which can be isolated, and these are indicated in the following examples which are examined from the point of view of handling industrial accounts.

SMALL AGENCY

The organization shown in Figure 17.1 might be typical of an agency employing up to around 25 people and having a turnover of up to and over £15 million. It is more than likely that the managing director will handle one or two accounts himself or herself, as indeed may the creative and media directors. This would leave each account executive with maybe £2 million of billing. The primary business of this kind of agency is likely to be heavily directed to business press advertising but it often possesses special skills in the particular requirements of its clients, perhaps in sales literature or direct mail. It may be necessary to sub-contract outside services even for creative work, and the amount of effort available for media planning, at least in the media department, will be limited. There is no built-in provision for press relations, exhibitions or research. The span of control is already approaching a maximum, especially if the managing director is handling accounts personally as well as running the business.

Most people in the agency will know and care about most of the clients. The staff will therefore be sensitive about the needs of clients and the organization will centre around these needs rather than expecting clients to fit into a rigid procedural pattern. The following are some of the advantages and disadvantages which may apply from a client's point of view.

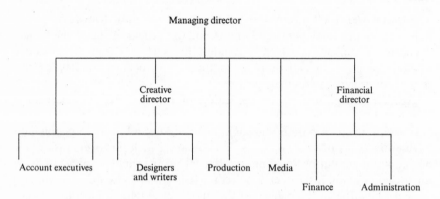

Figure 17.1 Small agency organization

1. Advantages:

   (a) Attention from top management
   (b) Quick response to needs
   (c) Short chain of command
   (d) Attention to personal details
   (e) Ease of identifying with clients' business
   (f) Often locally situated
   (g) Lower overheads, more economic costs

2. Disadvantages:

   (a) Lack of specialists
   (b) Difficulty in getting top calibre people to work in a small agency
   (c) Logistical problems in handling larger accounts
   (d) Over-dependence on a single person in the handling of an account
   (e) Lack of internal capacity, need to outsource
   (f) Lack of international connections

MEDIUM AGENCY

Such an agency may well be set up to handle medium-size advertisers and will employ people with appropriate talents and interests. The total number of employees may be a hundred or more with a billing of several tens of million pounds.

The organizational chart (Figure 17.2) shows a logical progression from Figure 17.1, with client service breaking into groups under the overall control of a director. Each group will contain three or four executives and be self-contained except for central services which may or may not include

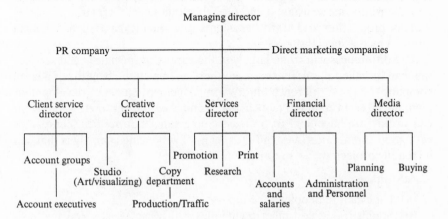

Figure 17.2 Medium agency organization

production and traffic. It is a matter of opinion whether there is benefit in the creative unit being centralized or integrated within each group. Whichever way it goes, however, it is important to have a creative director who can not only supply ideas and creative stimulus, but also ensure the maintenance of creative standards.

A feature in this size of agency is that it can justify the employment of specialists in media, research and print, as well as having associated companies to handle press relations and perhaps exhibitions, artwork, photography and so on.

1. Advantages:

  (a) Stable business of substance
  (b) Top people are likely to be able and experienced
  (c) Large number of account executives with a wide range of industrial experience
  (d) Availability of specialists
  (e) Access to associated services

2. Disdvantages:

  (a) Lack of personal attention from the top
  (b) Longer chain of command
  (c) Difficulty in getting instant response and attention
  (d) Extended and diffused internal communications
  (e) May not be fully resourced for the larger client

LARGE AGENCY

The kind of structure which may exist in a very large agency, is shown in Figure 17.3. There will be a group head with a number of account executives (usually with some assistants) and probably a number of creative people as well as production and traffic assistants and, in the case of a technical group, a media specialist.

The differences will come largely in the variety of specialists and services that can be called upon. Furthermore there will be all the benefits of a large company – a good reference library, a management and staff development plan, an IT section and a 'new media' section, eg the Internet. Most agencies of this size have not just overseas connections, but overseas companies with good communications, and the means of producing campaigns that can be readily projected on an international basis.

1. Advantages:

  (a) High calibre people at the top
  (b) Sophisticated consumer techniques which can be adapted for business-to-business advertising

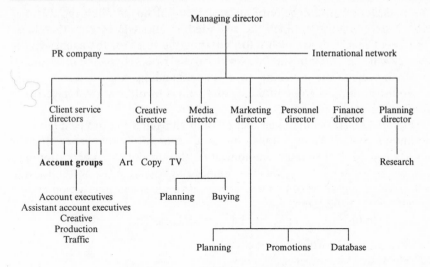

Figure 17.3   Large agency organization

    (c) Capacity to think big
    (d) Can provide virtually every service from within the company
    (e) Creative excellence

2. Disadvantages:
    (a) The business-to-business side may be regarded as the poor relation
    (b) Service is usually expensive
    (c) Work takes longer to produce, due to lengthy communications and internal procedures and disciplines
    (d) Staff are usually not so technical and have difficulty in interpreting a brief, particularly as regards copywriting
    (e) Smaller clients have to fit into agency organization rather than the agency changing to suit a client

Agency procedures

It is useful to examine the stages through which a typical job is likely to pass. It will be seen that, except in a small agency, there are a large number of people likely to be involved in the processing of a single advertisement. The question of effective communication becomes vital to ensure that the initial message and purpose are not lost or blunted, but rather sharpened and refined.

It is not always appreciated by the client how important the brief is to the agency. This, after all, is the raw material from which the advertisement or campaign is to be constructed. Inadequate briefing may be compensated by the persistence and tenacity of agency staff, but this is often the cause of high charges and jobs which are regarded as unsatisfactory by the client. The client must put as much into preparing the brief for the agency as the agency will subsequently put into its proposals. Briefs should be in writing in order to exclude the possibility of misunderstanding. A good starting point is to ensure that everyone in the agency who is involved should have had a thorough background brief.

Figure 17.4 shows the likely steps within an agency in the formulation of a campaign plan. Though appearing as a series of discrete steps, there is always a good deal of intercommunication throughout the preparation of a campaign. Media are very much influenced by research: the account group will have strong ideas of its own, and creative ideas will interact on almost every aspect of the campaign.

Points to be covered in agency background brief include:

1. Strategic and corporate objectives
2. Marketing objectives

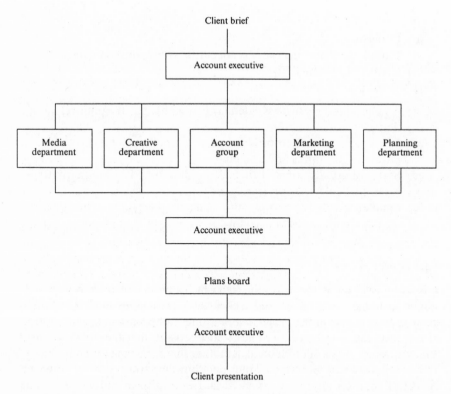

Figure 17.4   Agency procedural chart

3. Communications objectives
4. The market
5. The market need
6. The product
7. Competition
8. Price
9. Selling platform
10. Distribution channels
11. Pre- and post-sales service

First there is the brief from the client giving the objectives and requirements. The account executive is responsible for interpreting these to the various agency departments that are likely to be involved. The account group is shown as a separate function in this operation since while the account executive will bear the main load, there may be executives both junior and senior to him or her who will contribute to the plan. Research may be necessary to assist media planning and to provide intelligence for the marketing department. Creative personnel will not begin designing advertisements at this stage, but they should have the opportunity to express an opinion on whether press advertising is an appropriate vehicle from their point of view, or whether, for example, three dimensions are required: if press advertising, then does the nature of the objective indicate a need for double-page spreads, half pages or inserts? This will interact with media planning who may be concentrating on national dailies while creative want four-colour reproductions on art paper. The marketing department will examine the brief in a rather broader context and may be questioning the client's advertising brief in relation to its own marketing plan. There may be a call for a higher concentration on certain market segments – a proposition which if accepted will invalidate much of the media planning and perhaps throw the whole job back into the melting pot.

The planning of a campaign within an agency can be looked upon as a very intensive 'think' workshop: almost a long-drawn-out brainstorming session.

After the plan is agreed, it has to be implemented, and Figure 17.5 shows the stages through which a press advertisement is likely to pass.

This somewhat complex chart is an outline of what is probably a minimum of activity for an advertisement which develops without complication. At any stage there is likely to be a 'rejection' which can put the whole project back to an earlier stage, or even back to the starting point. The visual may be rejected by the creative head or by the group head or account executive. At the client end there may be two or three, or more, people who need to express an opinion. The artwork and sometimes the type mark-up may go through the same process, and the proofs may be subject to a number of revisions before everyone is satisfied. In the process of creating an advertisement there may well be two dozen or more points of decision-making

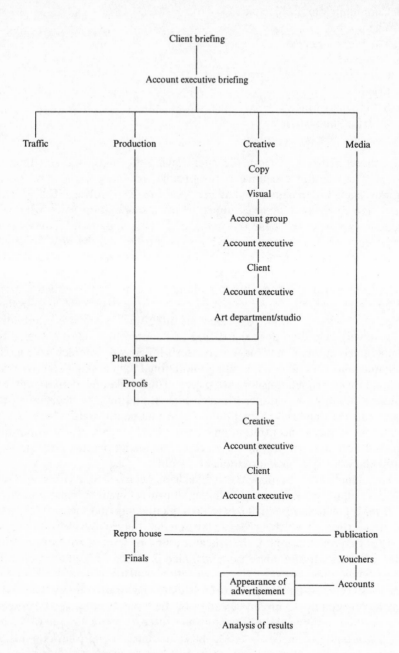

Figure 17.5   Advertising progress chart

before it is finally 'passed for press'. It will be seen that there is an uncomfortable similarity between this operation and a game of snakes and ladders!

Departments and functions

The functions and departments within an agency have been outlined, and their interrelationships examined. The roles of the principal ones are now considered in more detail.

ACCOUNT GROUP

Since there may or may not be an account group as such, it is the account executive or account manager who is considered principally under this head.

There are unquestionably some account executives (or supervisors, or associate directors) who are little more than message carriers between the agency and the client. At best such people might be regarded as liaison men or women. In business-to-business advertising, this is an unacceptable situation. The executive is the key person in the whole operation. He or she must understand fully the client's needs and interpret them with precision to the supporting staff at the agency. Thereafter the account executive must maintain a close watch on every stage of development, exercising direction and control where necessary, while retaining the respect and confidence both of the client and the agency personnel: he or she must mediate, persuade and enthuse colleagues, be a combination of diplomat, wet nurse, salesperson and dictator, and above and beyond all that must be a first-rate all-round business-to-business marketing executive.

MEDIA DEPARTMENT

The media department has two main operations, planning and buying. Both of these are important and call for a good deal of expertise.

Adequate data on industrial media are limited but growing in volume; also media planning is often highly superficial. General experience of industrial media is not enough in view of the large number of publications, and the large number of different products and markets which are all part of determining the media mix. A fully effective media planning operation is therefore likely to involve a good deal of investigation and research by very able specialists.

Media buying is not such an intangible business, but it is one in which significant sums of clients' money can be saved by careful planning and investigation coupled with ruthless negotiation and bargaining. Clients often measure the quality of a schedule by its 'added value'.

CREATIVE DEPARTMENT

This will usually comprise a mixture of writers, designers and typographers whose collective creative talents need to be welded into a cohesive team which will interpret product benefits into a visual selling proposition having impact upon potential customers. It is from this department largely that the spark of genius is needed to lift an advertisement out of the ordinary and into the outstanding.

It is basically 'ideas' which emanate from a creative department, not words and pictures. Its work therefore must be judged in terms of creative expression of a client's goods rather than by the graphic excellence of a final proof. It is also now increasingly the practice that an agency will use its own studio to produce finished artwork via IT equipment such as Apple Macs.

RESEARCH OR PLANNING DEPARTMENT

Too little research is put into industrial advertising, due often to the reluctance of clients to invest money in what at first sight seems a non-productive activity. Nevertheless, agencies are developing their research facilities which are being concentrated into media, advertisement and campaign evaluation.

Research departments are also able to carry out desk research themselves into markets both to supplement clients' own activities, and to provide data for the planning of campaigns within the agency.

Often a planning department will be a strategic point in an agency where the communications mix can be formulated.

MARKETING DEPARTMENT

Such a department usually exists only in the medium to large agencies, though some marketing expertise is usually available from other staff within an agency. There is also a trend to combine research and marketing into one 'planning' group.

Any agency marketing function can operate where the client has only a limited operation himself, or it can supplement it, or operate it as a second opinion. Furthermore it can work in conjunction with other agency departments during the preparation of an advertising plan. This will help to ensure that the advertising fits into the overall marketing strategy.

It is not uncommon for this department to be responsible for 'below the line' activities, that is those that do not bring a direct media commission.

PRODUCTION AND TRAFFIC

This is usually a central agency service often within the creative department but is sometimes carried out within an account group. The function, however, is to translate the 'creative' specification into print. That is to take the design, artwork, copy and type mark-up; order setting, obtain proofs, see to their progressing and eventual distribution. Production liaises here with the in-house studio.

Coupled with the production is the overall progressing of a job which begins when space is booked and goes on continuously, monitoring every stage until the advertisement appears and the invoices are cleared.

These are important services and are usually carried out very well by agencies: far better than a client could hope to do.

PRINT DEPARTMENT

A number of agencies providing a service for business-to-business accounts have found that there is a demand for sales and technical literature which can best be handled by a separate print department. This will usually include brochures, showcards and sometimes direct mail.

The writing and design work for literature will often be carried out by the main creative department, or perhaps by freelance people. The print department is then a specialized production unit which includes the function of print buying. Though the cost incurred may seem to be high, the result will usually show a good standard of professional workmanship.

PUBLIC RELATIONS

Most agencies do not have a public relations department, but rather an associated company which is thus enabled to take on business from companies not necessarily clients of the parent agency.

Editorial publicity in support of an integrated campaign will, in these circumstances, go through the separate company. Indeed, even where an agency has an integral PR department, it is more than usual to find that a separate executive has to be briefed on editorial publicity. Where this happens it is time wasted for a client, since the basic information is the same regardless of the medium. The selling platform, the product benefits, the creative expression, must be the same if a campaign is to have overall cohesion and impact.

EXHIBITIONS AND DISPLAY

As with public relations, it is not uncommon for exhibitions to be handled by an associated company. The same comments therefore apply as those on public relations.

One agency has a philosophy that an exhibition is only an advertisement with a third dimension. There is much to commend this attitude since many of the criteria for a good advertisement apply also to a good exhibition stand, for example stopping power, easy to read headline, punchy copy, and so on.

Methods of remuneration

As distinct from consumer accounts, which usually obtain their agency's services entirely out of the 15 per cent media commission, industrial advertising is usually undertaken only on the basis of an added fee. This may be to 'plus-up' all media commission to an agreed level, or it may be a flat rate per annum with or without media commission rebated. In between there are almost infinite variations, adjustments and understandings which enable an agency to recoup its expenses, though it is sometimes not realized how unnecessarily expensive the more complex payment systems are.

It is necessary to be clear about the method of remuneration for an agency. While, in the past, an agency was a representative for journals and newspapers, it was logical that it should be remunerated by a commission from the publishers.

If, however, an agency is operating on behalf of advertisers there can be no logical justification for payment other than from the clients it serves. The amount of space booked is quite irrelevant to the amount of work that is done by an agency either in terms of marketing communications as a whole or even press advertising alone. The creative time, the media planning time, the space booking time, the production, are the same whether for a 25 × 20 cm space in a plastics magazine or in a national daily. They are still the same if there is one appearance, or ten, and they are not much different whether they appear in one publication or a hundred. Furthermore, how can an account executive justify taking a briefing for a piece of direct mail when he or she is being paid out of commission from a magazine, for example?

Publications will continue to offer commission since in doing so there is a built-in attraction to agencies to place their business with them as opposed to other media. Agencies for their part are content to leave matters as they are since they can argue that only by using a 'recognized' agency can a client recoup the commission.

This is unsound practice from every business point of view and encourages inefficient operations and biased recommendations. The only basis upon which agency services can be justified is to pay for work done which, if not satisfactory, can soon be rectified by finding another supplier. It is difficult to see how the ending of the commission system could do other than benefit advertisers.

In the meantime it may be useful to give a detailed explanation of how agencies commonly 'plus up' their charges.

When an advertising agency places an order for an advertisement with a media owner, it will be charged the rate-card (gross) figure less an agency commission, commonly 15 per cent. Thus the client would pay £1000 for instance, but the agency only £850, ie it receives a commission of £150. This applies to all 'above the line' media such as press, TV, radio and posters. *NB*. Trade and technical journals only pay 10 per cent.

For non-commissionable services (below-the-line), an agency usually adds a sum as a handling fee. A bill for printing sent by a printer to an agency or consultancy will often be increased by 17.65 per cent. This may seem a very odd figure, and not many people know why. The reason is very hard to justify but comes about as follows:

£1000 + £176.50 = charge to client £1176.50 (gross)

Note: 15 per cent (the usual agency commission) of £1176.50 is £176.50 which when subtracted from the total leaves £1000.

So the charge of 17.65 per cent (of the net) enables the agency to recoup what would have been 15 per cent of the gross figure had there been a media commission. There is a trend, however to fee-only agreements.

Client–agency relationships

This is a problem which is written and talked about whenever advertising people meet.

It may be that the method of agency remuneration leads to clients being apathetic towards the quality of service derived from an agency, and this apathy encourages unwillingness to provide the material necessary for an agency to do a good job. The view often expressed by clients that an agency cannot produce good technical or industrial material is matched only by the view from the other side that clients seem incapable of providing a thorough and comprehensive brief. This is a failure in communications, and the failure is allowed to continue because neither side considers the real cost involved. The only other possible explanation for this communications gap is that the people concerned are inadequate, and if this is so, the solution is to employ people who are capable of doing the job properly.

If clients can obtain several designs and copy platforms 'free' they will not feel under pressure to ensure that they are precise in their briefing, nor will they put themselves out to spend time gathering background material which will enable agencies to hit the mark first time. Similarly there is no great pressure on account executives to put undue effort into projects since, if clients do not approve the first attempt, they can always have another. If, on the other hand, every advertisement design and copy was charged at market price, perhaps £1000 or so, and similarly every redesign, the whole procedure would necessarily tighten up considerably.

Over and above any considerations of the method of payment, most agencies can and will provide almost any service for which clients reasonably ask, providing there is a margin of profit. It rests then with the clients, who after all are the buyers, to demand the best standard of professional service, but to be prepared to pay for it. The mutual respect and confidence which must exist to obtain the best results will follow automatically.

Choosing an agency

The first question to be answered is why an agency should be necessary at all. The fact that almost all industrial advertisers use an agency does not necessarily prove that they are right.

The worst reason, but probably a common one, is that it is to obtain the benefit of the publishers' commission. The right reason has been summed up in an IPA publication.

The agency's most valuable asset is its objective and professional viewpoint. The analysis and assessment of a client's problems together with the unbiased, unemotional appraisal of specific market conditions, make a real contribution to efficient marketing and effective advertising.

An objective assessment of the need for an advertising agency leads to consideration of precisely which activities require servicing. This can then become the basis on which a choice is made. In other words a 'services specification' is required that will act as a coarse screen to filter out those companies that do not match requirements. Then their level of performance can be examined.

The objective assessment must come before involvement with the personalities concerned. Next comes the cost of the service, and the best value for money.

Finally, but in the end most important, are the personalities involved. The finest brains and the most businesslike organization are of little avail unless it is possible for the principals on both sides to establish an easy rapport which will enable them to work together as a team. The key figure here is the account executive who will ensure that the client receives the service he or she needs and demands. A weakness in creativity within the agency, for example, can be overcome by an effective account executive who will possibly insist on freelance services being used. As against this, an excellent creative team will find it difficult to produce effective advertising if the account executive is inadequate.

Perhaps it is appropriate at this stage to refer again to the role of the marketing communications manager. To obtain effective publicity, the manager must not only be professionally capable, but must be given real responsibility and authority. It follows that the appointment of an advertising agency is the responsibility of the marketing communications (marcom) manager. The marketing manager will certainly be involved, and is right to express his views, but the decision to hire and fire should rest with the chief communications executive. The results, good or bad, become his or her personal responsibility with all the advantages this brings. (See also Chapter 18.)

Checklist

In evaluating your present agency, or in making an assessment of a new one, have the following criteria been examined?

1. Agency management structure
2. Internal procedures
3. Basis of remuneration
4. Internal method of costing, plussing-up and charging: allocation of over-heads
5. Legal and financial status: major shareholders: issued capital: turnover
6. Clients – names, industry groups, billings, number of years, with named contacts for references
7. Experience in relevant industries and markets
8. Quality of advertisements in relation to brief of

   (a) Copywriting
   (b) Headline
   (c) Sign-off or action
   (d) Visual
   (e) Campaign continuity
   (f) Measurement of results

9. Campaign assessment in relation to brief of

   (a) Campaign plan
   (b) Copy platform
   (c) Media mix
   (d) Visual continuity
   (e) Measurement of results

10. Media services and expertise in

   (a) Press
   (b) TV
   (c) Direct mail
   (d) Merchandising
   (e) Packaging
   (f) Point of sale
   (g) Sales literature
   (h) Technical publications
   (i) Exhibitions
   (j) Photography
   (k) Press relations
   (l) Public relations

11. Research

    (a) Advertising
    (b) Media
    (c) Campaign
    (d) Market
    (e) Product
    (f) Other

12. Overseas connections
13. Regional connections
14. Personal compatibility with and professional capability of

    (a) Account manager
    (b) Account director
    (c) Creative head
    (d) Media manager
    (e) Research and/or market head
    (f) Managing director

18

OUTSIDE SERVICES

A changing feature of marketing activities is the extent to which outside services are used, as opposed to internal staff. This is partly due to a desire not to have a marketing department which is larger than absolutely necessary; due to the increasing specialisation of the marketing function, and the need for professional practitioners in each of the specialised areas. There are no absolutes in the sense of right or wrong, and perhaps it is best to first consider the strengths and weaknesses in very general terms.

Strengths and weaknesses

The first strength to consider of an advertising agency, a PR consultancy, or some such outside service is that it is likely to be far more professional than any in-company department. Whatever its size, the service will comprise a group of people whose sole activity is, and has been, in this one specialisation. And every day they are handling a range of clients with various objectives, plans, budgets, activities and evaluations. There is also the synergistic inter-relationship of the 'account-handling' staff who can refer to one another in arriving at solutions to their problems.

A second strength is objectivity. Outside advisers have no personal involvement; indeed, that is one of their weaknesses. They can look upon marketing problems and solutions completely dispassionately, uninfluenced by any of the factors which impinge upon an employee of a firm; 'what the boss thinks', or 'we tried it once, and it didn't work', will not cut much ice with a consultant. It might be said that client corporate culture will not necessarily have an overriding effect.

A third strength is the credibility of an outside organization, particularly if it is being paid a handsome fee. 'A prophet is without honour...' certainly applies to the way in which top management sometimes react to the recommendations of outside consultants as opposed to their own staff. It may not even be that the outside proposals are all that different to what has been said for years, but somehow the outsider seems to act as a more credible message source.

Finally, in the list of strengths, an outside service provides for a client company an expandable work force which can be increased or decreased substantially at very short notice. This is important in that no marketing campaign ever runs smoothly without peaks and troughs. There are frequently times when a much greater effort is required, just as there may crop up the need to stop an activity completely. The budget may have been cut for advertising, or all the campaign objectives are achieved prematurely. An agency will just stop work temporarily, whereas if such work is being carried out by one's own staff, what are they going to occupy themselves with now?

To counter the strengths of outside services it is necessary to consider their possible weaknesses, the first of which might be that their time is limited for any one client. They have other clients, each with their own priorities. Whereas with an in-house function a particular issue can be given a high priority like 'do it now', it may not even be possible to communicate with the client contact person, let alone obtain some service.

A second weakness, particularly in industrial marketing, is that the staff of outside agencies often seem to have merely superficial knowledge of the client's business, its markets or its products. How often does one hear of agencies submitting copy which has to be completely rewritten, or of a press release which has to undergo the same treatment? It may be due to inadequate briefing, poor communications, incompetence or lack of time, but it certainly happens.

A third factor is that outside services almost always seem to be far more expensive than expected. This is probably because the wrong criteria are used for comparison. A comparison might well be made between a PR consultancy with an average charge-out rate of £100 an hour, and an in-house person paid £25,000 pa which works out to £100 per day. This must be an unfair comparison since no overheads are included, but, in any case, an outside consultant can be hired in small increments as opposed to inside staff where one has an additional whole person or nothing at all.

A final weakness of outside services is that staff turnover seems always to be very high. No sooner has an account handler grown accustomed to the needs of a client, than he or she leaves or is transferred to another account. This leads straight away to the work being superficial which, in turn, must add to the expense.

There is thus no clear-cut answer in favour of or against a particular company using outside services. All that can be said is that their use is growing and that they are progressively becoming more and more capable. For efficient service it is necessary to pay special attention to the choice of an outside service, to its adequate briefing and, where necessary, to its evaluation.

It is useful at this stage to review the range of services on offer. Emphasis will be given to advertising agencies simply because they are the most frequently used service of all. Second place will be given to PR consultancies and thereafter all the others.

Advertising agencies

For the manufacturer of industrial products or for the supplier of services to business organizations, a special kind of advertising agency is required. Not everyone will agree with this proposition. Indeed, there are many who hold that since the advertising principles are the same for both consumer and industrial products, the practice is also the same and, therefore, any well set-up consumer agency can perform a thoroughly good job for an industrial client. There are three reasons why this is not the case.

1. Many industrial products and services are complex and specialized with the result that executives who are fully immersed in consumer products have difficulty in understanding the client's language, let alone interpreting it into a compelling and believable selling argument.
2. For the most part, the media are entirely different. Consumer marketing expertise in relation to television, newspapers and posters is of no value when what is needed is a broad knowledge of technical journals, exhibitions, literature, direct mail and the like. A further limitation is that consumer media planning is based upon extensive readership and market data. In the industrial sector the lack of information puts actual experience of industrial media at a premium.
3. Advertising budgets are relatively low, which leads to the necessity of charging a substantial fee, or alternatively providing a lower level service.

What are business-to-business agencies?

Quite simply these are what used to be called industrial agencies, but with a new name. There is good reason for this change in title since the expertise is not only in understanding industrial products, but more importantly the nature of the markets in which they are sold. And for the most part these markets are businesses or organizations. Indeed, there are some consumer products which also sell to industry, and here the expertise of a business to business agency is an important asset.

Otherwise the agencies operate as any other with a full service on offer, covering research, planning, creative, media and all the necessary administrative back-up. How do they differ?

BUDGETS

In industrial marketing, the balance between the cost of the sales force, product development, pre and post sales service, and advertising is quite different to consumer marketing. Advertising budgets are relatively small and considerable ingenuity is required to stretch them sufficiently to achieve the maximum effect. If budgets are small then income from media commission is even smaller. Thus a business to business agency has to be geared up to operate efficiently on a relatively low income. In many cases clients find it to their advantage to operate on a totally different financial basis, namely of paying an annual fee based upon the actual service provided. This has the advantage of ensuring that agency recommendations are totally unbiased, and even more importantly the agency is fully accountable for all the expenditure it incurs on a client's behalf. Media commission in this case is remitted to the client.

PLANNING

The first and vital stage of any advertising campaign is to produce the advertising plan. This requires an intimate knowledge of the marketplace. Industrial markets are not only extremely complex, but they also differ widely one from another.

The purchasing decision for a consumer product is relatively simple. When a company makes a purchase, however, the 'decision-making unit' is likely to be made up of technical specialists, purchasing executives, end users, and often several or even all members of the board. Identifying these purchasing decision-makers calls for an in-depth knowledge of industry and how it operates. Purchasing motives are also different. True, there are people involved who will each have personal reasons for wanting to make a purchase, and these may well be as subjective as any consumer purchase. But over and above these are objective and rational factors, with the buyer often in a position to evaluate fully and at length the performance of the product in question. The total number of prospects may number a hundred or so, and the value of the transaction may be of the order of hundreds of thousands pounds. All these factors require advertising to be planned in a completely different way for it to be really effective.

MEDIA

Since the markets are often numerous, and highly segmented, and since the managers making the decisions are likely to have completely different functions, it follows that matching the media to the markets is an intricate and specialized task. There is no room for the 'blunderbuss' approach of mass media; rather it is necessary to engage in precision targeting to ensure that advertising messages really do get through to the right people. A much wider range of media needs to be considered – trade and technical journals, management magazines, institution publications, sales literature, direct mail, seminars, conferences, exhibitions, sales aids, private shows, audio-visual material, editorial publicity, and so on. There needs to be within the agency a sufficient body of knowledge and experience to ensure that the most effective media mix is produced, having regard to the strengths and weaknesses of each medium.

CREATIVE

The creative magic is every bit as important in industrial advertising. Indeed, the creative opportunities from using such a wide variety of media are immense. But the creative inspiration must come across as authoritative and genuine, which calls for a knowledge on the part of the creative staff of the interests, motivation and terminology of the prospective customers they are addressing. In addition, there must be a realisation that the product benefits are likely to differ as between the financial director, the works manager, the purchasing officer and the chairman. Not only the media, but also the message, must match the market.

OBJECTIVES

Whereas in consumer advertising the primary objective may be to secure an increase in sales, in industrial advertising it is rarely that simple. More likely it is called upon to supply technical information and to generate enquiries. This can be followed up by mail, telephone and personal calling which will lead to a sale, but often after many months of careful negotiation. So the specific objectives are likely to be different.

TOTAL COMMUNICATIONS

The full service business to business agency plays an important role in a company's marketing operation, and for this reason its executives must have not only the necessary advertising skills, but also a working familiarity with the client's operations and the markets which they serve. More than that, it is not good enough to be restricted to the few major media channels which will suffice for a consumer campaign. It must be able to provide both counselling and executive action in any relevant channel of communication, no matter how unusual or difficult or financially unrewarding.

Media independents

These are a small number of organizations, sometimes known as media brokers. These companies set out to do no more than look after the advertising media interests of clients, ie excluding services in marketing, creativity (copy and design), research, production, etc. They are staffed by specialists in media and, thus, are able to provide a service, some say unequalled, in media planning and, in particular, media buying. They obviously have more muscle than any individual client when it comes to negotiating rates with the media. In relation to the needs of industrial advertisers, budgets are not usually high enough to make them interesting to a media independent, and they are probably not as knowledgeable about industrial media as the client.

Design studios

There are probably a thousand or more design studios, many of which will be individual consultants. They commonly provide design for a wide range of activities including press advertising, literature, direct mail shots, letter-heads, packaging, etc. Some of these businesses provide a broader 'creative' service, including creative ideas and copywriting. They are sometimes referred to as 'creative hotshops'. Design studios will not usually be geared up to handle media planning or buying, neither should they be expected to have any kind of marketing expertise.

PR consultancies

The term PR has been used deliberately in the sure knowledge that it is ambiguous. A number of outside services offer and provide a public rela-tions service, whilst a rather larger number offer press relations and nothing much more. The first step, then, is to decide exactly which service is required. If it is simply free editorial publicity that is required, the operation is very simple. Items of news and interest are found and delivered one way or another to the press to cover as they think fit. This is a vital, and probably the most cost-effective, channel of communications in the industrial market-ing plan. But it is not public relations. This is all about building a corporate reputation and developing efficient two-way communications between an organization and its publics. The latter will, of course, include customers and prospects, but they will also take in employees, shareholders, suppliers and, in fact, all the relevant stakeholders of a business.

PR consultancies are not, of course, consultancies at all. Some of them may set out to offer the kind of advice one might expect to receive from a consultant, but most of them are in the business of providing an executive service, just as an advertising agency or any other outside service. This raises an important issue since some client companies with particularly technical products or specialized services, may find that they are far better at putting together effective press releases and building up good relationships with industrial editors. But they can hardly fail to benefit from strategic PR advice and assistance in developing and implementing a PR plan.

Nevertheless, a PR consultancy will have all the strengths and weak-nesses described earlier. One can add to this a further benefit if it is needed. That is creativity. It is a fact that coverage in the press is dependent on the newsworthiness of the stories put out. With many firms in the technical/industrial/business fields, stories from new products alone provide more news than any one publication would be able to take in. Not much creativity is needed. With many consumer products, however, very little ever changes, and thus one needs a PR consultancy with lots of bright ideas on how to create news which will, in turn, publicise a product. There are, of course, numerous industrial products where things don't change too much – in basic raw materials, for example.

Most of the characteristics which have already been put forward in relation to advertising agencies are equally relevant to PR consultancies. There are about the same number of each in the UK, and they range from one-man/woman businesses to medium-size companies employing a few hundred people. There are some which specialize in industrial/business accounts, some consumer and some generalist. There are account handlers also, but here there is a difference in that these people have fewer back-up staff to call upon to help them. For instance, they mostly write their own copy, something which an agency contact person would never do. The other significant difference is that agencies are at least partly paid for out of media commission, whereas consultancies have no other income than the fees they charge.

Why are PR agencies hired?

The latest study by *PR Week* of why clients make use of a PR consultancy gives a breakdown as shown in Figure 18.1.

Why should I consider a PR consultancy?

Most public relations advisers are consultants: even the in-house professional acts as a consultant to his or her corporate and divisional colleagues. Public relations may be strategic, but it is not usually a line function. Organizations can use in-house or external (consultancy) professionals, or a mix of both.

WHAT MIGHT A CONSULTANCY OFFER?

Consultancies are as diverse as clients. Let us consider some factors that most have in common.

Independence

Good professionals should offer an unbiased perspective on the company and the issues it faces. Consultancy personnel can more easily offer candid views and say what needs to be said – not just what the client may wish to hear. Wise clients expect and recognize honest advice.

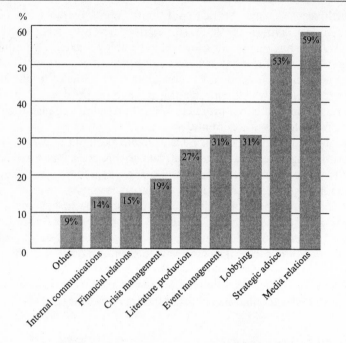

Figure 18.1   Why are PR agencies hired?

Expertise

Consultancy life is tough, and good people only succeed through real skill and talent. There will be few passengers in a consultancy, which means the quality of those working on the account should be assured.

Range of Skills

Many consultancies can employ a range of skilled executives beyond the realistic budget that might be available to staff an in-house function. Even if the budget were available, many talented consultancy people will *only* work in a consultancy because of the variety, pace and relative independence it guarantees.

Commitment

Ambitious people need to suceed and this can mean that a responsive client can get maximum input from consultancy personnel. Winning new business takes effort and holding this business requires great skill and considerable commitment. Good clients remember to praise good work (preferably in writing) which means the best consultancy people want to work on the account.

Continuity

The client should expect a named team to work on the business. There is no guarantee that personnel might not change – but the client could reserve the right to review the account should that happen.

Access

Sometimes (but not always), the consultancy may have clout in key sectors and even contacts that can be relevant, for example, in the media. An account director discussing three or four possible news stories weekly with the *Financial Times* may get better access than a smaller client company that might only handle this situation once or twice a year.

Resources

Many consultancies will have special departments, services or resources that can be called in onto the account where the need arises. These will only incur costs when they are utilised. Examples might include video production, internal communications or parliamentary divisions, regional or global offices and so on.

Economy

Consultancy is often seen as expensive. This is often because the true cost of the in-house department (with which the consultancy costs may be compared) are rarely calculated. Add in company pensions, cars, office space, support staff, training and so on, and the true difference is rarely more than 10 per cent, sometimes less. But remember, consultancy is bought as needed with the client paying for direct time with no unexpected costs.

Of course, there is the downside to each of these benefits. But consultancy is worth considering. The real skill is in selecting the right firm, getting measurable performance targets, agreeing a workable relationship then supporting the chosen team in your expectation of top performance.

PR distributors

A fast growing service sector is in providing distribution services from client or consultancy to the media. Activities can then be concentrated into preparation and writing of press releases, features and the like. Meanwhile their distribution can be left to specialist agencies who will provide a great deal of helpful reference, for example the names of the multitude of contacts to whom stories should be sent. This applies to the entire range of media – newspapers and magazines, as well as TV and radio.

Marketing consultancies

These are simply specialised management consultancies who, typically, are engaged on an ad hoc basis by a client company who requires top-level advice on some aspect of marketing. A major company will use the services of a marketing consultancy as an extension of its own marketing department; in effect, it buys in some extra time for a specific task. Alternatively, the client may require a second opinion on some aspect of strategic marketing. For the smaller client company, however, a marketing consultancy is often brought in to provide a level of marketing expertise which is not available amongst the permanent staff. It is not usual for a marketing consultancy to undertake executive work as against giving advice and drawing up, for instance, a marketing plan.

Direct mail houses

The whole direct mail process, which is growing in popularity, starts with the creative process of copy and design, then moves on to the provision of a suitable database. This is followed by the logistics of putting the scheme together and mailing it, and finally taking in the responses and handling them. Some direct mail houses will lay claim to handling the entire operation, and in consumer marketing this might be so. Chances are that in the field of industrial marketing, both the overall direction and also a great deal of the action will need to be handled by the client company itself.

The direct mail house excels when it comes to expediting the mailing. The mechanical processes of labelling and stuffing have been automated and can be carried out very efficiently and economically. It may be that creative services and the provision of lists had best be found elsewhere.

List brokers

These days, mailing lists or databases come from many sources including directories, journals, and company customer lists. List brokers make a business out of having access to large numbers of specialized mailing lists, which they will access for a handling fee. It is almost never possible to buy a mailing list, either direct from the original source or from a broker. Rather, lists are for hire and are supplied in such a way (eg direct to a mailing house) so that the hirer cannot get sight of the names and addresses.

As regards the quality of mailing lists, bitter experience leads one to the conclusion that considerable caution should be exercised when hiring lists. Many are considerably out of date and can result in major losses. If at all possible in industrial marketing communications, companies would be well advised to build their own mailing lists, and also make provision for keeping them up to date.

Telemarketing

Telemarketing is a fast-growing outside service in the UK, both for direct selling, market research, and other activities. It is well-established in consumer marketing, but in the industrial sector it has two disadvantages. The first is that it is probably unable to cope adequately with products, markets, or subjects which are technical. Secondly, it is likely to prove to be very much more expensive than an in-house exercise.

Other services

1. The outside service which almost all companies use is printing. There is always the option of putting printing through an advertising agency or PR consultancy, but the great disadvantage here is that of expense. The best solution is to build up an ongoing relationship with a particular printer who one learns to trust, both in terms of price and expertise. Even so, it is important that jobs should be periodically put out to competitive quotation.
2. Exhibitions are another activity in which outside services have a role to play. Choice of exhibition and location in the hall are matters which just have to be looked after by the client company itself, but when it comes to stand design and then stand construction, it is mostly beneficial to use outside services but always going through the procedure of competitive quotations.
3. The growing importance of audio-visual material has led to the growth of specialist outside services here. This is important since it is difficult for the non-specialist to produce material which is up to the required professional standard. Care must be taken to shop around for a supplier who can meet the requirements of the budget, since many AV suppliers are accustomed to doing business with clients in consumer marketing where budgets are higher, eg by a factor of ten or more.
4. Market research is an activity for which very few firms employ a specialist. As a result, any major research is usually contracted out whilst much minor research work is conducted in-house but, even so, this can be much better than no research at all provided that one is aware of the possible shortcomings. It is worth bearing in mind that a good number of research consultancies specialize in industrial and business markets and products.
5. A further outside service which is mentioned for the sake of completeness is that of commando sales. Here one can hire an outside sales force to supplement one's own. Such a facility is often used for a product launch so as to get to a large number of customers in a short period of time. As with telemarketing, the limitation lies in the ability of the sales force to take in the technicalities of an industrial or business product. This is essentially a consumer service.

Other outside services which can offer important benefits are:

Photographic agencies
Model agencies
Conference organizers
Translation services
Sales promotion agencies
Merchandising agencies
Recruitment agencies
Training organizations

Use of outside vendors

The latest study of the use in the US of outside marketing communications agencies showed the following:

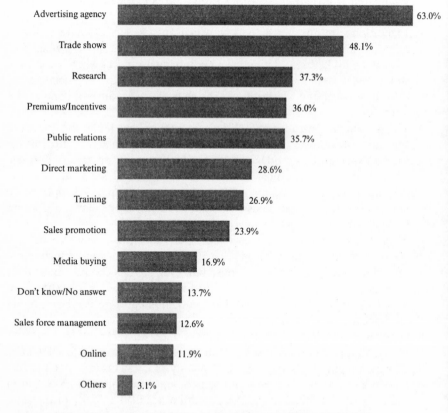

Figure 18.2   Use of outside marketing communications agencies
(*Source*: Outfront Marketing Study)

Using outside services efficiently

Particular reference here is made to advertising agencies and, to some extent, PR consultancies. The key to obtaining efficient service has to lie in the quality of the brief from the client company. It is convenient to consider the briefing as having two stages – the tactical brief, and the background brief. It is important that the tactical brief should be well thought out and should cover the complete story or message to be put across, together with a fine definition of the target audience. This should be in writing, and should have been approved by everyone who has a say in the matter. It is just not good enough to wait until the advertisement is proofed, or the press release written, before getting approval since this is a waste of time and, thus, money. Indeed, poor briefing is one of the reasons why agencies and consultancies are sometimes accused of being over-expensive.

Over and above ensuring that a sound tactical briefing system is in place, it is necessary to ensure that all the involved personnel have a thorough knowledge of the company. This calls for a comprehensive background brief, and for preference this should be no less than the whole marketing plan as described in Chapter 2.

Table 18.1   Tactical advertisement brief

---

1. Product/service details
2. Specific objective(s)
3. Market segments: DMUs (quantify), geographical location
4. Product benefits: (prioritize)
5. Competition
6. Selling proposition/copy platform/illustrations
7. Media:
     Frequency
     Size
     Colour
     Special requirements
8. Action – response mechanism
9. Timing
10. Budget:
     Space
     Production
11. Other marcom activities

CHOOSING OUTSIDE SERVICES

The most difficult outside service to choose is probably an advertising agency, followed by a PR consultancy. These two will be looked at in some detail.

Changing an advertising agency – selecting a new one – has always been a major, sometimes massive, and often traumatic process. And yet if anything, it happens more often these days and has become even more complex due to the wider variety of available choice and the confusing rate of change of people, organizations, services and, not least, the names of agencies themselves.

Why change?

Since a change of agency brings with it considerable upheaval for everyone involved, the decision is obviously not lightly made. Why then, does it happen? A special study suggested that the reasons could be divided into 'minor irritants' and major or fundamental facts. Irritants include poor reception/telephone contact problems; non-availability of agency people; invoice errors; late invoices; budget control problems; and staff changes. These factors, it was suggested, tended to cause a client to become more concerned with or aware of more fundamental failures such as over-spending, strategy disagreement, disenchantment with agency teams, advertising execution problems, and so on.

How Often?

A study by the writer of the frequency of change showed that over a ten-year period exactly half the respondents changed their agency once, a quarter made no change and the remainder had made up to three or more changes. Comparing these results with a similar survey done seven years previously, it appeared that agency changes were less frequent then as indicated by the fact that half the clients had made no change at all over five years and one-third no change over ten years.

It is difficult to quantify agency changes with any accuracy, but taking an average of five years and assuming 10,000 accounts/clients, there must be some 2,000 agency changes a year. Interestingly, the latest report from the US shows an average 'agency life' in the consumer field of three years, and of seven years for business or industrial agencies.

What to look for

Each client company will have its own very specific requirements, but the starting point for any new agency search must be to formalize and identify these so that some order and method can be introduced into what must always be a highly subjective and personalized judgement.

A piece of research into the selection of agency showed the most important factor to be creativity in design and writing, with particular references to the products and markets in question. Other factors were:

Quality of staff	000
Knowledge of 'our' business and an interest in it	000
Good service	000
Professionalism	00
Within easy reach	00
Competent media selection	00
Enthusiasm	00
Experience on similar accounts	00
Evidence of good work on other accounts	00
Organization and administration	00
Knowledge of marketing	0
Wide range of services	0
Cost consciousness	0
Small agency	0
Length of service of staff	0
Integrity	0
Overseas connections	0
Service fee	0
Personal interest	0

Key: 000   Highest significance
       00   Moderate significance
        0   Of some significance

The first and most important step is to draw up a specification. This must outline the complete range of activities which you will require, together with the 'profile' of the ideal organization, eg location, size, other clients, method of charging, etc. The choosing process can then be examined in three stages – coarse screening, fine screening, and the pitch.

The coarse screening stage starts with the identification of, say, a dozen agencies which would appear to be candidates for further scrutiny. Obvious sources of names are one's existing file of likely agencies that have sent in details over the past few years. To this can be added any that one has heard about in a favourable light, and any which may be recommended by colleagues and acquaintances. The really serious work, however, must be done with a directory, which might be the *Advertiser's Annual* or, alternatively, the quarterly (small) edition of *BRAD* (British Rate and Data). In both these publications there is a comprehensive list of advertising agencies together with their clients. It is relatively easy to identify those which are likely to have ongoing knowledge of at least the relevant markets, if not products, providing they are not competitive. Alternatively, there are one or two companies who specialize in agency selection, such as the Advertising Agencies Register. Another important source of information is the IPA (Institute of Practitioners in Advertising). For existing advertisers, of course, it is worthwhile consulting advertisement sales representatives, many of whom have an intimate knowledge of agencies with expertise precisely in the areas in which one has an interest. Thus, one compiles a coarse screen list of candidate agencies. Write a personal letter to the managing director, together with the specification, asking if there would be any interest in taking on a new account. At this stage it is best to keep a distance away from a dozen or so candidates and get them to outline their suitability by post. This avoids lengthy meetings and, from experience, it is usually found to be easy to make a rough choice from the information which will be supplied. The objective here is to arrive at three or four agencies which, on the face of it, might be able to handle your account.

With the short-listed agencies the fine screening is reached. The first step is to visit each and receive a 'credentials' presentation. This is where the agency will put up its very best work for inspection. For some this will be the most important part of the selection process, since this is work actually completed together with some indication of the results achieved. There is no reason why the clients themselves should not be contacted in order to get their opinions on the campaigns which have been presented, not to mention for some comment on the agency in question. The next step will be for the agency to visit you and to meet all the various people they would have to do business with, should they be appointed.

For the agencies which survive the fine screening stage comes the pitch. Here a detailed brief is given on some real marketing communications problem, or even the entire company programme for the next year. Each agency is given a fixed amount of time to come up with their proposals – the overall plan, media, budget, and, very often, first creative thoughts. In some cases, a nominal charge will be made. On the basis of such a series of competitive presentations, probably to a number of senior company managers, the final choice will be made. For industrial advertisers, some thought must be given to the validity of the final selection process. Can a candidate agency really gain an adequate knowledge about a client company in the few weeks allowed to it to make a presentation which will do justice to the problem? Or will it lead to the very weakness that many agencies are accused of, namely, of being superficial and lacking in technical knowledge? It is for this reason that the credentials presentation is so important.

The choice of a PR consultancy follows exactly the same path, but with a few minor differences. At the coarse screening stage, the directories to use are the *Hollis Directory* and the *PRCA Year Book*. Advice on matching a consultancy to a client specification can be obtained from the PRCA (Public Relations Consultants' Association) and the IPR (Institute of Public Relations). A very useful rundown on choosing an agency is given in a paper published jointly by ISBA, DMA and IPA which is reproduced below, with kind acknowledgements.

ISBA/IPA/DMA pitch guide

Joint guidance note for clients and agencies – best practice in the management of the pitching process.

FIVE CONSIDERATIONS BEFORE UNDERTAKING A PITCH

1. The selection and retention of the right agency is critical for a client because of the key role that the advertising agency is able to play in promoting the company's brands and enhancing its ultimate profitability. Long-term relationships benefit the health of the brand. Try to make the existing relationship work rather than thinking that a move is necessarily the answer.
2. If there is a requirement for a new advertising campaign, it will not always be right to pitch. An alternative is to approach an agency with whom the client is already familiar, perhaps through work on another brand.
3. If the client proceeds to a pitch, it is not always appropriate to have a full creative pitch: strategic direction may suffice.
4. Throughout the process of the pitch both client and agency need to establish agreement on copyright and confidentiality on material that is produced by the agency or supplied by the client for the pitch.
5. The objective of the ten stage pitch process outlined below is to optimize the quality of response and the likelihood of selecting the ideal partner.

THE TEN-POINT PITCH GUIDE

1. Prepare all the necessary background information

Prepare an outline brief.

Consider the role of advertising and other marketing communications and the potential contribution of the agency.

Consider the type of agency required (eg in terms of size relative to budget, location and specialization).

Many of the following notes assume that the client is looking for a full-service or creative agency – but the essential advice applies to specialist media agencies too.

Study the trade press.

Identify relevant existing advertising which you rate highly.

Talk to colleagues in other companies.

Seek credentials information from, and possibly talk with, selected agencies which match the criteria in your outline brief. Be aware, however, of the dangers of information on your search becoming widely known.

Approach ISBA and IPA for confidential information and detailed advice if appropriate.

Consider other professional, objective and confidential sources of information for the search (list available from ISBA, IPA and the DMA).

Evaluate the information against your checklist.

2. Invite up to three agencies to pitch (or up to four if incumbent included)

Decide on a positive list of up to three agencies only.

If the incumbent agency is invited, the list can go up to four.

Don't be seduced into lengthening the list.

Competing agencies should be aware of the number on the list and whether the incumbent agency is included. The client should confirm in writing whether the pitch process and the names of participants are confidential.

3. Think of the response required and prepare a written brief accordingly

Prepare a concise but thorough written brief for the competing agencies.

Identify and make clear all aspects on which the agencies' presentations will be judged and advise the approximate duration of the pitch presentation period.

It must be clear from the brief whether strategic proposals alone are required, or whether some creative ideas or a full creative pitch are expected. Agencies should respect the client's wishes in this.

Be explicit about the nature of the services which you expect to use.

Indicate proposed remuneration and contract terms.

4. Consider the time necessary for response to the brief

Prepare a firm timetable for the total pitching process and stick to it.

Time must be allowed for constructive ideas between brief and presentation.

A minimum of four weeks is suggested for work to a full creative pitch (after all, in an ongoing relationship proper proposals take weeks or even months to develop).

5. Help the process by demonstrating commitment with some financial contribution

The client should decide whether to make a contribution to the pitch.

Some financial contribution (announced upfront and the same offer made to all agencies on the short-list) shows commitment and the seriousness of your intent. The objective is to motivate the agencies: the contribution is not likely to cover all the third-party, staff and associated costs.

6. Give background market data, interpretation and clarification

The client should be willing to share, on a confidential basis, market data and other relevant research and allow agency personnel access to people in the company with whom they would work if appointed.

Ensure that there is always a specified senior member of the client's company to handle all enquiries and meet requests of the agency – to ensure consistency of response. Allow the same rules of access to all those pitching.

7. Understand the roles of all those involved on both sides, and set up an objective evaluation system

Ensure that all the decision-makers have been fully briefed and that they are all present at each pitch.

Advise the agencies of the job titles and roles of those attending for the client.

Establish an objective evaluation system for assessing each pitch.

Ensure that the agency presentation teams include people who will actually work on the business.

Allow enough time (perhaps two working days) for participants to attend, ask questions and discuss the presentations.

8. Insist on necessary business disciplines before an appointment is made

Ensure that the business side (contracts, remuneration and the management of the relationship) are discussed before an appointment is made.

Help in the form of information and relevant courses is available from the ISBA, IPA and the DMA.

9. Decide quickly and inform fairly

As soon as possible after all the presentations, normally no more than one week (except in those special cases where it has been agreed to put competing creative work out to research), decide on the winning agency. Establish a firm procedure for notifying (both successful and unsuccessful) agencies of the decision.

Ensure that all pitching agencies learn of your decision on the same day.

Immediately issue a press release to the trade press.

10. Embrace the new agency into a long-term relationship and treat the losing agencies courteously

After the pitch, give the losing agencies the courtesy of a full 'lost order' meeting.

Any losing agency must return all confidential material and information provided for the pitch to the client and the client, on request, must return the losing agency pitch presentation.

Honour the incumbent agency's contract, particularly with regard to the agreed notice period and payment of outstanding invoices.

Ensure that they co-operate fully in a handover to the new agency, making sure that all materials belonging to the client, in accordance with the contract, are handed back to them.

Welcome the winning agency into the start of a long-lasting and mutually satisfying relationship.

Advertising agency audit

One of the most elusive factors in the whole advertising process is finding some effective means of assessing an advertising agency's performance. A tried and tested method is to set up a structured annual agency audit which will give an immediate measure in absolute terms, as well as providing an excellent bench mark for measuring change in the level of client satisfaction. The same methodology can obviously be used for assessing a PR consultancy. The key to setting up an agency audit is to draw up a list of, say, ten criteria against which an agency's performance is to be judged. This will naturally vary from one client company to another, as will the particular importance of each item.

The criteria then go to form the basis of an annual review meeting in which the client gives an assessment of the extent to which the agency has provided the service required. This can be simply against a semantic rating, such as 'very good', 'average', or 'completely unacceptable', or it can be against arithmetical ratings in which a mark is allocated against a total possible score.

The format is very simple, quick and, most importantly, inexpensive. A meeting is set up in which the key people from both agency and client come together to give a frank exchange of views. Against the client's appraisal, the agency will have the opportunity to give explanations, and agreement can be reached on a course of action.

This process should not be seen as a preamble to the agency being fired. On the contrary, by highlighting dissatisfactions before they reach a critical stage it is at the very least a way of avoiding such terminal action. Indeed, the agency audit should be seen as a way of applauding good service, and of giving credit where it is due.

The following is intended to serve as a checklist on the whole range of agency services. Each in turn can be examined in order to identify the need for change, if any, and to pinpoint areas of satisfaction and dissatisfaction. The figures in brackets are given as a guide to quantifying the audit by allocating marks of satisfaction against a possible weighting. They will obviously vary from client to client, but they have been chosen such that the total possible ratings add up to 100. Thus the allocated ratings when summated represent a percentage in which 100 per cent indicates complete satisfaction, and any lower score shows a measure of dissatisfaction, with an immediate indication of where remedial action is required.

1. Basis of remuneration (5)
2. Methods of costing, plussing-up, and charging: allocation of overheads (10)
3. Knowledge of relevant industries and markets (10)
4. Quality of advertisements in relation to brief of (15)

    (a) Copywriting
    (b) Headline
    (c) Sign-off or action
    (d) Visual
    (e) Campaign continuity
    (f) Measurement of results

5. Campaign assessment in relation to brief of (15)

    (a) Campaign plan
    (b) Copy platform
    (c) Media mix
    (d) Visual continuity
    (e) Measurement of results

6. Media services and expertise (planning and buying) in (15)

    (a) Press
    (b) TV
    (c) Direct mail
    (d) Merchandising
    (e) Packaging
    (f) Point of sale
    (g) Sales literature
    (h) Technical publications
    (i) Exhibitions
    (j) Photography
    (k) Press relations
    (l) Public relations

7. Research (5)

   (a) Advertising
   (b) Media
   (c) Campaign
   (d) Market
   (e) Product
   (f) Other

8. Overseas operations (5)
9. Personal relationships and professional capability of (15)

   (a) Account executive
   (b) Account director
   (c) Creative head
   (d) Media director
   (e) Chairman
   (f) Managing director

10. Meeting scheduled dates (5)

A good target to be set for absolute excellence is a score of 80 per cent or more.

Part 6

A LOOK TO THE FUTURE

Segmentation: marketing way
marketing comm.

bus – bus
bus – customer } externally

bus } internally ▷
↳ job des
▷ prog – adv
▷ customer info
▷ role o
▷ concept of

bus
str
↳ return

~ customer ▷ xpectations
~ faster
~ ind./personal

Selling
product message (promotion)
price
competition customer
↳ overseas market

19

RELATIONSHIP MARKETING

Relationship marketing is a developing marketing discipline, combining many activities which have been in place for years with some newly-emerging facilities primarily involving the increased accessibility of IT, both hardware and software. Its inclusion as a separate chapter in this book is due to the fact that it depends for its successful implementation on marketing communications, both traditional and also new and specialized.

The starting point for this development is to obtain a new balance between efforts to hold on to existing customers and setting out to find new ones. Whilst both objectives have always been in place, the fact of the matter is that the balance of a firm's activities, and in particular its marcom spend, has recently been heavily in favour of attracting new customers.

Then there has been the change in the role of marketing itself, which is moving into a role superior to selling. Managers are considering, and indeed measuring, customers' needs and wants and adapting their offerings to meet them, then making this the basis of their messages, as opposed to concentrating on the products themselves and their attributes.

Another aspect of the widespread acceptance of the marketing concept has been to regard all employees as being in marketing, the only differentiation being that there are broadly two groups – customer-facing, and those providing service and support to the customer-facing group. Thus the messages transmitted by an organisation are the sum total of all message sources, both people and other.

On top of all this is the attention being given to customer turnover, whereby a measurement is made and targets set for the number of retained customers per annum (or other period), the number lost and the number of new ones acquired. This is coupled with a measure of customer satisfaction, and evaluation of the 'lifetime customer', all set against the very much higher cost of attracting a new customer as against holding on to an existing one.

The spur to take some new action comes from ever-increasing competition, particularly from international sources, which is attacking both home and overseas markets. Relationship marketing, then, is a cocktail of strategic marketing, database marketing, customer satisfaction, customer retention, public relations, corporate image, information technology and TQM. It takes in closer scrutiny of the decision-making unit (DMU) and more narrowly-defined market segmentation to the extent that it aims for 'people segmentation'. In communications there may well be a movement from marcom support for the sales force, coupled with the provision of leads, to a state in which, in many instances, marcom becomes the *only* sales effort. After all, a sales representative in the field can cost well in excess of £150,000 pa, and will maybe make an average of three calls to secure an order. That represents a massive cost compared with other channels of communication. Even if in industrial and business-to-business marketing face-to-face contact still remains necessary to clinch a deal, the role of marketing communications must be to strive increasingly to filter through only those prospects who *will* buy, rather than those who just *might*. The final factor in this equation is that the cost of deploying people in the field is rising, and will continue to rise faster than all those channels which fall under the aegis of marketing communications.

The ladder of customer loyalty

Relationship marketing strategy can be said to be based on a somewhat amplified 'ladder of customer loyalty', as shown in Figure 19.1. Here, the starting point is with all those people (not firms or organizations – one can only communicate with people) who go to make up the 'suspects' in a particular market segment. They may or may not become customers – establishing this requires some form of filtering mechanism. Thus the first step in marketing communications is to obtain enquiries, which can then be followed up to see if they qualify as 'prospects', ie there is a good chance that they will place an order within, say, 12 months. The full sales armoury is now brought to bear by way of visits, demonstrations, quotations and personal advocacy.

The placing of the first order changes a prospect into a 'customer', from which point one of two things can happen over the course of time: either a repeat order is placed and the customer becomes a 'client'; or the customer can begin to have doubts about the supplier, ie suffer from a condition known as cognitive or post-purchase dissonance. If this condition is allowed to fester, not only will the customer place business elsewhere, but may also turn into a 'critic'. So 'reassurance' is a major task for marketing communications if customers are to move upwards on the loyalty ladder.

A client becomes a 'supporter' when, if asked, a positive, supporting view is given of the product. But this is reactive. What one must aim for is a pro-active situation in which a customer insists on telling all and sundry what a success a product has been, ie the customer becomes an 'advocate'. This stage requires a first-class product, of course, coupled with competitive price, better than

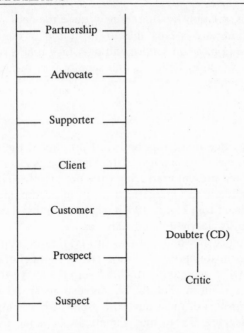

Figure 19.1 The Ladder Of Customer Loyalty

expected delivery and outstanding service, but even then a continuous supply of information is required to cultivate the growth of a vocal partisan.

The final stage in climbing the ladder of loyalty is where the customer develops a mutually beneficial 'partnership' such as happens with a JIT (just-in-time) delivery service, or joint advertising, or even joint R&D.

Transaction marketing

In laying down a marketing strategy there are two routes to be considered – a 'conquest' strategy, and/or a 'retention' strategy. Most firms will choose a combination of both, ie aiming to add to the total number of customers as well as devoting some resources to maintaining business from existing customers. It is, then, simply a question of degree, and the concept of relationship marketing is that there should be a heavy emphasis on the latter. Transaction marketing is simply another term for a conquest or offensive marketing strategy, where a campaign is concerned primarily with acquiring new customers. So the focus may be on a single sale over a short time-scale, with maybe little emphasis on customer service, and no more than the minimum required customer contact. The selling messages are based on product features or attributes, and quality is primarily the concern of production.

As against this, relationship marketing is quite the opposite. It focuses on customer retention, and is thus able to justify a high degree of customer contact with an emphasis on service and on a long time-scale. The orientation is towards customer benefits, and quality is a prime concern of all aspects of the business.

Conquest strategy

Already, leading edge marketers both in Europe and the US are holding that transaction marketing is out of date. Since this is clearly not so, it is as well to set down the present marketing structure, if only to make a comparison with what is likely to emerge as a result of all the changes which are slowly taking place. From Figure 19.2 it can be seen that a conquest strategy breaks down into six clearly-defined activities.

Personal selling is shown as the first function, as in industrial marketing this is seen as the most important, if most costly, channel of communication. This is followed by all the media which fall into the above-the-line category. This is where the main marketing communications spend is concentrated, and takes in all groups of press advertising but with an emphasis on trade, technical and business. There may sometimes be some use of television, radio, outdoor and posters, and even cinema. The remaining media, almost by definition, come under the heading of below-the-line. The largest spend here is on sales literature, and other collateral or deliverables. Expanding fast are exhibitions, both public and private, together with seminars and conferences. Strictly, publicity is a below-the-line channel of communication (it has nothing to do with public relations), and there is a wide range of merchandise and sales promotion.

Direct marketing is, strictly, below-the-line, but is now so important as to justify a heading of its own. The term is sadly very confusing and is short for 'direct response marketing', which in turn means any system of marketing (not marketing communications) which results in the product going *direct* to

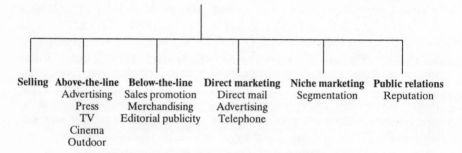

Figure 19.2 Conquest strategy (offensive marketing)

the customer, ie without going through an intermediary such as a wholesaler, retailer, business partner or other agent. In practice, however, it has come to mean any direct contact, including enquiries and leads, which more properly come under the heading of 'direct response advertising'. Another term is now coming into place, namely 'database marketing'. Whatever the terminology, this category covers direct mail followed by telephone calls under the heading of 'telemarketing', and any other form of advertising, above- or below-the-line, which sets out to generate some kind of response.

One of the latest marketing buzzwords is 'niche marketing'. This term actually starts to move towards relationship marketing, since it is all about narrowing the focus of communications to those who can be said to be 'hot' prospects. In other words, it is no more than market segmentation taken to its narrowest bandwidth.

Finally, in transaction marketing public relations has an increasingly important part to play in overlaying product perception with corporate image or reputation.

Retention strategy

The strategy here is to achieve the objective of getting more business from existing customers by means of exceeding customer expectations. Thus we set about establishing the various criteria which must be met in order to provide the right level of 'customer satisfaction'. For this to be able to be monitored, a 'customer satisfaction index' is set up, and this measures all of the many factors which will lead to a targeted level of satisfaction, pleasure, or even delight.

Once again, this process has been broken down into its component parts (Fig. 19.3), but this time it doesn't start off with the sales force, since this is regarded as an element of relationship marketing. As with a conquest strategy, any above- and below-the-line communications to prospects (acquisition strategy) may also be received by customers, thus contributing to any retention strategy. Public relations is shown here in rather more detail simply because this does not often include face-to-face communications but, rather, relies upon other channels. Reputation is clearly most important, and this is shown as coming from three centres: the corporate culture of the organisation ('do I feel happy about buying from such a company?'); the corporate identity in all its forms; and from what has been referred to in the 'Public Relations' chapter (14) as message sources. Service now appears as a separate function, and at this stage is broken down respectively into services provided by processes and those provided by people.

Conceptually, relationship marketing which makes its first appearance, is no more than external people (customers) communicating through all appropriate media to as many internal people (employees) as are likely ever to be in a position to transmit (and receive) favourable messages.

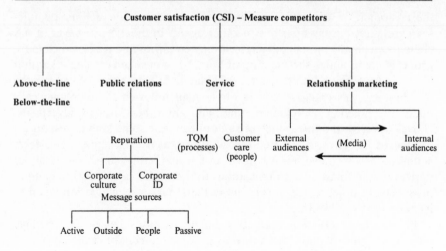

Figure 19.3   Retention strategy (the lifetime customer)

Service

In relationship marketing, the service element changes from sending out service engineers to put right something which has gone wrong with the product, to a procedure which becomes a vital contributing factor in competitor differentiation. It provides an additional competitive edge, or differential advantage.

In Figure 19.4, service is shown as breaking down into three parts. Pre-sales service may start off with an organization's reputation for giving advice and solving problems in a particular field. Then there are 14 principal types of contact with customers, which all contribute to the growth and development of the customer's perception of an organization which is a leader in its field and safe, or even a pleasure, to do business with. The actual 'sales' stage is shown as being a lot more than just delivering the goods, and can only be regarded as complete when the customer is entirely satisfied or even delighted with the product.

'Post-sales' is where relationship marketing comes to the fore in that the concept of the lifetime customer is introduced. A major factor is providing reassurance to overcome any post-purchase dissonance, and in sending reminder communications which, among other things, will take in new products and new applications. The customer satisfaction index will show how well the service factor is contributing to the well-being of the relationship.

Total quality management (TQM)

This concept now changes from being one which deals principally with

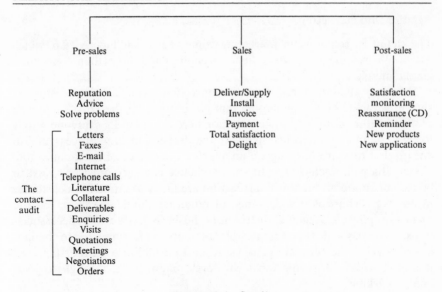

Figure 19.4   Service

manufacturing to one which comes into force in all aspects of an organization's business, involving both processes and people. It means very simply that at every interface between a company and its customers both the practice and the perception of quality will be involved. This will take in research and development, raw materials, packaging and presentation, and distribution. And the latter will involve all direct contact (eg direct marketing) as well as indirect contact such as occurs in the use of intermediaries such as business partners and, where applicable, wholesalers and retailers.

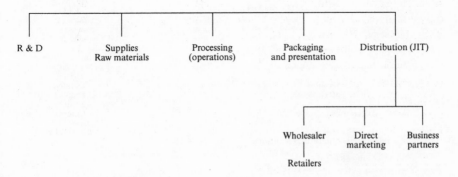

Figure 19.5   TQM (total quality management)

Relationship marketing

The detail of relationship marketing comes across in Figure 19.6, which essentially examines the two audience groupings and shows their connection via the media.

External audiences are first demonstrated, with existing customers shown as including all the people that go to make up the DMU, and also past and future customers. The intention here is to identify everyone who is likely to be in any way concerned with the decision-making process, and to ensure that they are lined up for an appropriate degree of communication. The media will be chosen to fit each audience category precisely. Next to be examined are all the third parties who are likely to influence a customer in any way. There is a wide range of potential candidates here, but the main groupings are agents, distributors, business partners, trade associations, the press and, where applicable, retailers. Referring back to the ladder of loyalty, the ultimate goal has to be to establish a partnership, and this is shown as involving technical development, even through to joint bench-marking.

At the other end of the scale are internal audiences, where the marketing concept needs to percolate through from top management to all employees – but obviously with special concentration on all customer-facing people.

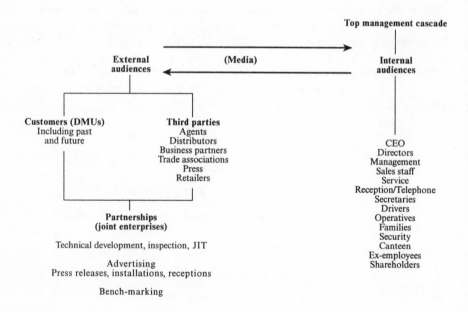

Figure 19.6   Relationship marketing

Provision is also made here for shareholders who can play an important role in transmitting favourable messages.

Notice that media, ie communication channels, work in two directions. So the final outcome is a good number of people at the supplier end communicating with a good number of people at the customer end: hence the term 'relationship'.

Media

The essence of external media planning is to move right away from above-the-line 'blunderbuss' media to those which facilitate precision marksmanship. Whilst the sales representative must stay at the head of the list, he or she will be followed closely by direct mail of one sort or another, together with an equally planned programme of telephone contact – the latter, of course refers to both incoming and outgoing calls. The following is a list of all the media which can be called into action to reach individuals with precision:

Salespeople
DM, fax and e-mail
Telephone
Exhibitions: public and private
Seminars and conferences
AV
Presentations
Road shows
Works visits
Sales aids
Disks
House magazines (internal, external, audio)
Customer user panels
Dealer panels
Letters
Gifts
Sales service actions
Help lines
Competitions
Social events
Corporate hospitality
Books
Newsletters
Complaints
Mailing: ads and press releases
Training
Literature
Case studies

Programme planning

Just as with relationship marketing there is a change in emphasis from obtaining new customers to developing existing ones, so there is a change in the methods of maintaining contact. For reasons of economy, customers are grouped together depending on what is considered to be their lifetime value. Then each group is allocated a well thought-out degree of contact. So, for the highest group (eg national accounts) there might be six personal visits supported by a monthly mailer, and regular telephone calls. Added to this might be any of the media listed above. In a second category level there might be just one visit a year, but four dedicated telephone calls as well as mailings. A final category of customer might justify no personal calls unless reactive, but rely on telephone and mail. The whole idea is to maintain or improve the perceived level of contact whilst reducing costs.

As regards internal media, most firms will already have in place a variety of employee communications channels. These will start with what has been referred to as the top management cascade and will comprise person-to-person, and face-to-face, with heavy responsibility falling upon managers at all levels. The following is a list of the more obvious internal media which can be used in order to inform all internal people of the facts they need to acquire in order that they can be in a position to transmit favourable messages towards customers whenever the need arises. It should not be forgotten that many external channels like the distribution of press releases or cuttings, advertisement proofs, and so on, can also be utilized.

Notice boards
Pay packet inserts
Special launch brochures
Training sessions
Trades union representatives
Campaigns presentations
Static displays
Special competitions
Congratulations boards
'Big boss' visits
Award ceremonies
Company magazines
Manager/employee team talks
Senior management presentations
Mass meetings
Specialist consultants
Videos/Audio cassettes
Posters
Information on personal computers

Attitude surveys
Local newspaper articles
Sports and social activities
Literature
Annual reports

Verbal and non-verbal communications

Over and above written and what might be termed audio-visual communications, an important part of communications in building good relationships with customers comes down to verbal and non-verbal communications. In speaking, as well as in writing, there are many factors which can make or mar a relationship. These include accent, clarity, speed, knowledge and vocabulary, enthusiasm, use of clichés, and indeed establishing a rapport through listening and having a friendly manner, but not through over-familiarity. It is also important to plan and structure what one is going to say, for there to be a logic about one's presentation, and not to take too long to say it. The speech may well also be accompanied by appropriate visual aids.

Attention must be given to body language which, some hold, has a far more important part to play than is generally realized. What about appearance? Think about physique, dress, hair, clothes, feel, and even smell. Even your job title and the mode of travel you use will be sending messages which may be favourable, neutral or unfavourable.

Summing up

A few factors to take note of are:

- The customer base is a major economic asset
- Up to 90 per cent of profit may well come from existing customers, ie repeat purchases – but not all customers repeat
- It costs up to ten times more to find a new customer than to keep one
- Readership of direct mail and advertisements is higher among existing customers
- The objective is more than just 'retention': it is to convert light users to medium and medium to heavy.

BENEFITS

The following are some of the changes brought about by relationship marketing and the benefits they bring:

- Greater demand leads to a reduction in price elasticity
- Reduction in marketing spend to achieve the same result

- Competitors have to fight harder to lure satisfied customers away
- Sales administration costs are lower
- Decrease in customer turnover
- Satisfied customers send positive messages – third party endorsement.

20.

THE IMPACT OF NEW MEDIA ON INDUSTRIAL MARKETING
by Blackett Ditchburn, Deputy Managing Director, Carat Insight

And so the computer began to speak...

Life for a marketing person in the late twentieth century can be characterized by a single word – change. The cause of a great deal of that change can be attributed to the influence of the computer on the way the society we live in communicates. Marketers have coined the phrase 'new media' to act as a catch-all. But it seems inadequate. In many senses, media is far too limiting a concept to get across the way in which the computer is affecting communication in our daily lives.

Naturally, there is a huge amount of jargon obscuring the true significance of the changes. Bits, bytes, webs, e-mail, Internet, Intranet: all are words new to our language in the last few years. All are picked up, used and abused as attempts are made to describe the changes in soundbites for general consumption. Unless you make a sustained attempt to find out more, you could be forgiven for dismissing all the hype as a passing fad.

Every now and then every market goes through rapid change. As the change evolves, there is usually no consensus as to where it will end. One can think of the uncertainty about the future of newspapers as Eddie Shah and then Rupert Murdoch sought to introduce new working practices, or the confusion among computer manufacturers as networked personal computers began to threaten the established order of mainframes. Such uncertainty is now growing at an unprecedented rate in the media market. Although they may be neither sudden nor dramatic, users of media – viewers, readers and advertisers – nevertheless face a series of changes that will alter the delivery of media beyond all recognition. The only problem is that we don't know quite how the changes will manifest themselves, nor how soon they will begin to challenge the established order.

What we are seeing today is but a dirt track compared to the information superhighway that will emerge as the rise in computing and communications power increases. Although the hype is easy to dismiss, the power of digitization that lies behind it is hard to ignore. Without wishing to be too technical, different forms of information have always been reproduced in different ways. Words are printed on paper. Photographs are taken using light-sensitive chemicals. Sound is transferred by vibrations transmitted through a needle (remember records?), or through radio waves. Television is broadcast to receivers capable of receiving radio waves of a different frequency, and so on. Each kind of information has developed its own technology.

Now, however, any form of information can be reduced to digital language – the language of the computer. Thus the different information technologies we have grown used to have been reduced to a single form. Text, graphics, voices, music and video images can all be received and decoded by a single tool, the computer.

Those with responsibility for marketing are thus caught up in these changes. Marketers turn to all kinds of media to communicate their brands, and so it is inevitable that the impact of these changes to the delivery mechanism of all media should therefore affect how marketers think. But we must not be constrained by thinking along the lines of 'conventional' media. After all, television, radio, cinema, press and outdoor media are all products of their own economic and technical frameworks. The digitization of all forms of communication undermines both those types of framework – so when we begin to consider the possibilities raised by 'new media', we must think in terms of what might be possible, not simply in terms of what is presently available.

As the popular encyclopedia CD-ROM *Encarta* demonstrates, it is now possible for words, pictures, sound and video all to be incorporated in a single storage mechanism, and retrieved in any combination at the user's discretion. Not so long ago, such a confection would have required an enormously complex range of differing technologies for its creation and then recreation. Today a simple PC can do it all for us. And in the not-too-distant future the same combination of words, pictures, sound and video will be available, if needed, simultaneously anywhere in the world.

It has been observed many times that the speed and nature of the changes taking place to the flows of information in late twentieth-century society bear a considerable resemblance to the changes brought about by the Industrial Revolution. The Industrial Revolution had a profound effect on the society of the time, changing it in a short period to an almost unimaginable degree. That revolution, of course, also generated almost unimaginable wealth for the country. While the wealth creation of the information revolution will be spread more widely around the globe, the social changes in western society at least will be just as profound.

The Internet has taken the brunt of the attention. But it has to be seen as but one part of the whole. It may be by far the most tangible expression of the changes thus far, but marketers can leverage the digital revolution in many ways. Think of the commercial stationery company that very early on transferred its catalogue on to CD-ROM. They realized at the time that most of the secretaries responsible for ordering stationery did not have a computer capable of reading the disk – but they had a hunch that their bosses would all be in the front line for higher-specification machines. And the hunch proved correct – secretaries took the disk to their bosses' machine to see what it contained and how it worked. The company had therefore managed to draw its services to the attention of the very people who were almost unreachable by conventional means. Sales grew very satisfactorily...

What drove this particular success is probably the novelty value of the method of presentation, rather than any intrinsic benefit. But the speed of technological advance is generating such novelties at a constantly escalating rate. Behind the wheezes, however, there is a more fundamental series of questions that need to be addressed by today's marketer.

As the means to distribute television signals is commoditized, even business-to-business marketers can consider not merely advertising on television, but utilizing a whole channel. Already there is an organization that can organize the broadcasting of your own television programme to a national network of hotels. What might that do to the sales conference? And at least one car manufacturer has installed its own satellite television channel in its dealers' showrooms. News of new models can be conveyed, of course, but how much easier is it to make technical points when you can show the assembled technicians how to do something, rather than be constrained by having to describe it in dry terms in a manual? This system is still using analogue, conventional television signals. But even with that constraint it is a viable commercial proposition. With the advent of digital television, the possibilities become almost limitless.

Key to a great deal of this new digital freedom is the concept of interactivity. Rather than having to use broadcast signals at the time they are broadcast, it is increasingly possible for them to be played at the timing and discretion of the user. This eliminates the need for careful timetabling. The user has control.

As is pointed out by those closest to the technology, the future electronic media landscape cannot be determined through analysis – to know what the future will be like, you have to invent it. Through the rest of this chapter you will find today's manifestations of technology described. But advantage will be gained only by understanding what's possible, creating a solution that suits your needs, and then going out there and doing it.

There is one further aspect to the information age that has enormous implications for marketers: more data than ever before will be available on the behaviour and preferences of the customer. As more transactions transfer into a digital environment, so it becomes possible to build up a more comprehensive picture of the average customer. In theory, we will see the preferences and expectations of customers being held alongside their names and addresses. A forerunner of this already exists in the shape of contact database software, but the future holds the possibility of this file being built up automatically and, indeed, triggering the owning organization to be able to make timely and accurate offers.

Such imaginings are not yet mainstream, but we will gradually see their emergence into the process of business. In many cases, however, we must recognize that new media offer the opportunity to be a distribution mechanism as much as a means for promotion. New media decisions thus take place in a wider context than conventional above-the-line media decisions.

Despite the huge volume increase in data, skilled interpretation will still be required if companies are to make any sense of what is available. A strategy for information management thus becomes a prerequisite for exploiting the new opportunities.

The Internet

The Internet is the first and most tangible manifestation of the digital age. The idea of a complex, continually growing mesh of computer networks that share a common language and can thus talk easily with one another makes for an attractive and tantalizing story for the pundits. This 'network of networks' is truly global. All you need is a PC, a modem (the bit that connects the PC to a communications line), and a telephone line. Armed with these bits of kit, and the right software, you can send and retrieve just about any information you can imagine.

The Internet is actually a relic of the 'Cold War' between Russia and the US. It was originally called Arpanet, after the Defense Advanced Research Projects Agency, and was established in the 1960s to enable collaborative research projects, and to provide a more secure alternative to the one-site super computer. The idea of distributing computer power across a wide geographical area meant that if any one installation were crippled, the network could still continue without undue disruption. In order to realize this dream, Arpanet designers invented a common language called Transmission Control Protocol/Internet Protocol (TCP/IP) to allow linked computers to communicate with one another. As commercial networks began to emerge in the 1980s, the need for a common language was vital. TCP/IP fitted that need, and thus it was a short step from having a commercial network to joining up with the Internet itself.

Internet growth and accessibility has accelerated with the advent of 'user friendly' and more intuitive software familiar to users of Microsoft's Windows operating system. Hitherto, Internet access had been available only through the use of complex code, and the information returned in unattractive computer script. The growth in processing power and memory allowed the creation of easy-to-use access software such as Netscape,

Mosaic and latterly Microsoft Network. This liberate(
allowed it to become a widespread phenomenon.

Until the early 1990s, computers in educational bodi
ties were the largest single group of users connecte
Through the network, academics were quick to realize t!
mic papers anywhere in the world at the touch of a ke
breakthrough. Between July and October 1994, howev(
overtook those of educational establishments. With continuous compound
growth since then, commerce has arrived with a vengeance.

Gaining access to the Internet is simple. There are a number of Internet
Service Providers (ISPs) who offer connection to the Internet. Software is
loaded on to your PC enabling it to dial up the Internet Service Provider. In
turn, the ISP provides access to the Internet. Thus the cost of Internet connection is presently the cost of a (usually monthly) subscription to the ISP,
coupled with the cost of a local telephone call for the duration of the con-
nect time. Once connected, browsing software allows you to 'surf' through
vast quantities of information. One of the technical issues that every user
encounters very quickly is the speed with which information is transmitted.
This is very dependent upon the speed of the slowest link in the chain, usually the speed of the modem and telephone line.

So once you have access, what does it provide? There are two sides to the
Internet. The first is the e-mail facility, and the second is the World Wide
Web (WWW). While the latter has been the focus of much media attention,
the former should not be overlooked.

E-mail is now a fairly familiar concept. Put simply, it is merely a way of
transferring messages and files between PCs. Armed with your e-mail
address it is possible to join any one of a number of 'newsgroups'. A newsgroup is a group of people who have some form of shared interest (there
are presently an estimated 8000 such groups). By joining such a group you
'tap in to' regular correspondence on the topic in question. Once tapped in
you can participate, asking any question you like. Answers may be provided
from anywhere in the world. Many newsgroups cover extremely esoteric
subject areas, and to a large extent they are a reflection of the beginnings of
the Internet – the days when its appeal was limited to those fascinated by
the technology rather than the function. It was these people who were, and
remain, extremely vocal in terms of what is acceptable behaviour. For
instance, sending unsolicited and unwanted information to a newsgroup or
even an individual is regarded as bad behaviour, and the response of the
recipients can be a chorus of abuse and derision – a process known as 'flam-
ing'. There are now sophisticated programmes available to help users retali-
ate against those who dare to send unwanted e-mail. E-mail for commercial
purposes is thus an instrument that must be treated with respect.
Newsgroups do not simply provide ready-made mailing lists.

he World Wide Web is a relative newcomer to the Internet, emerging its present form in 1992. But the WWW is the vehicle that has transformed the Internet from a network for boffins and enthusiasts into one that has promise for a wider and more general audience. The WWW made the information-delivering ability of the Internet searchable and accessible. The WWW allowed the point-and-click approach so familiar to users of today's PCs to be used to surf through pages and pages of richly-formatted text and colour pictures. It even allowed for the downloading of video and sound. This new freedom meant that commercial organizations could begin to express themselves online in far more familiar graphic and visual ways.

Access to the WWW is through some form of browsing software – a set of clickable icons surrounding a screen familiar to anyone used to Windows-based PC operating software. It was probably the development of this sort of browsing software that lead to the huge growth in the Internet we have seen in the past five or so years. In 1991 there were no 'host' computers attached to the WWW, that is computers capable of sending and receiving data. By the end of 1996 the figure had reached 16 million worldwide – many of which are being used by several people. So far, this translates as a doubling in the number of connected computers each year.

There are one or two issues that have emerged in the face of this tremendous growth. First, as the Internet becomes more and more widely available, so it has been subject to a hardening of attitudes towards the level of service delivery. Where once enthusiastic trailblazers were prepared to tolerate slow or intermittent connection, those taking out a subscription today expect the same smoothness and slickness they get with other new products.

Secondly, the sheer growth in connections and usage has resulted in pressure on the network of telephone lines that carry Internet traffic. As a user, therefore, there are times of the day when the delivery of information – particularly of graphic files that take up significant file space – becomes quite slow. This problem has been compounded by the new content providers offering ever more complex graphic presentations which make their Web sites more attractive, but also has the negative effect of increasing the size of the file that has to be sent.

Both these issues are being dealt with, however. Speed of access is increasing as the cost of faster modems tumbles, and there has been great progress in 'file compression' techniques that allow the same quality of graphic delivery but with far smaller overall file sizes.

So who is using the Internet? This is where the Internet is at present fairly poorly served. There is relatively little audience data available, and many of the definitions used to describe audience achievement are yet to be defined with the accuracy we associate with other media measurement. Potentially, however, the Internet could deliver almost perfect audience data – for every page of information accessed there is a computer record.

Collecting all these records could in theory result in perfect access data that could never be replicated by conventional survey means.

In the UK, conventional survey data have provided us with a reasonable fix on the typical user. In mid-1996, 64 per cent of Internet users were under 35 and relatively upmarket – 36 per cent AB and 43 per cent C1. As would follow from such a profile, they are relatively wealthy and light viewers of commercial television. Seventy per cent of users are male, although recent reports from America suggest that this imbalance is being redressed as the Internet's popularity increases. Fifty-nine per cent of all use took place either at work or at college, with 25 per cent taking place in the home.

From the perspective of the industrial marketer, the high proportion of Internet usage generated through the workplace must represent an opportunity. The PC – for the office worker at least – is a very pervasive presence in the work environment. Information delivered through the Internet could therefore reach directly into the decision-making arena.

The Internet is characterized by the speed with which it changes. There is a saying that during one calendar year the Internet experiences seven years of change, such is the scale of development. It is also very difficult to be sure about where it all ends, if indeed it does. Many organizations are making huge investments in developing Internet services – and as yet there is no real evidence as to when the payback begins to emerge. So those developing the services are taking the view that they are very much creating the future, rather than merely aligning their organizations with what they know will happen.

One of the debates that is raging fiercely as this chapter is written is that of the PC versus the network computer. The PC has made all the running so far. But the unit cost is significant. After all, you need a high-end PC with a great deal of software preloaded. There is a counter view, propounded vigorously by Larry Ellison of Oracle, that the mass audience for the Internet will actually be better suited to a dumber terminal, with all the clever software loaded from the Internet each time it is needed. In this way, the occasional user can be confident that they will always have state-of-the-art access, and not have to worry about continual upgrades to the software they are using. Additionally, the cost of entry is therefore reduced and thus the potential mass audience could be brought a little closer. As yet, the network computer has to make its appearance. When it does, we will see which vision of the future has proved to be the correct one.

CD-ROM

CD-ROM (Compact Disc-Read Only Memory) is the technology that gives us a taste of what a multi-media world might be like. The disc itself is identical in appearance to the familiar audio CD – but it is technically different. The benefit of a CD-ROM is that it offers vast amounts of storage space for a very low price. When installed in your PC you can therefore enjoy high-speed reproduction of video, audio, graphics and text files. The reason for the speed advantage is that the internal speed of data transmission within a PC is far higher than when an external data source is involved.

Given that speed of delivery for external data is coming down all the time, there will come a time when the CD-ROM is technically redundant. Until that time, however, CD-ROM remains a very powerful expression of multimedia. As such, it represents a big opportunity for the marketer. Many PCs – particularly those destined for use in the home – are now sold with a CD-ROM drive as an integral part of the package, thus creating an installed base of significance. Evidence also suggests that CD-ROM drives are becoming more prevalent in the office environment, particularly as CD-ROM is becoming a far easier vehicle on which to transport complex software programmes. So instead of a huge number of floppy disks to install a piece of software, a single CD-ROM is far more convenient. Since a CD-ROM drive only adds a relatively small amount to the cost of a PC, it is easy to understand why there is a growth of such machines in the office environment.

The CD-ROM offers marketers – especially those with a complex story to tell – the opportunity to present themselves attractively, and yet still tailor the story to the needs of the customer. The huge storage capacity, aided by easy searching, means that just about every aspect of your company and range of products can be captured on a single disc. Sound and video can be introduced as well as the conventional words and pictures. With such limitless opportunity, of course, comes a new challenge for the authors of such material. Writers and creators of conventional marketing and sales support material understand how the particular item will be used. A brochure, for instance, may be an attractive reminder of the key points used during a sales visit – and thus will be designed to dramatize the key benefits in a way that the potential customer can reflect on in private and at his own pace. To communicate effectively a video may choose to portray the single overriding benefit of the product – and leave the viewer in no doubt as to the principal reason for purchase.

With a CD-ROM, however, the rules change. So much can be presented that the eventual use of the disc – so vital for the creation of message – cannot be determined with the same precision as indicated above. If you are considering using CD-ROM to support your marketing, these points must be considered – you have such freedom that you must design the medium as well as the message.

CD-ROM can also be used in conjunction with the Internet, and thus overcome some of the present deficiencies in speed. Why not have the big files of video or sound held on the CD-ROM, and then the more transient information (prices or delivery dates, for instance) delivered from the Internet? The technology exists to be able to offer such a proposition.

Floppy disks

When considering CD-ROM it is worth mentioning the conventional floppy disk. Familiar to any PC user, they have been the means by which information has been transferred between different machines that don't share a network. Their advantage is that the user can save information on them (unlike the current generation of CD-ROM) as well as read information from them. Their disadvantage is that their capacity is relatively limited – they aren't big enough for many graphic files, and certainly not big enough for video. But they are, without doubt, absolutely universal. And if you resist the temptation to create complex graphics, then there is still enough file space for vast amounts of information. If you have a PC, you have the means to save to and retrieve from a floppy disk. From an industrial marketing perspective, this means that virtually every customer can be presented with a disk that can tell him or her the details of your product. Screensavers have been an early innovation, and have been very successful in getting messages into potential customers' buildings. Fearful of viruses, however, many companies are now clamping down on information being brought in on unchecked disks supplied by outsiders.

CD-ROM or floppy disk – both offer the chance to put complex information into the hands of your customers. Back them up with an Internet service and you could be on the path to offering a powerful new dimension to your marketing.

Intranets

We've had the Internet, now for the Intranet. The Internet is an open network, accessible to anyone. Intranets are exactly the same, and use the Internet as a carrier, but they are closed networks, only accessible to specified machines or users. Intranets can thus facilitate the exchange of information between any identifiable group of users.

Once more, new media create an opportunity for the imaginative marketer. If your business involves customers that regularly require new information, could this be provided through an Intranet? Could your help desk improve its service if it had the ability to swap complex information on-line? As companies are having to become ever faster in their delivery, how would it be if you could let people know almost immediately of changes to product specifications, or even progress reports? Many of the international courier companies have Internet services that tell their customers exactly where their package is: in the air, at the airport; or in road transit. For many industrial marketers, with fewer customers and the need for a little more privacy, an Intranet could become a valuable way of building a closer relationship with their key customers. Would an Intranet make life easier for those customers who need to place regular orders? The possibilities are vast – so vast that the marketer has to be creative as to how such technology could be applied to and benefit his business, and then take steps to realize the vision.

Video-conferencing

They have been doing it in science fiction movies for years, but in real life the telephone that lets you see who's on the line has never really taken off. Some video-conferencing has taken place in multinational companies, but it has been expensive and has required complicated, fixed installations. But the possibilities created by the advent of multi-media-capable PCs mean that an Internet-connected PC can also become a means for video-conferencing at very little extra cost. So sitting at your desk potentially gives you a window into the offices of your clients – or potential clients. Although the picture has yet to reach television quality, such packages do provide an added dimension to the communication that is possible in the business environment.

Of course, we are not used to using or communicating through such means, and the idea feels strange. What benefits will there really be when we can see as well as hear? It is hard to imagine how things might change: but don't forget Alfred Hitchcock's reaction when the first movie with sound, *The Jazz Singer,* was premiered. Sound, he said, would 'ruin the dramatic effect' of film. Alexander Graham Bell also predicted wrongly when he thought that the greatest benefit of his invention of telephony would be the ability to enjoy opera without having to attend. Man has a poor track record when it comes to predicting the consequences of technological innovation when applied to communication. But the marketer will see this as an opportunity and, in part, will invent the future for himself.

Implications for industrial marketing

We began this chapter by describing the digital revolution that has so characterized change during the latter part of the twentieth century. Almost as this chapter is written, it will become out of date as today's new ideas succeed yesterday's new ideas. Change, however, is a tremendous generator of opportunities – and seizing and making the most of opportunities has to be one of the preoccupations of the marketer.

 The supply of a means of distribution for information in all its forms has remained expensive and technically restricted up until now. As a consequence, the marketing business is structured in the way it is. But digital technology looks set to bring down those barriers for distribution, and threaten the structure we have created for marketing.

The marketer can either be an active partner in the creation of the future, or he can bury his head in the sand and hope that it all goes away. Should he choose to participate, then it's worth establishing a few ground rules:

1. Make sure your planning is as imaginative as it is thorough. In the conventional planning process we are constrained by our past. As the digital revolution gathers pace, possibilities emerge that our past does not prepare us for. We must therefore use our imaginations at the planning stage to make sure that we consider every opportunity.
2. Establish clear goals and objectives. Just because the plan might not have a precedent does not mean that we can be fuzzy about why we propose a particular course of action. Establishing clarity, however, will demand a clear and informed understanding of the whole new media mix. The difficulty in setting goals is that there is nothing to go on – so the goal setting must be based upon your understanding of the potential of what you are attempting. Ruthless objectivity will be useful, but hard to achieve. Many companies today are looking at their site on the WWW and wondering why it's there, because they did not set sufficiently clear objectives before allowing the hype to get the better of them.
3. Careful costing remains essential. It is harder to prepare a new media budget than it is a conventional one. After all, when you are in relatively uncharted territory, it is easy to overlook that crucial (possibly expensive) step. As anyone who has worked with technology will testify, estimating how long it might take or how much it might all cost is a difficult business. When you enter the new media world, you are dealing with some of the most up-to-date technology there is. Of gremlins there will be many.
4. Allocating a budget to new media is also tricky. If you can't be sure of its delivery, it's difficult to predict what it is worth. As with so many marketing decisions, however, you must also consider the cost of not participating.
5. Regard new media as marketing's research and development cost. The 'steady state' model of marketing that we have had for so long has resulted in relatively little being spent on its own research and development. But new media has destabilised things – so we must return to first principles. We are in an age of discovery and you should regard the new media budget as part of the discovery process.

Is the digital revolution just another example of the 'let them eat cake' school of marketing we have come to expect from new technology? Is it all technological wizardry, chasing no real social or human need? Or is it a development of similar significance to that which Gutenberg had for the written word? By the turn of the millennium, we should be getting closer to finding answers to these questions. But by then, of course, we will be facing yet more questions.

21

13 WAYS OF STRETCHING THE MARKETING BUDGET

This final chapter sets out to identify the principal areas in which major savings can be achieved. No one can doubt that a massive waste of money can result from not having acquired all the facts about marketing and communications. Sometimes companies are not even aware of the money that is being wasted. This is, after all, the only significant activity which is not in some way accountable. When money is spent on raw materials, on employees, on process equipment or new machinery, the likely outcome is always known, and with some degree of precision. With marketing, and in particular with marketing communications and public relations, no one seems to bother. There is a general malaise which holds that none of it is measurable, so why bother? As readers of this book will have gathered, just about everything is measurable – sometimes without much cost, and to a remarkable degree of accuracy. But even when it is not, the time for relying on hunches is past.

There are many ways of setting about reducing the marketing spend without reducing effectiveness. These are just a few of the most important ones, and should result in savings which are really significant.

1. The sales force

The single most expensive item in the industrial marketing budget is the sales force, with the cost of a single visit amounting to well over £200, and with a number of sales calls often necessary to clinch a deal. This all detracts from profit, as does advertising and all the other marketing expenses. Since the sales force is a vital element, its function must be as cost-effective as possible. The answer is to be found in two ways. In the first place all the channels of marketing communications must be used to act as a very narrow band-pass filter to identify 'hot' sales leads which are likely to be converted into sales in the near future. Cold calling, and even warm calling, must be a thing of the past. The second action necessary is to be found in the chapter on 'Relationship Marketing'. Here, emphasis is put on the need for a new communication channel mix, in which a planned cocktail of visits (both ways), post (letters, quotes, leaflets, etc) and telephone calls are planned in advance according to the importance of each customer or prospect. This, then, will be accompanied by a marked change of emphasis from getting new business from new customers on to getting more business from existing customers. Back-up from inside sales staff is important here.

2. Set quantified objectives

This starts with marketing objectives and goes on to those for all the elements of marketing communications. Only by quantifying all the objectives can there be any final evaluation, but even more important is continuous tracking as the campaign proceeds. With sales, and thus market share, there must be a sales forecast based on past and anticipated performance, which makes use of a SWOT and a PEEST analysis. The vital step now is to change the forecast into a target which everyone is charged to aim for. Then set marcom primary objectives followed by secondary objectives. Even if these prove to be highly inaccurate for the first year, they will gradually become more precise as time goes on, to such an extent that 'marketing ratios' can be established in which, for a given product in a given market, the ratios of enquiries to leads, to visits, to quotations, and to sales can be established along with cost per enquiry, and eventually cost per sale.

3. Produce a marcom plan

In marketing communications the single most important action is to produce a marcom plan along the lines set out in Chapter 3. It is just not acceptable that a sum of money be allocated arbitrarily on any basis other than the 'task method'. No one of the ten steps given can be left undone without seriously affecting the efficient operation of marketing communications. This obviously points to the need for a dedicated specialist with a professional understanding of the function. The marcom plan must, of course, be a sub-set of a marketing plan which, in turn, is part of the business plan.

4. Audit the agency

Or the consultancy. There is widespread discontent with the performance of both advertising agencies and PR consultancies. So often the first ideas are not acceptable, the copywriting needs changing, the media plan shows a lack of knowledge and the production charges are astronomical. A regular agency audit must be the answer to achieving major changes in the way that the account is handled. This takes just a few hours but can result in major improvements, and thus major savings. The key to the use of outside marketing services is to identify precisely what added value is achieved, eg the copywriting must be significantly better than the client could produce. This simple process is not intended to be the preamble to firing the agency – quite the opposite – but if things do not improve, then a competitive pitch once in a while is no more than good business practice: rather like going out on open tender from time to time with print work.

5. Change agency remuneration

The system of allowing an agency to take a 15 per cent media commission (or 10 per cent with trade and technical journals) is highly inefficient and out of date. It is inefficient because the agency does not have to be accountable to the client for doing its job properly since it will get paid anyway. It just doesn't make sense for one party (the agency) to do a job for another (the client) and to be paid by a third party (the media), regardless of how well – or badly – it does the job. It is out of date now since the commission can be claimed directly from the media by the client because the commission system is no longer legally enforceable. The solution, which is rapidly being adopted, is simply to change over to a fee basis negotiated in advance for the work to be done, with all media commission refunded to the client. The agency staff immediately become accountable to the client for everything they do, and the outcome is an improved service. A further possibility which has to be looked at is to consider the services of a media independent or media broker where, perhaps, the media commission will be remitted except for maybe a much reduced figure of, say, 2½ per cent. It may be that for business-to-business media planning this is too specialized for a media broker, but they will certainly be expected to buy more aggressively since they have both the muscle and the professional expertise to get the best possible financial deal as against basic rate card prices.

6. Staff productivity

Marketing, being one of the newest management functions, is staffed by many people who are not always as proficient as they might be. The starting point is to draw up a list of the required marketing competences and to assess each member of staff against a checklist. Gaps in knowledge and experience can be identified and corrective action such as training put in place. The following is such a checklist (overleaf):

Marketing competences	None	Some	Adequate	Strong
Advertising (above-the-line)				
Analysing annual reports and financial data				
Brand management				
Budgeting and budgetary control				
Business writing				
Campaign evaluation				
Cinema advertising				
Codes of practice and legislation				
Competitors and the market place				
Conferences and seminars				
Consumer behaviour				
Copywriting				
Customer relations and customer satisfaction				
Delegation and supervision				
Direct mail				
Direct marketing				
Ethics and social responsibility				
Event management				
Exhibitions and trade shows				
Forecasting				
Integrated marketing communications				
Internal communications				
International marketing				
Interviewing and staff selection				
Macromarket factors – political, economic, environmental, sociological and technological				
Marketing concept				
Marketing functions				
Marketing mix				
Marketing organization				
Marketing planning				
Marketing research				
Media buying and planning				
Media relations				
Meeting technique				
Merchandising				

Marketing competences	None	Some	Adequate	Strong
Motivation and leadership				
Negotiation skills				
New media, eg Internet				
Outside services – choosing, using and auditing				
Packaging and presentation				
Physical distribution and customer service				
Point of purchase (POP)				
Portfolio management				
Poster and outdoor advertising				
Pricing				
Primary research				
Print advertising				
Product development and life cycle – quality				
Public relations				
Public speaking and presentation technique				
Qualitative research				
Quantitative research				
Radio advertising				
Relationship marketing				
Sales literature				
Sales management				
Sales promotion (below-the-line)				
Secondary research				
Sponsorship				
Strategic marketing				
Team-building and management				
Telemarketing				
Telephone technique				
Test marketing				
Time management				
Trade marketing				
Training and development of individuals and teams				
TV advertising				
Understanding and design of financial controls				

The above checklist could form the basis for drawing up a job specification which represents the formula for staff recruitment, as well as a training programme. It is a simple gap analysis. Another key factor nowadays is marketing qualifications. This applies both in recruitment and in staff development. There are very many excellent first degrees in business studies which have a substantial marketing element, and then there are any number of post-graduate qualifications which can be taken part-time or by distance learning. The widely accepted professional qualification is the post-graduate Diploma of Marketing offered by the Chartered Institute of Marketing. A further qualification is the Certificate of Marketing Communications offered by the CAM (Communications, Advertising and Marketing) Foundation. This is followed by the Advertising Diploma and the Public Relations Diploma. The latter is now a requirement for membership of the Institute of Public Relations.

7. Measure journal readership

Hardly any of the 4000 or so trade, technical and business journals are able to provide reliable readership data. Forty per cent offer circulation data which have been audited, while the rest just give figures which are no more than a publisher's statement. Even if circulation figures and readership information were universally available it still would not be sufficient for reliable media selection. Every advertiser is concerned with a number of market segments, and within each the individual people who go to make up the decision-making unit. It is vital to know precisely what publications are read regularly and the extent to which they are held in high regard. Without this information an efficient media plan cannot be produced, and the only way to obtain this information is to carry out a tailored readership survey. This can increase the value for money obtained from the media budget by a factor of two or more, and should be done for each campaign. Even so, this only shows the reading habits of a journal's audience as a whole. What the advertiser needs to know is more than just how many people had an 'opportunity to see'. The important question is, 'Was my advertisement actually seen (or noted, read)?' and, if so, by what proportion of the readership, and then by what proportion of the target audience, ie what was its real 'reach'?

8. Strengthen response mechanism

Every advertisement has an objective: make it, or add to it, to obtain responses. There are two reasons for this: first, to obtain the names and addresses of potential customers in order to amplify or update the database and to follow through into qualified sales leads; and secondly to increase the impact of the advertising. Instead of the best that can be obtained by a prospect looking at an advertisement and then turning to the next page all in a matter of, maybe, ten seconds, with a response, the time taken to respond – maybe a telephone call, a letter or a coupon can be added on to that ten seconds: at least 30 seconds extra. Also, on the arrival of whatever has been requested, the prospective customer will spend further time, say, reading a brochure, or using or referring to some kind of 'deliverable': this could be a matter of hours, or even act as a constant reminder. The impact on one's memory can be greater by a factor of ten; equally, the actual response can be increased by another factor of ten. The necessary action is to offer something which the reader really wants to acquire, and to offer it boldly. The other vital ingredient is to ensure that any offer is made in such a way that its origin can be identified. So the response mechanism must be coded, but in such a way that it is not obvious to the enquirer. A coded leaflet number can be used, or a dedicated telephone number.

9. Cut media schedule

As will have been seen, in a homogeneous market segment with a large number of journals available, no more than three are necessary to give optimum reach. After this, the incremental increase from adding a fourth is so small as to make it of no significant value. Having reduced the schedule in this way, and maybe made a very large saving, the next step is to look at the size of the advertisements themselves. A surprising piece of research shows that, if enquiries are the object of advertising, then the size of the advertisement is not a major factor. The answer may not be so radical as to reduce from whole page to quarter page, but there could certainly be merit in changing from a whole page to, say, two-thirds of a page, or from a double-page spread to one-and-one-third, running across the gutter – this would also have the benefit of the higher page traffic for the remaining two-thirds of the page, which would be taken up by editional. An alternative approach to take with full-page advertisements is to change them all to bleed. This should not involve any extra expense (in spite of rate card hopes), and will provide a much larger area, giving higher impact and making the advertisement much more noticeable. Finally, on advertisements, the wear-out factor tends to be underestimated. An advertisement can almost always be used up to ten times before it loses its effectiveness. If in doubt, try it out.

10. Greater use of case studies

At last research is beginning to come to the fore which shows that advertorials are more effective than conventional display advertisements, though not as effective as editorials. Page traffic scores are somewhere in between. A highly cost-effective procedure is to commission a case study which is already spoken for as an exclusive article in a leading journal. This is then run-on and used as a mailer and a handout for the sales force and at exhibitions. It is very inexpensive, and involves no design charge. It can then be used directly as an advertorial. So for the cost of writing a page or two, with no layout or production costs, one obtains a feature article, a direct mail piece and an advertisement.

11. A wider use of direct mail

There is plenty of evidence that an advertisement in a journal will be seen by only a small percentage of readers. The solution here is to hire the journal's database and mail out the advertisement, which will thus achieve a 100 per cent reach. A similar treatment can be afforded to a press release. The objective of sending it to a given publication is to get it reproduced for the readers to see. Do that by all means, but just to make sure it is seen, send it out too, again to that journal's database.

12. A greater use of publicity

The impact of an editorial as opposed to an advertisement on the same subject is many times greater. Not only does it have a larger readership, but it will appear in more publications. The most obvious course of action is to reduce the expenditure on display advertising and transfer it to publicity. While you're at it, a further useful action is to set a minimum standard for the conversion of releases into mentions of at least 40 per cent.

13. Measure advertisements

It is no longer necessary to rely simply on guesswork when approving advertisement proposals. An advertisement can be measured, as can a direct mail piece, a brochure and even an exhibition stand. In this way, minimum standards can be set below which one is not prepared to go (see page 192).

Research into advertisers and agencies and their respective practices

This is the fourth piece of research conducted as the basis for commenting on current practices in marketing communications in the UK. The current survey is intended to provide input for the sixth edition of *Business-to-Business Marketing Communications*, published by Kogan Page.

In most cases the actual percentage response is given, and sometimes the equivalent figure for the previous study. Questionnaires were sent to agencies and to advertisers with budgets in the order of £500,000. The total number of clients handled by the responding agencies amounted to 541, which compares with 563 for the previous study conducted in 1993.

RESULTS OF ADVERTISER SURVEY

1a. Do you use an advertising agency?
     YES   89 per cent
     NO   11 per cent
Comment: It is clear that the vast majority of advertising is still being placed through advertising agencies.

1b. If yes, is your agency:
     Industrial/business only?   33 per cent
     Mainly industrial/business?   20 per cent
     About half industrial/business?   33 per cent
     Mainly consumer?   14 per cent
Comment: A substantial proportion of advertisers use agencies with B-to-B experience and therefore expertise – 86 per cent.

1c. Approximately how many people does your agency employ? Is it nearer to:
     10   35 per cent
     20   12 per cent
     30   6 per cent
     60   41 per cent
     100   6 per cent

Comment: This is statistically unsound due to the small sample. From the responses to the agency questionnaire it is clear that the situation remains the same as at the time of the last two studies, ie that most industrial/business agencies employ fewer than 30 staff.

1d. Does your agency have overseas connections?

     YES   78 per cent

     NO   22 per cent

Comment: Even more agencies now offer international coverage than in any previous studies.

1e. Does it handle your export advertising?

     YES   23 per cent

     NO   77 per cent

Comment: This result provides more evidence that, whilst clients may look for agencies with international connections, in practice they tend not to use such facilities.

2. If you are not in the London area, do you prefer using:

     A London-based advertising agency?   25 per cent

     A local advertising agency?   75 per cent

Comment: Confirmation of the two previous reports which showed exactly the same proportions, namely that provinial agencies are preferred.

3. Do you pay your advertising agency a service fee?

     YES   33 per cent

     NO   67 per cent

Comment: A surprising number of accounts still based upon media commission.

4. Do you favour remunerating an agency by:

     A flat annual fee?   56 per cent

     Commission, or commission plus related fee?   44 per cent

Comment: There is a major change here, showing for the first time a preference for fee payments. A decade ago it was almost unheard of.

5. Are you satisfied with the calibre of your agency personnel?

     YES   89 per cent

     NO   11 per cent

Comment: Clients have consistently shown a high degree of satisfaction with their agency people. Yet this conflicts with the answers given to face-to-face questioning, where the responsible managers are almost always critical of agency services, particularly copywriting.

6. Is your account executive a director or associate director of the agency?

     YES   78 per cent

     NO   22 per cent

Comment: This figure has remained constant over the past ten years or so.

7. Does the agency's creative team have as much direct contact with you as you would like?

YES   78 per cent
NO   22 per cent

Comment: This response also confirms the views of previous respondents.

8. Please assess your agency's service in relation to the following activities, scoring 5 if completely satisfied and 0 if the service is unsatisfactory or non-existent. *NB* The following scores represent the arithmetic average of the responses, and are listed in descending order of preference. Scores for the previous research (1993) are shown in brackets.

Photography	4.3
Sales literature	4.1 (3.7)
Market research	4.0 (3.7)
Media relations	3.9 (3.4)
Direct mail	3.5 (3.3)
Data sheets	3.5 (3.5)
Media evaluation	3.3 (3.7)
Media buying	3.3 (3.9)
Press advertising	3.3 (3.9)
Planning	3.2 (3.5)

Comment: A number of other services were included but the response has not been large enough to be statistically reliable. Generally, there can be seen an improvement in below-the-line services, reflecting the growing requirements of the clients. Direct mail and media relations have improved significantly over the past two surveys. As against this, clients seem to make more demands of above-the-line media, reflecting perhaps the growing dis-illusionment with conventional display advertising.

8. Approximately how many changes of agency have you had in the past five to ten years?

	Five years	Ten years
No change	47 per cent	33 per cent
One change	20 per cent	27 per cent
Two changes	27 per cent	20 per cent
Three or more	6 per cent	20 per cent

Comment: If anything, there seems to be greater stability than in previous years with changes of agency being less frequent. There seemed to be some uncertainty in the responses, particularly in relation to what had happened ten years ago. This is perhaps due to the fact that managers do not stay with a particular employer for as long as they used to.

9. Have you ever dismissed an agency, and if so, can you say why?

Answers here tend to confirm the findings of previous years, and are more or less predictable; namely, service, high costs and lack of creativity.

10. What factors would be most likely to influence your choice if selecting another agency?

The most important factor seemed to be a good personal relationship coupled with a real understanding of the client's markets, products and technology.

11. Approximately what is your expenditure on all forms of marketing communication (excluding staff overheads)?

The question was broken down into five expenditure groups, ranging from 0 to £500,000+. 83 per cent of respondents were spending £500,000 or more, compared with 65 per cent at the last survey.

12. Approximately what percentage of your appropriation is allocated to the various media?

Press advertising	25 per cent (33 per cent)
Direct mail	11 per cent (14 per cent)
Sales literature	30 per cent (28 per cent)
Exhibitions	17 per cent (13 per cent)
Public relations	17 per cent (9 per cent)

Comment: There were very wide differences as between one account and another, indicating greater creativity in media selection. In particular, the proportion of spend on press advertising reduced yet again, whilst at the same time the figure for public relations (by which the respondents clearly meant press relations) increased compared with the two previous studies. The figure for direct mail is surprising, and must be due to the small statistical base.

13. Is your marketing communications budget arrived at as a percentage of sales turnover, a calculated cost related to objectives, or as an arbitrary sum fixed on past practice?

Responses here were difficult to analyse, but the overall conclusion has to be that an arbitrary sum is still a frequent basis, though it is often mixed with a variety of other criteria. Compared with earlier years, there is no doubt that the client side of the business is becoming more and more professional, but this does not usually extend to top management, where marketing communications is still not being seen as being vital to business success.

14. Your position within the company?

The title 'Advertising Manager' has almost disappeared but has been replaced by a very wide range of titles, mostly including the word 'communications' somewhere. There is a clear indication that all forms of communication, including public relations, are being conducted by one person who therefore has a much broader brief than just 'marketing'.

15. To whom does the marketing communications function report at board level?

Chairman	15 per cent
Managing director	25 per cent
Marketing director	25 per cent
Sales director	20 per cent
Other	15 per cent

Comment: With some 40 per cent still reporting to the CEO, there is little change here. The surprising outcome was the continuing importance of sales directors, a title which, by comparison with the last survey, seemed largely to have disappeared.

RESULTS OF AGENCY SURVEY

1. In which of the following areas do you provide a comprehensive service?

Sales literature	93 per cent (100 per cent)
Press advertising	89 per cent (96 per cent)
Media buying	82 per cent (96 per cent)
Planning	79 per cent (83 per cent)
Media evaluation	71 per cent (96 per cent)
Direct mail	71 per cent (87 per cent)
House journals	64 per cent (83 per cent)
Data sheets	61 per cent (91 per cent)
Television	57 per cent (30 per cent)
Sales promotion	57 per cent (57 per cent)
Trade shows	57 per cent (65 per cent)
Media relations	54 per cent (83 per cent)
Video production	46 per cent (57 per cent)
Private exhibitions	46 per cent (57 per cent)
Conferences	46 per cent (48 per cent)

Comment: The same – very wide – range of services are still being offered, though from the advertisers' survey it is clear that not many of them are being used. Also, a good proportion of the services claimed are in fact outsourced. The biggest difference of note is the large increase in television facilities.

2. In the scheduling of trade, technical and business media, who is mainly responsible?

The agency	63 per cent (82 per cent)
The client	7 per cent (4 per cent)
About equal	30 per cent (14 per cent)

Comment: This might be a biased result, but nevertheless shows greater client involvement than before.

3. If mainly carried out by the agency, is the planning done by:

Media department?	32 per cent (33 per cent)
Account executive?	28 per cent (24 per cent)
A combination?	40 per cent (43 per cent)

Comment: No significant change, though if we look back at even earlier survey results, the account handler is becoming more involved, as indeed is the client.

4. What sources of reference do you use in planning media, on a scale of 0 to 5?

	Average
Calls by representatives	2.5 (3.0)
ABC Certificates	3.7 (3.7)
BRAD/rate cards	3.7 (3.4)

Comment: Response here was very varied, with sales reps highly rated by some agencies, and the very opposite by others. The surprising outcome was that, in spite of an 'other' category, few agencies seem to rely on any other sources of information, including any work that they might have done themselves on the clients' behalf.

5a. In how many of the following areas is the advertising (marketing services, etc) manager able to make a decision?

Reject an ad	79 per cent (52 per cent)
Accept an ad	65 per cent (43 per cent)
Reject a schedule	71 per cent (50 per cent)
Accept a schedule	55 per cent (48 per cent)
Reject a campaign	47 per cent (44 per cent)
Accept a campaign	36 per cent (32 per cent)

5b. In how many of these does an ad have to be approved by:

Client's MD?	44 per cent (39 per cent)
Another director?	45 per cent (34 per cent)

Comment: There is some conflicting evidence here which, on the one hand, shows an involvement by some other 'authoriser', whilst indicating that the marcom specialist is freer than heretofore in the taking of tactical decisions. Going back over ten years or so, we can see clearly the emergence of communications specialists, having more and more responsibility. But there is still a long way to go, this really being due to the lack of objective evaluation procedures; decisions are often based on personal likes and dislikes.

6. From what number of clients do you receive an adequate briefing in relation to:

Campaigns?	32 per cent (31 per cent)
Individual ads?	37 per cent (41 per cent)

Comment: Agency people still seem to have a low regard for their clients.

7. How many clients would you say have a thorough understanding of the value of:

     Industrial (business) advertising?   44 per cent (52 per cent)
     Marketing?   37 per cent (59 per cent)

Comment: Further confirmation of the above comment. It might be argued that agency executives are hardly in a position to judge; but their perceptions are important.

8. How many clients pay a service fee?   29 per cent (46 per cent)

Comment: This discrepancy is probably accounted for by the number of accounts which actually combine media commission with some element of service fee top-up.

MARKETING

Marketing Management and Strategy

A most authoritative book on the marketing scene	Doyle, P	Prentice-Hall

Marketing Plans

A marketing best-seller	MacDonald, M	Butterworth-Heinemann

The CIM Marketing Dictionary

A very comprehensive glossary of marketing, public relations, advertising, sales and related subjects	Hart, N A	Butterworth-Heinemann

Marketing Management

The world textbook	Kotler, P	Prentice-Hall

The Fundamentals & Practice of Marketing

Outstanding basic book	Wilmshurst, J	Butterworth-Heinemann

Marketing Management

A British equivalent to Kotler	Lancaster & Massingham	McGraw-Hill

Marketing Communications

A very comprehensive text	Smith, P R	Kogan Page

How to get on in Marketing

A guide for new entrants	Hart, N A and Waite, N	Kogan Page

ADVERTISING

The Effective Use of Advertising Media

A basic text on the use of media Davis, M Business Books

Advertising: What it is and How to do it

New edition of a successful White, R McGraw-Hill
introductory text

Spending Advertising Money

A 'classic' on how to spend money Broadbent, S Business Books
on advertising

Below the Line Promotion

New addition to popular Wilmshurst, J Butterworth-Heinemann
CIM/Butterworth-Heinemann Series

The Practice of Advertising

Well-established work, completely Hart, N A Butterworth-Heinemann
revised and updated

Advertising World-wide

A new book on international De Mooij, M K Prentice-Hall
advertising and Keegan, W

PUBLIC RELATIONS

Company Image and Reality

A comprehensive review of Bernstein, D Holt, Rinehart and
creating a corporate image Winston

All about PR

Generally the most popular book Haywood, R McGraw-Hill
amongst practitioners

The Practice of Public Relations

The standard introduction to Howard, W Butterworth-Heinemann
PR: commissioned by the
CAM Foundation

Survey Research for Managers

Of particular use to PR managers Hutton, P Macmillan

How to Manage Public Relations

| The first really serious book on PR management | Stone, N | McGraw-Hill |

Strategic Public Relations

| Sixteen chapters each written by an acknowledged expert in the field | Hart, N A | Macmillan |

Principles of Corporate Communications

| A comprehensive conceptual text with very practical implications | Cees van Riel, B M | Prentice Hall |

INDEX

References in italic indicate figures or tables